access to history

Britain 1900–51

access to history

Britain 1900–51

Michael Lynch

HODDER
EDUCATION
PART OF HACHETTE LIVRE UK

For Peerson Lynch, born 2002

Study guides written in 2008, by Sally Waller (AQA) and Geoff Woodward (OCR).

The Publishers would like to thank the following for permission to reproduce copyright material:

Photo credits
p.11 People's History Museum/Labour Party; **p.14** The Library of the London School of Economics and Political Science Ref: COLL MISC 0519/81; **p.15** Printed and published by the Daily News, Ltd/National Archives/Solo Syndication; **p.16** © Political Cartoon Society; **p.24** © Getty Images; **p.42** © 2001 Topham Picturepoint, TopFoto.co.uk; **p.47** (top) The Illustrated London News Picture Library, London, UK/The Bridgeman Art Library; **p.47** (bottom) Facsimile of poster, National Library of Ireland; **p.73** Photograph used with the permission of The Trustees of the Imperial War Museum. © IWM. Q 3257; **p.85** Mirrorpix; **p.92** © Mary Evans Picture Library; **p.103** © Punch Limited/TopFoto; **p.122** Cartoon by A.W. Lloyd published in the *News of the World* on the 11th October 1931. British Cartoon Archive, University of Kent/NI Syndication Ltd; **p.149** (top left) © Lordprice Collection/Alamy; **p.149** (top right) © Lordprice Collection/Alamy; **p.149** (bottom left) © Lordprice Collection/Alamy; **p.149** (bottom right) © John Robertson/Alamy; **p.151** © Mary Evans Picture Library/Simon Roberts; **p.160** Cartoon by George Whitelaw published in the *Daily Herald* in 1944. British Cartoon Archive, University of Kent/Mirrorpix; **p.161** Cartoon by George Whitelaw published in the *Daily Herald* on the 2nd December 1942, British Cartoon Archive, University of Kent/Mirrorpix; **p.167** © Mary Evans/Rue des Archives/Tallandier; **p.171** Cartoon by David Low published in the Evening Standard on the 14th May 1940. British Cartoon Archive, University of Kent/Solo Syndication/Associated Newspapers; **p.173** © Mirrorpix; **p.184** © Illustrated London News/Mary Evans; **p.188** © Punch Cartoon Library; **p.193** National Library of Wales/Solo Syndication/Associated Newspapers

Acknowledgements
p.35 Manchester University Press for an extract from D. Brooks, *The Age of Upheaval*, 1995; **p.79** Hodder Education for an extract from V. Ullswater, *A Speaker's Commentaries*, 1925

Every effort has been made to trace all copyright holders, but if any have been inadvertently overlooked the Publishers will be pleased to make the necessary arrangements at the first opportunity.

Hachette Livre UK's policy is to use papers that are natural, renewable and recyclable products and made from wood grown in sustainable forests. The logging and manufacturing processes are expected to conform to the environmental regulations of the country of origin.

Orders: please contact Bookpoint Ltd, 130 Milton Park, Abingdon, Oxon OX14 4SB. Telephone: (44) 01235 827720. Fax: (44) 01235 400454. Lines are open 9.00–5.00, Monday to Saturday, with a 24-hour message answering service. Visit our website at www.hoddereducation.co.uk

© Michael Lynch 2008
First published in 2008 by
Hodder Education,
Part of Hachette Livre UK
338 Euston Road
London NW1 3BH

Impression number	5 4 3 2 1
Year	2012 2011 2010 2009 2008

Cover photo courtesy of the Mary Evans Picture Library
Illustrations by GreenGate Publishing Services and Derek Griffin
Typeset in New Baskerville 10/12pt by GreenGate Publishing Services, Tonbridge, Kent
Printed in Malta

A catalogue record for this title is available from the British Library

ISBN: 978 0340 965 948

Contents

Dedication

Keith Randell (1943–2002)

The *Access to History* series was conceived and developed by Keith, who created a series to 'cater for students as they are, not as we might wish them to be'. He leaves a living legacy of a series that for over 20 years has provided a trusted, stimulating and well-loved accompaniment to the post-16 study. Our aim with these new editions is to continue to offer students the best possible support for their studies.

1

Pre-War Britain, 1900–11

POINTS TO CONSIDER

In 1900 there were two major parties competing for power in Britain – the Conservatives and the Liberals. There were also two smaller parties – Labour and the Irish Nationalists – which were to have an important influence on affairs. This chapter examines the progress and fortunes of these parties as they attempted to respond to the major problems facing Britain at the beginning of the twentieth century. The analysis is developed under the following headings:

- Britain in 1900
- The Conservative Party, 1900–06
- The Liberal Party, 1900–06
- The Labour Party, 1906–11

Key dates

1899–1902	The Anglo-Boer War
1900	Khaki election victory for Salisbury's Conservatives
	LRC formed
1902–05	Balfour led Conservative government
1903	Lib–Lab pact formed
1905	Liberals in office under Campbell-Bannerman
1906	Liberal landslide electoral victory
1908–11	Asquith led Liberal Reform programme

1 | Britain in 1900

Key question
What were the major problems and questions facing Britain in 1900?

Britain in the late **Victorian** and **Edwardian** years faced great economic, social and **constitutional** difficulties. These may be listed and examined as:

a) the problem of poverty
b) Britain's economy

c) the crisis in industrial relations
d) Britain's role as an empire
e) the question of the franchise
f) the position of the House of Lords
g) the Ulster question (see pages 45–48).

Table 1.1: Governments of the late Victorian and Edwardian eras

1895–1902	Conservatives under Lord Salisbury
	(Queen Victoria died in 1901, succeeded by Edward VII)
1902–05	Conservatives under Arthur Balfour
1905–08	Liberals under Henry Campbell-Bannerman
	(Edward VII died in 1910, succeeded by George V)
1908–14	Liberals under Herbert Asquith

a) The problem of poverty

By the early twentieth century Britain had experienced a remarkable increase in the size and the concentration of its population. This was largely a consequence of **industrialisation** and was strikingly evident in the growth of towns and the formation of the great **conurbations**.

Table 1.2: The growth of population in the conurbations

	Greater London	South East Lancashire	West Midlands	West Yorkshire	Mersey-side
1871	3,890,000	1,386,000	969,000	1,064,000	690,000
1901	6,856,000	2,117,000	1,483,000	1,524,000	1,030,000
1911	7,256,000	2,328,000	1,634,000	1,590,000	1,157,000

In the 40 years after 1871, the population in those areas virtually doubled. This created a need for key resources such as water supply and sanitation that simply did not exist. The result was the intensifying of such social ills as:

• overcrowding
• malnutrition
• ill-health.

It is true that central and local government in the Victorian age had begun to take measures to alleviate the worst of the conditions but their efforts fell far short of what was required. The rudimentary welfare and relief schemes that existed in the towns and cities were simply overwhelmed. It was also the case that although wage rates had risen they were not at a level where the majority of workers had sufficient surplus cash to improve their living conditions. Poverty was widespread.

Key terms

Victorian
Relating to the years of Queen Victoria's reign (1837–1901).

Edwardian
Strictly speaking, the adjective 'Edwardian' refers to the reign of Edward VII (1901–10). However, the term is often extended to include the early years of George V's reign between his accession in 1910 and the outbreak of the First World War in 1914.

Constitutional
Issues relating to the conventions and methods by which Britain was governed.

Industrialisation
The spread of manufacturing plants and factories, invariably accompanied by urbanisation.

Conurbations
Concentrated urban areas of high population density.

Key terms

Poor Law
As amended in 1834, a scheme for providing relief by taking the destitute into workhouses where the conditions were made deliberately grim so as to deter all but the most needy from entering them.

Eugenics
The science of improving the quality of a race by allowing only couples of a high level of physical and mental health to produce children.

Left-wing intellectuals
Writers and thinkers who believed in radical social and economic change along socialist lines.

Key date

The Anglo-Boer War: 1899–1902

Key figure

George Bernard Shaw (1856–1950)
A celebrated playwright and social commentator.

The only major scheme for dealing with poverty was the **Poor Law**, which had been introduced in an earlier age when it was believed that poverty could be contained by dealing with it on a local basis, parish by parish. However, the enormous increase in population made this system of parish relief inadequate to deal with the problem.

The wretched conditions that shaped the lives of the mass of the people who lived in the towns and cities were graphically revealed in a series of carefully researched public reports. Outstanding pioneering studies were produced by Charles Booth and Seebohm Rowntree; their meticulously detailed analysis of social conditions in London and Yorkshire respectively gave evidence of appalling squalor and deprivation.

> We are faced by the startling probability that from twenty-five to thirty per cent of the town population of the United Kingdom are living in poverty.
>
> In this land of abounding wealth, during a time of perhaps unexampled prosperity, probably more than one-fourth of the population are living in poverty ... There is surely need for greater concentration of thought by the nation upon the well-being of its own people, for no civilization can be sound or stable which has at its base this mass of stunted human life.
>
> Seebohm Rowntree, *Poverty: A Study of Town Life*, 1901

National efficiency

The sheer extent of the poverty and distress in Britain that such stark details provided convinced all but a few that something had to be done. All the parties agreed that government and parliament had a duty to tackle the deprivation that afflicted so many in the nation. This was not merely for humanitarian reasons. In 1902 it was officially reported by the Army high command that nearly two-thirds of those who had volunteered to join the services at the time of the Anglo-Boer War of 1899 to 1902 (see page 8) had failed to pass their basic medical test.

Such revelations strengthened a widespread conviction, current in the Edwardian period, that Britain had to recreate 'national efficiency'. This was a term often used at the time to denote the level of well-being and health that it was felt the British people needed to achieve if their nation was to sustain its strength industrially and militarily.

The notion of national efficiency was closely linked to **eugenics**, a science that attracted many adherents, particularly among **left-wing intellectuals**. A prominent voice among these was **George Bernard Shaw** who spoke in favour of what he called 'selective breeding'.

Charles Masterman, an influential Liberal writer, represented the basic concern of the national efficiency campaigners in Britain when he described the unhealthy conditions in which the mass of the people who had migrated from the countryside to the industrial towns now lived. He wrote of their 'cramped physical accessories [quarters], hot, fretful life and long hours of unhealthy toil' and warned:

The problem of the coming years is the problem of this New Town type; upon their development and action depend the future progress of the Anglo-Saxon race, and for the next half-century at least the policy of the British Empire in the world.

C. Masterman, *The Heart of the Empire, Discussions of Problems of Modern City Life in England*, 1902

In 1904, a specially appointed Interdepartmental Committee on Physical Deterioration delivered a formal report to parliament. Among its recommendations were:

- the appointment of full-time medical officers and health visitors in urban areas
- local authorities to lay down standards of purity for all food and drinks
- regular medical examination of all school children
- urban overcrowding to be studied and addressed
- laws against smoke pollution to be introduced
- basic hygiene to be taught in schools
- local authorities to provide meals for school children.

Not all these proposals were acted upon straight away, but they had helped to define and clarify the problems.

One particularly interesting response to the need for national efficiency was the creation of a youth movement which continues to thrive in Britain today – the Boy Scouts. Its founder, **Lord Baden-Powell**, left no doubt as to the purpose of the movement:

Remember, whether rich or poor, from castle or from slum, you are all Britons first, and you've got to keep Britain up against outside enemies, you have to stand shoulder to shoulder to do it. If you are doing harm to yourselves, you are doing harm to your country.

Robert Baden-Powell, *Scouting for Boys*, 1908

Yet, while there was general agreement that Britain had to address its severe social and economic problems, there were deep disputes between the parties and also between different factions within individual parties as to how these problems should be tackled. The disputes over this were to be a prominent feature of pre-1914 Britain.

b) Britain's economy

Between 1870 and 1914, Britain's trade and industry appeared to be shrinking relative to those of other countries such as Germany and the United States (see graph on page 5). The British industrial growth rate of 2.3 per cent was only half that of the United States. By the turn of the century Germany and the USA had overtaken Britain in the volume of their iron and steel production. By 1910, British industrial exports made up only ten per cent of the world trade compared with figures of twenty per cent for German goods and forty per cent for American.

Key figure

Lord Robert Baden-Powell (1857–1941) Had a successful military career and proved to be one of the heroes of the Boer War. He wrote *Scouting for Boys* in 1908. By 1914 the movement he had started had spread nationwide, and by 1920 worldwide.

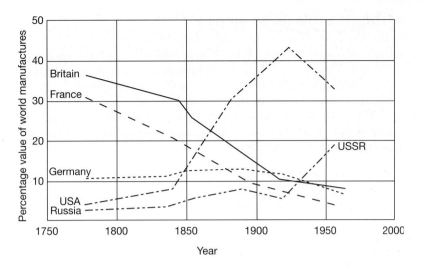

Figure 1.1: World trade, 1750–1955.

Key terms

Revisionist historians
Those who challenge the accepted interpretation of events.

'Old' unions
Established organisations representing skilled workers.

'New' unions
Represented large groups of workers, such as dockers, transport workers and miners.

Modern **revisionist historians** have argued that the decline was exaggerated by contemporaries who were unnecessarily frightened by the growth of Germany and the USA. They suggest that, in fact, British industry was still growing healthily and was more cost effective than American and German industry, even though total output in those two countries was higher. Revisionists further argue that it was the First World War which caused Britain's twentieth-century industrial decline by shattering the international economy in which Britain had held such a predominant place.

While noting the revisionists' argument, it has to be emphasised that late Victorian and Edwardian industrialists truly believed that the trade figures showed that they were losing out to their American and German rivals in the open market.

c) The crisis in industrial relations

For much of the nineteenth century the trade union movement had been dominated by the **'old' unions**. But the last quarter of the nineteenth century witnessed a rapid growth in the number of mass-membership trade unions, composed largely of unskilled or semi-skilled workers. These **'new' unions** were eager to use their collective strength in a campaign for better wages and conditions. By 1890 they had already won some major victories; the gas workers had successfully struck for an eight-hour day, and the 'dockers' tanner' (sixpence a day basic pay rate) had been reluctantly granted by the port authorities.

The employers had attempted to counter what they saw as a major threat to their interests by forming federations aimed specifically at resisting the strength of organised labour. The scene was set for major conflict on the industrial front. So strong was the threat of industrial disruption that it raised the issue of whether it was the role of government or parliament to intervene in worker–employer relations. This was to prove a critical question in the pre-1914 years.

d) Britain's role as an empire

In the last thirty years of the nineteenth century Britain had rapidly increased the size of its existing empire. This was largely the result of its participation in the European **scramble for Africa**, which had begun in the 1870s. The Conservatives had been particularly associated with the development of this new phase of imperialism. Although there were also some Liberals, known as liberal-imperialists, who supported overseas expansion, the Liberal Party itself strongly opposed it.

By the end of the century there was considerable dispute between and within the parties as to whether Britain should continue to pursue expansionist policies or whether the view, espoused earlier by such great Liberal figures as W.E. Gladstone, that imperialism was both immoral and a threat to international peace, should prevail. The two opposed viewpoints were to be bitterly and violently expressed at the time of the Anglo-Boer War fought between 1899 and 1902 (see page 8).

e) The question of the franchise

At the beginning of the twentieth century, Britain was not yet a democracy. Nevertheless, significant steps had been taken since 1832 to extend the **franchise**. By 1900, some sixty per cent of adult males had the vote. The question now arose: should the nation become fully democratic? This would involve not only granting full adult male **suffrage**, but also, far more controversially, the enfranchising of women. All the parties were worried over the political implications of extending the vote to the female population. For which party would women actually vote? It was a leap into the unknown. The battle over this issue became a dramatic feature of pre-1914 politics.

f) The position of the House of Lords

The issue of democracy lay at the heart of another of the major controversies of the time. The **two-chamber structure** of the British parliament meant that the House of Lords was constitutionally able to block the legislation sent up to it by the House of Commons. In practice, it was only measures presented by Liberal governments that the Lords chose to reject. This was because Conservative peers were in an overwhelming majority in the Upper House, which enabled the Conservative Party to reject Liberal measures of which it disapproved. The most striking example of this had occurred in 1894 when Gladstone's Irish **Home Rule** Bill (see page 45), having passed through the Commons, was then thrown out by the Lords. As Britain moved towards democracy, the question was how much longer the anomaly of an unelected assembly having an absolute veto over the elected chamber would be tolerated.

Key terms

Scramble for Africa
Between the 1870s and 1914 the major European colonial powers, France, Germany, Belgium, Portugal and Britain, separately took over large areas of the African continent.

Franchise/suffrage
The right to vote in parliamentary elections.

Two-chamber structure
The elected House of Commons and the unelected House of Lords.

Home Rule
An independent government in Dublin responsible for Irish affairs.

Key terms

Middle class
The comfortable, moneyed section of society.

Conservative and Unionist
The party had added Unionist to its title after 1886 in order to indicate the strength of its opposition to Home Rule for Ireland.

The issues and problems which have been discussed in the preceding sections, a) to f), may be expressed as a series of demanding questions confronting the Government, parliament and the political parties in the period between the beginning of the century and the outbreak of the Great War in 1914:

- How could poverty be tackled?
- How far should the Government be responsible for running the economy?
- By what means could Britain best earn its living?
- How much power should the State have over ordinary people's lives?
- Should wealth be redistributed by the Government taking it from the wealthy in taxes to give to the poor?
- How far should the Government be involved in industrial disputes?
- What was Britain's relationship to Ulster? (see pages 45–48)
- Was the House of Lords in need of radical reform?

It is interesting to note how modern these questions seem. They are the issues which were to continue to demand attention throughout the twentieth century and into the twenty-first.

Summary diagram: Britain in 1900

PROBLEMS
- Poverty
- A declining economy
- Crisis in industrial relations
- The disputed role of empire
- The franchise
- The anomalous position of the House of Lords

Key question
What was the character of the Conservative and Unionist Party at the start of the twentieth century?

2 | The Conservative Party, 1900–06

Nineteenth-century Britain had seen the rise of a powerful **middle class** which had grown wealthy on the profits of commerce and industry. Much less wealthy, but no less important politically, were the industrial workers who had grown in number as industry expanded. The majority of the men in both these classes had gained the vote. They now had an electoral importance no party could afford to disregard.

The **Conservative and Unionist Party**, which had traditionally been the party of the landed classes, had skilfully modified itself in the nineteenth century in order to appeal to both middle- and working-class voters. Its outstanding leader, Benjamin Disraeli, had accepted that if the party was to survive as a political force it had to adapt itself to the changes that industrialisation had brought about. Disraeli's recognition of this was made clear in a series of important social reforms that his Conservative government introduced.

By 1900 the Conservatives had been in power under their leader, **Lord Salisbury,** for all but three of the previous fourteen years. It has been said that under Salisbury Conservatism became 'an organised rearguard action' to prevent the growing democracy of the times from becoming too disruptive. Yet this view needs to be balanced against the fact that Salisbury came to accept the wisdom of Disraeli's belief that it was possible to win over the enfranchised working classes to the Conservative side. That is why Salisbury put great stress on party organisation. It was under him that the Conservative Party machine, with its emphasis on recruitment of supporters in the constituencies, began to take its modern shape. His success in this was shown in Conservative victories in the general elections of 1885, 1895 and 1900.

However, the dominant issue in Britain preoccupying Salisbury's government when the century opened was not a domestic but an imperial one: the Anglo-Boer War.

a) The Anglo-Boer war, 1899–1902

The war arose from a dispute between the British and the Dutch **Boer** settlers as to who controlled southern Africa. In 1884 Britain had agreed to a division which gave it Cape Colony and Natal and granted the Boers the Transvaal and the Orange Free State. However, although Britain formally recognised Boer rights of self-government in the Transvaal, it illogically continued to claim that it had authority over the region.

Key figure

Lord Salisbury (1830–1903)
He led three governments (1885–86, 1886–1892, 1895–1902) and was the last peer to be a prime minister. He was renowned for his contribution to foreign affairs.

Key question
How did Britain become involved in the Anglo-Boer war?

Key term

Boer
Afrikaans (Dutch) for farmer.

Key figure

Joseph Chamberlain (1836–1914)
A prominent radical in the Liberal party until he fell out with Gladstone over Home Rule in 1886, when he joined the Conservatives as a 'Liberal Unionist'. A fervent believer in empire, he first became Colonial Secretary in 1895 under Salisbury.

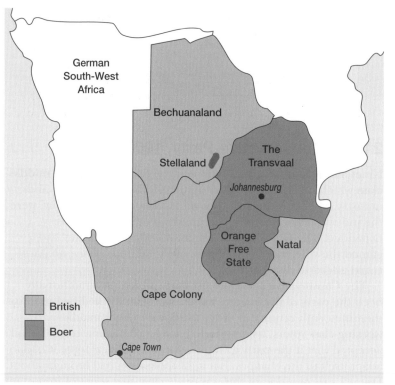

Figure 1.2: Southern Africa on the eve of the Anglo-Boer War.

Key date

Khaki election victory for Salisbury's conservatives: 1900

Key term

Khaki
British forces adopted this as the colour of their standard uniform during the Boer war.

Key figures

Henry Campbell-Bannerman (1836–1908)
Led the Liberals from 1899 to 1908, was prime minister from 1905–08, and was the first British premier to be officially entitled 'prime minister'.

David Lloyd George (1863–1945)
Was involved in every major political issue from 1900 to 1945; he held government posts continuously from 1905 to 1922, the last six of those years as prime minister.

Arthur Balfour (1848–1930)
An MP 1874–1922, Secretary for Ireland 1887–91, Prime Minister 1902–05, leader of the Conservative Party 1905–11 and Foreign Secretary 1916–19.

There is now little doubt that Britain deliberately provoked the war that broke out in 1899. For **Joseph Chamberlain**, the Colonial Secretary, British supremacy in southern Africa was essential in order to maintain Britain's strength as an empire. He held that unless Britain was a powerful empire it could not be a powerful nation. So he plotted with the aggressive British High Commissioner in the Cape to make such unreasonable demands on the Boers that they would have no choice but to fight.

From the beginning there was a significant group in Britain who were deeply unhappy with the war. Referred to as 'pro-Boers', they questioned the morality of Britain's position as aggressors who had started the war. Initially, however, the war was widely popular in Britain, and Prime Minister Salisbury sought to exploit this by calling an election in 1900. The Conservatives deliberately played upon the patriotism of the electorate in what became known as the **Khaki** election. Salisbury's government was returned with a very comfortable majority over the Liberals.

Table 1.3: 1900 election results

	Votes	Seats	% of total votes cast
Conservatives	1,797,444	402	51.1
Liberals	1,568,141	184	44.6
Labour (LRC)	63,304	2	1.8
Irish Nationalists	124,586	82	2.5

However, thereafter things went badly for the Government. Although the war was eventually won, with the surrender of the Boers in 1902, the Conservatives' handling of it proved dismal. The pro-Boers drew constant attention to the failure of British forces to win the war quickly. Still more unsettling for the Government were the reports of the extreme measures that the British forces employed in trying to break Boer resistance. The most notorious of these was the internment of civilians in 'concentration' camps, where the cramped and unhygienic conditions frequently led to the spread of fatal diseases.

Henry Campbell-Bannerman, who had become Liberal leader in 1899, accused Salisbury's government of employing 'the methods of barbarism'. **David Lloyd George**, a dynamic young Liberal, declared: 'we have now taken to killing babies'. Britain's inhumane strategy against Boer civilians, added to the fact that it took the might of the British imperial army three long years to overcome an outnumbered and outgunned group of farmers, caused embarrassment at home and aroused ridicule abroad.

When **Arthur Balfour** succeeded Salisbury as prime minister in 1902 he inherited the poor reputation that the Conservatives had earned over their embarrassing Boer-war record. But his troubles did not end there. Despite the credit his party had earned since the mid-1880s for their progressive reforms, in which he had played a prominent part, Balfour's years in office from 1902 to

1905 were overshadowed by a set of problems that would lead to the crushing defeat of his party and a landslide Liberal victory in the 1906 election.

Balfour led Conservative government: 1902–05

Key date

b) 'Chinese slavery'

Africa again came to haunt the Conservatives. Balfour's government was accused of having permitted large numbers of Chinese labourers, referred to as 'coolies' or slaves, to be brought from Asia to work in appalling conditions and for pitiful wages in the gold and diamond mines of southern Africa. It was widely felt that the Government's claim that this was a matter for British officials in Africa to sort out was an inadequate response. Opponents suggested that Balfour's government was simply passing the buck, and that its moral authority was compromised.

Key question
Why did problems mount for the Conservatives during this period?

c) The Taff Vale decision, 1901

The significant part industrial relations now played in British politics was evident in this landmark case. In June 1900, the employees of the Taff Vale Railway Company in South Wales went on strike with the full backing and financial aid of their union, the Associated Society of Railway Servants (ASRS). The Company tried to break the strike by bringing in non-union labour and by taking the ASRS to court for illegal **picketing**. The tactics worked and the strikers reluctantly returned to work with nothing gained.

Boosted by its victory, the Company again took the union to court, claiming damages for the financial losses caused by the strike. The first court hearing went in favour of the Company but, on appeal by the ASRS, a higher court reversed this decision in November 1900. The Taff Vale Railway Company was not prepared to give up. It presented its case to the House of Lords, the highest legal authority in the land. The Lords overruled the appeal court decision and found for the Company. The Lords' ruling, delivered in July 1901, came at the end of many months of legal wrangling. The time span meant that the issue excited the widest interest; both the unions and the employers knew that it was a test case in industrial relations. The key part of the Lords' decision, delivered by the senior judge, Lord Macnaughten, read:

Picketing
Strikers' stationing themselves at the gates of a factory or work place so as to deter other workers from entering.

Key term

> Has the legislature authorised the creation of numerous bodies of men, capable of owning great wealth and of acting by agents, with absolutely no responsibility for the wrong they may do to other persons by the use of that wealth and the employment of those agents? In my opinion Parliament has done nothing of the kind ... to warrant such a notion.
>
> Quoted in Vivien Brendon, *The Edwardian Age*, 1997

The ruling was accompanied by the awarding of substantial damages and costs against the ASRS. It was now clear that the unions' right to strike and to picket had been effectively destroyed by the Lords' decision. Only an Act of Parliament could reverse this. But, when Balfour declared in 1902 that his government had no intention of formally reversing the Taff Vale decision against the trade unions, it reinforced the conviction among the workers that Conservatism was wholly unsympathetic to their interests.

A Labour poster of 1906 depicting the oppression suffered by the unions. How accurate a depiction of the situation is this cartoon?

WHIPS FOR LABOUR'S BACK.

d) Balfour's Education Act, 1902

Key question
Why did Balfour's Education Act cause such anger among religious groups in Britain?

The measure which bears Balfour's name, since he was largely responsible for its drafting and introduction, is now regarded as an important and progressive step. It:

- raised the school-leaving age to twelve
- granted subsidies to church schools from local rates
- abolished the locally elected School Boards, and passed the authority over schools to the county or borough councils.

However, at the time, the credit Balfour might justifiably have expected was largely lost because of the furious row that broke out among religious rivals over the nature of the schooling to be provided. Ever since educational reforms had been attempted in earlier decades there had been a stand-off between the **Anglican** and **Nonconformist** churches.

Historically, most of the schools in England and Wales had been set up and run by the Anglican Church. When the nineteenth-century reformers sought to extend state education to all, they had to use the existing Anglican schools otherwise schooling simply could not have been provided on a big enough scale. It followed that schools teaching the Anglican faith now received state funding. It was this that offended the Nonconformists, who complained bitterly of heresy (false religious doctrine) being taught on the **rates**. For their part, Anglicans were unhappy at the thought that as state education was extended they would lose their traditional hold over it. These anxieties and resentments were intensified by Balfour's 1902 measure.

e) The Licensing Act, 1904

It was also angry Nonconformists who were the most vociferous in attacking the Government's Licensing Act which was introduced in 1904 to regulate the sale and consumption of liquor. The aims of the new controls were to protect children and to prevent the adulteration of alcoholic drinks. However, the Nonconformists were unimpressed by this. They chose instead to condemn the clauses in the act which provided generous compensation to the brewers and landlords who stood to lose their licences under the new liquor regulations. Why, the Nonconformists asked, should the Treasury use its funds to reward vice?

Their objections were not simply kill-joy puritanism. All the prominent movements dealing with social distress, such as the **Salvation Army**, testified that drink was a major factor in deepening the poverty from which so many families suffered.

f) The Irish Land Act, 1902

Another Conservative measure which was well intended but which brought the Government more scorn than praise was the 1902 Irish Land Act, often referred to as **Wyndham's Act**. The reform is now seen as a very enlightened move, which went a long way towards finally solving the land problem in Ireland. It made £100 million available to tenants to buy out their English landlords and thus become owners of the land that they farmed, something for which the Irish peasantry had yearned for centuries.

However, Ireland's sense of grievance, recently intensified by the English parliament's rejection of Home Rule, was too ingrained for one measure, no matter how enlightened, to end Anglo-Irish bitterness. The Act received only grudging thanks from the Irish Nationalists who regarded it as a belated recognition of their long-withheld rights, while the Irish Unionists dismissed the measure as a craven submission to Nationalist pressure. It is notable that although Balfour as Irish Secretary had often taken a very progressive attitude towards Ireland, as in his support for land reform, he had combined this with tough measures to control disorder. For this, the Nationalists had given him the title 'bloody Balfour'.

Key terms

Anglican
The established English Protestant Church, the nation's official religion.

Nonconformist
Those Protestant churches which refused to accept the doctrines and authority of the Anglican Church. Nonconformists tended to regard themselves as the conscience of the nation and had become an influential moral force in Victorian Britain.

Rates
Taxed levied on householders to pay for local government services.

Salvation Army
A religious movement founded in 1878 by William Booth to put Christian values into practical form by directly helping the unfortunates of society, including the destitute, orphans, prostitutes and the victims of drink.

Wyndham's Act
Named after George Wyndham, Secretary for Ireland, 1900–05.

g) Tariff reform (imperial preference)

Damaging as the problems listed above (2a to 2f) were, it was the question of tariff reform that most seriously weakened the Conservatives. In a misguided attempt to outmanoeuvre the Liberals on economic matters, Balfour's government adopted imperial preference as its official economic programme in 1903. It was a policy most closely associated with Joseph Chamberlain, the former radical Liberal who had joined the Conservatives in 1886. Chamberlain's objective was to protect home-produced food and manufactured goods by placing restrictive duties on imports unless they came from the British dominions and colonies. These countries would receive preferential treatment; their goods would enter free of duty. British exports would be granted a corresponding preference in the colonies. The idea behind this was to develop the British Empire as a worldwide **protectionist trading bloc**.

Key question
How were the Empire and protection combined in Chamberlain's thinking?

Chamberlain's motives

There was a still deeper intention behind Chamberlain's thinking. He was not seeking to maintain Britain's prosperity simply for its own sake. He believed that so great were the poverty and destitution blighting the nation that, unless these were remedied, the grievances of the poor would lead to widespread social violence. National efficiency had to be restored. Money had to be found and distributed to raise people from the squalor in which so many lived. But how was the money to be found? One simple answer was through taxation.

Chamberlain found this unacceptable; he argued that the taxing of one group in society for the benefit of another would encourage **revolutionary socialism** and class war. His proposed answer was imperial preference. If the empire was developed through protection into a worldwide trading association it would bring Britain the wealth it needed to cure its social ills. And all this would be achieved without recourse to unjust and disruptive taxation. This was why Chamberlain was such an ardent imperialist. His belief in the maintenance and extension of the Empire came together with his belief in the need for social reform.

Key terms

Protectionist trading bloc
A modern parallel is the European Union which is based on the notion of free trade between its own member states and firm protection towards non-member nations.

Revolutionary socialism
A radical movement that wanted to overthrow the existing state and replace it with a worker-led government.

The battle over protection

Chamberlain's dream of empire was never to become a reality, but he argued his case with such persuasive force that if any one person could be said to have made tariff reform a national issue it was he.

It is certainly the case that few issues in any age have excited so much interest in the British people as tariff reform did in the Edwardian era. Although to later generations it may seem a rather dry topic, in its time it was seen as vitally important. Ordinary people saw it in terms of whether or not they could afford to feed themselves and their families. Manufacturers and industrialists saw it as a question of whether they could survive in a competitive trading world. Workers felt somehow that their jobs and wages depended on it. While few of the electorate had the knowledge of economic theory to enable them to follow the tariff-reform debate in detail, they were well able to grasp that it was about choice between dear food and cheap food, between having a job and being out of work.

Despite their official adoption of it as a policy, few Conservatives were genuinely happy with the tariff reform programme. They accepted it because it seemed to offer a means of raising revenue without resorting to taxation, to which, as a party of the moneyed classes, they were obviously opposed. A notable feature of Conservatism was that it was not, as its critics often tried to make out, against social reform in principle. Indeed, from Disraeli on, Conservative governments had introduced many significant reforms in this area (see page 18). The problem for most Conservatives was that they were unwilling to increase taxes to pay for reform, their argument being that heavy taxation imposed an unfair burden on those who were efficient and successful.

Tariff reform. What message are the tariff reformers endeavouring to put across in this poster regarding the results of free trade?

A free trade poster, 1905. What basic message is the 'big loaf, little loaf' illustration attempting to put across?

Key question
What strategic mistakes did Balfour make in preparing for the election?

The 1906 election

In the passionate national debate that followed over free trade, the electorate judged that the protectionists had lost the argument. Apart from Joseph Chamberlain himself, there were few advocates of imperial preference who were able to put over a convincing case or conduct a successful campaign. Sceptical observers said it was clear that the Conservatives did not understand, let alone believe in, the tariff reform policy with which Chamberlain had saddled them. As one contemporary put it, 'the Conservatives went into the polling booths with the albatross of tariff reform about their necks'.

The result of all this was a sweeping victory for the Liberals in the 1906 election held in January and February 1906. Henry Campbell-Bannerman, who had already become prime minister of a minority Liberal government two months earlier, now headed a Liberal ministry with a majority of 243 over the Conservatives. That the Liberals were already in government when the election was held was the result of a failed ruse by Balfour.

STEPPING STONES TO OFFICE.

A cartoon illustrating the problems confronting the Conservatives between 1900 and 1906. Which of the problems has the cartoonist chosen to include and which to omit?

Conscious that matters were not going well for his government and party, Balfour had resigned as prime minister in December 1905 and advised the King, Edward VII, to dissolve parliament, knowing that this would oblige the Liberals under Campbell-Bannerman to form an interim government before an election was held. Balfour's intention was to play upon the divisions among the Liberals over Irish Home Rule and over the leadership of Campbell-Bannerman. He hoped that the Liberals would either be unable to form a government at all or to be so divided when in government that this would hand the initiative back to the Conservatives who would then doubtless win an ensuing election.

It is also likely that Balfour was engaging in what would now be called a 'damage limitation exercise'. By forcing an election earlier than was necessary, he hoped his party might suffer less badly at the polls than if he waited until 1907 when, under the **seven-year rule**, an election would have to be held.

Key dates

Liberals in office under Campbell-Bannerman: 1905

Liberal landslide electoral victory: 1906

Balfour's scheming let him down. The Liberals were far from being as disunited as he had believed. Campbell-Bannerman accepted office enthusiastically and had no problems in forming a loyal cabinet. He and his party went into the election with a confidence that the results showed had been entirely justified.

Table 1.4: 1906 election results

	Votes	Seats	% of total votes cast
Conservatives	2,451,584	157	43.6
Liberals	2,757,883	400	49.0
LRC (Labour in 1906)	329,748	30	5.9
Irish Nationalists	35, 031	83	0.6

Key question
In what sense may the Conservatives be said to have been the victims of the electoral system in 1906?

h) Electoral problems for the Conservatives

It is often said that in British politics oppositions do not win elections, governments lose them. That could be certainly applied to 1906. It was not so much the attraction of the Liberals that won them the day as the dissatisfaction felt by the electorate towards the Conservatives.

However, a note of caution should be sounded here. When dealing with the results of elections it is perhaps too easy to talk of sweeping victories and landslide triumphs. Such dramatic terms tend to distort the real picture. The truth is that the result of an election is invariably the consequence of a slight shift in public attitude. A striking feature of the British electoral system is that parliamentary seats are awarded not in proportion to the number of votes a party receives overall, but according to how many individual constituencies it wins. Since each elected MP gains his seat simply by being '**first past the post**', he could win by a very large majority or a very small one. So whether a party wins or loses is not a matter of how many votes it gets nationally, but how those votes are distributed.

Key terms

Seven-year rule
At this time, the law required that a general election be held at least once every seven years.

First past the post
A candidate winning an election simply by gaining more votes that any of his challengers individually.

This can be seen by comparing the figures in Tables 1.3 (page 9) and 1.4. Across the two elections the Liberals more than doubled their number of seats, while the Conservatives saw their number more than halved. However, in terms of overall votes the returns were nowhere near as dramatic; there had been a marginal shift in the popular vote, not a landslide.

This is not to argue that the Conservatives had not lost support or that the Liberals had not gained it. Between 1900 and 1906 there certainly had been a major movement from the Conservatives to the Liberals. The former had improved their vote by only 654,140, while the Liberals had picked up an extra 1,189,742. Yet the Liberals' popular vote majority over the

Conservatives was only 306,299, hardly sufficient in proportional terms to justify a majority of 243 in the House of Commons. To put it as a ratio, in 1906, it required 15,615 votes to return a Conservative, and only 6,894 to return a Liberal.

This imbalance would not always work in the Liberals' favour. It is one of the ironies discussed later in the book (see page 91) that although the Liberals gained from the oddity of the British electoral system in 1906, they were to become its victims after 1918 when they consistently failed to turn their popular vote into parliamentary seats. That development, however, lay in the future. In 1906 their great moment had arrived. They were in power with a massive majority, which gave them the freedom to turn their political ideas into practical policies.

i) The Conservative record

Key question
How successful had the Conservatives been in their period of office?

Six years after winning a handsome victory in the 'Khaki election' the Conservatives had squandered that supremacy and suffered a crushing electoral defeat at the hands of the Liberals that was to keep them out of office until 1922. It appeared to the electorate in 1906 that the Conservatives had been unsuccessful in tackling the great questions facing Britain. Their measures and policies had aroused more enemies than they had won them friends. It was now the turn of the Liberals to test whether their ideas and programmes were better fitted to the times.

However, before turning to consider the Liberals, it is to be noted that historians now are far less willing to accept the traditional depiction of the Conservatives of this era as reactionaries vainly trying to hold back the forces of progress. The record of the Salisbury and Balfour governments shows a willingness to entertain reform.

The major social reforms of the Conservative governments, 1886–1905, were:

- provision made to improve working-class housing
- steps taken to prevent cruelty to children
- landlords rather than tenants to be responsible for paying tithes
- Factory Act, 1891, improved safety conditions in the mines
- Education Act, 1891, established free elementary education
- measures to improve the conditions of shop assistants and mill hands
- factory acts tightening safety regulations
- Workmen's Compensation Act, 1897, provided payments for injuries sustained at the workplace
- Factory and Workshop Act, 1901, improved working conditions
- Education Act, 1902, extended compulsory education for all into the secondary area
- Wyndham's Land Act, 1902, settled the landlord–tenant problem in Ireland.

While these may not represent a systematic programme of reform, they do indicate a readiness by the Conservatives to contemplate progressive legislation in key social areas. When the Liberals came into office in 1905 intent on reform they would be working on prepared ground.

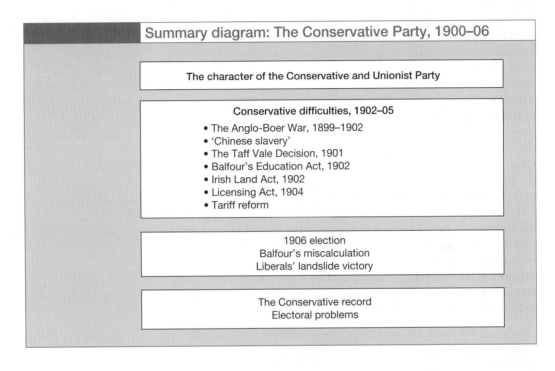

Summary diagram: The Conservative Party, 1900–06

The character of the Conservative and Unionist Party

Conservative difficulties, 1902–05
- The Anglo-Boer War, 1899–1902
- 'Chinese slavery'
- The Taff Vale Decision, 1901
- Balfour's Education Act, 1902
- Irish Land Act, 1902
- Licensing Act, 1904
- Tariff reform

1906 election
Balfour's miscalculation
Liberals' landslide victory

The Conservative record
Electoral problems

3 | The Liberal Party, 1906–11

a) New Liberalism

Key question
In what sense were these years the age of 'New Liberalism'?

The electoral landslide of 1906 was not simply a victory for the Liberal Party after a decade in the wilderness; it was a victory for '**New Liberalism**'. To understand that, we have to remember that in the last part of the nineteenth century the Liberal Party had faced a crisis of identity. Its traditional character was Gladstonian; that is to say it had developed into a major party in accordance with the ideas and attitudes of its leader, William Ewart Gladstone, the towering figure of late Victorian politics. The policies and principles that the Liberal Party had come to represent under him were succinctly captured in Gladstone's own slogan, '**Peace, Retrenchment** and **Reform**'.

A prominent feature of these policies was that while they included the principle of necessary change, they excluded the idea of the state's undertaking a comprehensive programme of social and economic reform. This was because traditional Liberalism championed the cause of the individual. It was very reluctant to allow the state to intrude on the economic and social liberties of the people. That was why it supported free trade.

Key terms

New Liberalism
The movement among progressive Liberals who wanted their party to commit itself fully to social reform.

Peace
The avoidance of war and unnecessary foreign entanglements by embracing the concepts of internationalism and anti-imperialism.

By the 1890s, however, such an approach was too restrictive for the progressive, radical Liberals who began to chaff against the limitations Gladstone's pervading presence imposed upon their party. Although none dare say it openly, in their eyes Gladstone had lasted too long. Despite retiring on a number of occasions, he had never truly left the political scene. Deaf and near blind during his last years, Gladstone continued to dominate the Liberal Party until his death in 1898. This effectively prevented the younger members from pushing their ideas onto the party agenda.

Joseph Chamberlain

The major victim of this was Joseph Chamberlain, who was unable to persuade the Liberal Party to accept his radical ideas (see page 13). Frustrated by the seeming unwillingness of a party led by Gladstone ever adapting itself to the real needs of the nation, Chamberlain took the dramatic step in the late 1880s of abandoning the Liberals and joining the Unionists. His decision was motivated in part by his anger at Gladstone's attempt to grant Home Rule to Ireland (see page 45), but he was equally concerned about pushing his schemes for dealing with national poverty. Chamberlain feared that if the plight of the industrial masses was left untouched they would turn to socialism. In 1885 he had challenged Gladstone by presenting his own radical 'Unauthorised Programme', advocating an extensive scheme of social reform. Chamberlain explained the driving conviction that inspired his programme in these terms:

> Politics is the science of human happiness, and the business of a statesman and of politicians is to find out how they can raise the general condition of the people; how they can increase the happiness of those who are less fortunate among them.
>
> Joseph Chamberlain quoted in *The Times*, October 1885

By the beginning of the century Gladstone was dead and Chamberlain had joined the Conservatives. The question was now which of them had left the greater mark upon the Liberal Party. Events were soon to show that it was Chamberlain. It was his legacy that was turned into New Liberalism.

The outstanding representative of this new force in the party was David Lloyd George, to whom Chamberlain was a political hero. Sharing Chamberlain's dislike of socialism, Lloyd George also wished to prevent its rise and believed this could best be done by the Liberal Party widening its political appeal by adopting social reform as its principal objective. Lloyd George's great ally in this period was **Winston Churchill**, who was destined to be the greatest statesman of the twentieth century. In 1906 Churchill gave a precise definition of the practical need for New Liberalism:

> No view of society can be complete which does not comprise within its scope both collective organisation and individual incentive. The evergrowing complications of civilisation create for us new services which have to be undertaken by the State.

Key terms

Retrenchment
Saving public money by tightly controlling central-government expenditure.

Reform
Allowing for necessary changes to be introduced by government so long as they do not encroach on the freedom of the individual.

Key figure

Winston Churchill (1874–1965)
Entered the Commons as a Conservative MP in 1900, fell out with his party over tariff reform and, in 1904, joined the Liberals.

'The sovereignty of social welfare'

There were liberals who saw New Liberalism not as a break with the party's past, but as a continuation of it. They argued that the progressive elements in traditional, Gladstonian Liberalism could be expanded to embrace the demands of the times. An important voice in the formulation of such thinking was J.A. Hobson. Writing in 1909, he summed up the essential change of attitude:

> Liberalism is now formally committed to a task which certainly involves a new conception of the State in its relation to the individual life and to private enterprise. From the standpoint which best presents its continuity with earlier Liberalism, it appears as a fuller appreciation and realisation of individual liberty contained in the provision of equal opportunities for self-development. But to this individual standpoint must be joined a just apprehension of the social, viz., the insistence that these claims or rights of self-development must be adjusted to the sovereignty of social welfare.
>
> J.A. Hobson, *The Crisis of Liberalism*, 1909

What Hobson meant by 'the sovereignty of social welfare' was that New Liberalism had accepted that social reform was now its paramount policy. Personal liberty and freedom of enterprise remained valid objectives, but the rights of the individual must not be pursued at the expense of the general social good. Equal opportunity through social reform ought now to be the goal of Liberal policies.

Writing in 1909, Hobson had the luxury of knowing that in the three years since their victory in the 1906 election the Liberal Party had clearly committed itself to 'the sovereignty of social welfare'.

Key term

Mandate
Authority from the people to follow a particular set of policies.

Key question
In what ways were the reforms the implementation of New Liberalism?

Key figure

Herbert Asquith (1852–1928)
Home Secretary 1892–95, Chancellor of the Exchequer 1905–08, Liberal Party leader 1908–1926, Prime Minister 1908–1916.

b) The social and economic reforms of the Liberals, 1906–11

It was Campbell-Bannerman, prime minister from 1905 to 1908, who set the Liberals on the path to reform by claiming that the 1906 election had given the party a **mandate** to pursue the radical policies for which the New Liberals had pressed. The pace of reform quickened still more in 1908 when Campbell Bannerman retired and was replaced by **Herbert Asquith**, who was to remain Prime Minister for the next eight years. What proved to be one of the new leader's shrewdest moves was the appointment of the radical David Lloyd George as Chancellor of the Exchequer. Lloyd George brought a bustling energy to the Government's programme. He and the equally dynamic Winston Churchill, who took over from him at the Board of Trade, were largely responsible for the reputation that the pre-1914 Liberal government gained as a great reforming ministry.

The main Liberal social reforms, 1906–11

1906   *Trade Disputes Act* – reversed the Taff Vale decision by protecting union funds from claims for damages arising from strikes.

1906   *Education Act* – empowered local education authorities (LEAs) to provide school meals for 'needy' children. Yet, since the measure was not compulsory, only a third of LEAs were providing meals by 1911.

1907   *Education Act* – introduced compulsory medical examinations; children had to be examined at least three times during their school years.

1907–12 A set of measures improved conditions in prisons, created the probation service and ended imprisonment for debt.

1908   *Children's Act* – created special provisions for young offenders by setting up juvenile courts and remand homes. This measure became known as the '*Children's Charter*' because, along with the Education Acts of 1906 and 1907, it helped to establish the principle that the needs of children were to be separately examined and treated. The belief was that it was by improving the conditions of the young and treating their offences in a specially understanding way that 'national efficiency' was to be achieved.

1908   *Old Age Pensions Act* (see below).

1909   '*The People's Budget*' (see page 23).

1909   *Trade Boards Act* – laid down minimum wages in the notorious **'sweated'** industries.

1909   *Labour Exchanges Act* – provided easily accessible centres where employers could advertise jobs and workers could go to be advised on what positions were available. The aim was to take away the uncertainty and hit-and-miss nature of the job market.

1909   A *Development Commission* was set up to organise the funding of State welfare.

1911   *National Insurance Act* (see page 24).

1911   *Shops Act* – established the legal right of shop workers to a weekly half-day holiday.

Asquith led Liberal Reform programme: 1908–11

Key date

'Sweated' Unhealthy, overcrowded premises where unscrupulous employers running businesses, such as clothing manufacture, exploited cheap, often immigrant, labour.

Key term

Inspiring much of the legislation introduced in this period was the Royal Commission on Poverty, which sat between 1905 and 1909. It was this body that collected and presented to parliament the evidence on which the reforms were based.

In the list above there are three particular measures that most directly illustrate the character of the Liberals' approach to social welfare: old age pensions, 'the People's Budget' and National Insurance.

Old age pensions, 1908
- Granted 5s (25p) a week to people over 70 years of age who had incomes of less than £31.10s (£31.50) a year and who had not previously received help from the Poor Law.
- The pension was non-contributory, i.e. it was funded entirely from government revenues.

Key question
Why did the 1909 budget cause fierce controversy?

'The People's Budget', 1909

Paying pensions to the elderly was not a new idea. Other countries, Germany and New Zealand, for example, had already adopted them, and they had been considered by all the parties, including the Conservatives, during the previous twenty years. It could be argued, therefore, that far from being a dramatic new move, the introduction of pensions was a long overdue measure. But what made them so contentious in 1908 was not the principle behind them, but the method of paying for them. To meet the cost of the old age pensions Lloyd George planned to raise revenue by increased taxation of the propertied classes. This was the purpose of his 1909 budget, which became known as 'the People's Budget'.

The main terms were:

- standard rate of income tax to be raised from 9d (4p) to 1s 3d (7p) in the pound on incomes up to £3,000 p.a.
- a new 'super tax' of 6d (3p) in the pound on incomes over £5,000 p.a.
- death duties to be paid on estates valued at over £5,000
- a twenty per cent levy on the unearned increase in land values
- increased taxation on the sale of alcohol, tobacco and motor cars.

It was the proposal to impose death duties and to tax increases on land values that aroused the bitter opposition of the propertied classes. The Conservatives attacked the budget by asserting that in taxing the landowners so heavily Lloyd George was deliberately waging class war. He retaliated by claiming that it was indeed a war budget, but not of the kind described by the Conservatives:

> This is a war budget. It is for raising money to wage implacable warfare against poverty and squalidness. I cannot help hoping and believing that before this generation has passed away we shall have advanced a great step towards that good time when poverty and wretchedness and human degradation which always follow in its camp will be as remote to the people of this country as the wolves which once infested the forests.
>
> From a speech in the House of Commons, 1909

Yet his incensed opponents claimed that there was hypocrisy behind his passionate words. They had a case; only a portion of the proposed revenue from the budget was earmarked for pensions. The greater part of the £16 million that Lloyd George was hoping to raise was to go towards the cost of new warships that were being built for the navy.

What intensified the battle between the parties was the free trade versus protection argument, which was still the dominating economic issue of the day. To maintain themselves as a free-trade party it was essential for the Liberals to be able to pay for their welfare programme without resorting to trade tariffs. For their part, the Conservatives realised that they would lose the protectionist argument if the Liberal government were to succeed in raising the necessary revenue through domestic taxation.

The Conservatives therefore organised a Budget Protest League in the country, while in the Commons they delayed the budget in a long ten-week debate. Even though the Government eventually pushed it through, the Conservatives were far from broken-spirited. They took comfort from knowing that their colleagues in the House of Lords would throw the budget out when it reached them there.

The National Insurance Act, 1911

The principal terms of the Act:

- It covered workers aged between 16 and 60 who earned less than £160 a year against sickness and unemployment.
- It did not apply to all industries, but only to building, engineering and ship building – covering three million workers.
- Sickness benefit of 10 shillings (50p) for men, and 7s 6d (35p) for women was to be paid for a period of 26 weeks.
- A maternity grant of 3s (15p) was set up.

How the money was to be raised:

- The scheme was to be funded by compulsory weekly contributions: 4d (2p) from the employer, 3d (1.5p) from the employee and 2d (1p) from the state.
- Contributions were to be paid by buying adhesive stamps which were then affixed to a card.

Key question
Why did the intended recipients of national insurance initially oppose it?

National Insurance: The Dawn of Hope – Liberal Party poster, 1911. Lloyd George in his best bedside manner shows the sick patient that National Insurance will protect him. What point is the cartoon making by portraying Lloyd George as a doctor?

Interestingly, the National Insurance Act met strong resistance from the very people it was intended to benefit. Its compulsory character was particularly disturbing to the five-and-a-half million people, many of them working class, who already paid privately into schemes run by insurance companies, **friendly societies** and trade unions. The workers doubted that they were going to gain more from an imposed State plan than from their own private insurance. The popular press attacked the compulsory contributions as theft from the workers' pay packets.

Lloyd George responded by claiming that the workers were 'getting 9d for 4d'. As the originator of the scheme, Lloyd George showed remarkable skill in meeting the objections to it. He quietened the protests from the insurance companies who feared losing out to the State scheme by making them an integral part of the operation of the new plans. He was also able to overcome the complaints of the Labour Party, who had wanted national insurance to be paid for by higher taxes on the wealthy. Lloyd George pacified Labour by promising to introduce payment for MPs, a commitment which he honoured in 1911 (see page 38).

The resistance of the workers and the Labour Party to measures, which were supposedly in their interest, is at first sight surprising. What it shows is that attitudes to welfare reform in the Edwardian period were often complex. It is notable that Churchill's Trade Boards Act of 1909, which aimed at providing minimum wages in the 'sweated' industries, was also initially opposed by the unions because they feared that the effect of a minimum wage would be job cuts by the employers. The minimum wage was also seen as undermining the customary right of unions to negotiate **differentials**. It was a similar dislike of the State's interference between employer and worker that led the unions to look suspiciously at the labour exchanges introduced by Churchill in 1909.

The suspicious reaction of the working-class people was understandable. They had a well-founded distrust of State intervention, which they saw as patronising and disruptive. Their practical experience of officialdom in the nineteenth century, in such developments as the workhouse, compulsory education and vaccination, had seldom been a happy one. Too often they felt they were being pushed around by State-employed snoopers. Workers suspected that State welfare was primarily intended to keep them in their place and make them conform. R.H. Tawney, one of the outstanding social historians of his day and a strong Labour Party supporter, explained the workers' reasoning:

> The middle- and upper-class view in social reform is that it should regulate the worker's *life* in order that he may *work* better. The working-class view of economic reform is that it should regulate his *work*, in order that he may have a change of *living*. Hence to working people licensing reform, insurance acts, etc. seems beginning at the wrong end.
>
> R.H. Tawney, *Ethical Socialism*, 1920

Key terms

Friendly societies
Non-profit-making bodies which pooled contributions from members and paid out when members were in need.

Differentials
Separate rates of pay for different levels of skill.

c) The Liberals' achievement

The Liberal social-reform programme has come to be seen as a key stage on the path to the modern **welfare state**. Introduced in the face of strong opposition, and in some cases rejected by the people they had been primarily intended to aid, the reforms were not as sweeping or as radical as some new Liberals had wanted. Nevertheless, collectively they were a considerable achievement. They had established that it was the responsibility of government to provide for people who could not provide for themselves. They had pointed Britain in the direction it was to follow for the rest of the century.

It is worth restating the main Liberal social reforms: old age pensions, labour exchanges and National Insurance. These did not create a full welfare state; the resources simply did not exist for that, but the Liberals had taken significant steps towards what has been termed 'the social service state', a centrally organised administration capable of improving the living and working conditions of large portions of the British population.

Yet we must be careful not to confuse intention with achievement. We must not assume that the Liberals dealt effectively with poverty simply because that is what they set out to do. It may be that we have been too impressed by the amount of legislation they introduced and have not paid sufficient attention to how well it actually worked. That is a point strongly made by a modern analyst, David Vincent, who suggests that, despite the good will and energy that the Liberals put into their reform programme, little real improvement had occurred in the conditions of the nation's underprivileged.

> The incidence of poverty and the basic strategies the poor adopted to cope with their problems changed very little between the end of the Boer War and the outbreak of the Great War. The neighbourhood remained for the poor as essential and inadequate a means of support as it had done in the latter part of the nineteenth century. **Pawnbroking** reached its peak as the Edwardian period came to an end. The concept of 'foundations' [of the welfare state] which is so often deployed in accounts of poverty legislation before 1914 is in many ways inaccurate.
>
> Quoted in P. Burgland, *Poor Citizens: The State and the Poor in the Twentieth Century,* 1991

Key question
Did the Liberal social reforms mark the beginning of the welfare state in Britain?

Welfare state
A fully funded state programme to provide the essential social, health and educational needs of all its people, regardless of their income or social status.

Pawnbroking
Exchanging items for money in the hope that they can be later reclaimed by paying back the original sum with interest added.

Key terms

Summary diagram: The Liberal Party, 1906–11

The Liberal party's crisis of identity
New Liberalism v Gladstonian Liberalism

The character of New Liberalism
The sovereignty of social welfare

The definitive reforms

Old age pensions   The 'People's Budget'   National Insurance

The battle over the People's Budget
↓
Reactions to the National Insurance Act
↓
The Liberal social reforms in perspective
↓
How successfully did the Liberals' welfare programme tackle poverty?

4 | The Labour Party, 1906–11

Key question
What were the main features of the Labour Party in 1900?

Key date

LRC formed: 1900

In the second half of the nineteenth century, parliamentary reform had extended the vote to a growing number of working men. The Liberals had been confident that these new voters would support them as the only party in parliament who understood the workers. Initially, this tended to happen. However, by 1900 a view had developed among working-class organisations that the Liberal Party represented too many interests to be able to concentrate fully on the needs of the workers and, in any case, as an essentially middle-class party, did not really understand the problems faced by ordinary working people and their families.

What was needed, therefore, was a completely separate political party devoted solely to representing and defending the working class. The result of such thinking was the coming together in 1900 of a variety of reforming and radical groups to form the Labour Representation Committee (LRC). Six years later, the LRC adopted the title of the Labour Party.

Principal groups that merged to form the Labour Party in 1906:

- the trade unions, which wanted a distinct political party to represent them
- the Social Democratic Federation (SDF), led by **H.M. Hyndman**, which wanted class war against the ruling establishment
- the Socialist League, similar to the SDF in its revolutionary aim
- the Fabians (intellectuals such as George Bernard Shaw), who wanted to spread socialism not by revolution but through propaganda and education
- the Independent Labour Party (ILP), founded by **James Keir Hardie** in 1893 and strongly influenced by Christian values in its desire to change Britain into a fair and moral society
- the **co-operative societies**, set up to protect the working class against capitalist exploitation by operating a wholesale system in which any dividends (profits) were shared among the customers.

Of the groups that made up the Labour Party, the trade unions were the most significant. It was they who provided the bulk of the funds and the members. Without trade union backing there would not have been a viable Labour Party. It was the formal resolution of the **TUC**, in 1899, to work for the organisation of a parliamentary party specifically for workers that enabled the Labour Party to become a reality in 1906.

Not all the unions had accepted the move; some doubted the wisdom of following the parliamentary path. However, the anti-union Taff Vale decision (see page 10) appeared to be a dramatic vindication of the TUC's decision. It greatly strengthened the argument for a new political party to plead the unions' cause. By 1903, 127 unions had **affiliated** to the Labour Representation Committee. The Taff Vale decision had stifled the doubts regarding the wisdom of unions engaging in political as opposed to industrial action and had forged the historic link between the trade union movement and the Labour Party.

Some historians suggest that this marks the beginning of 'class' politics in Britain; the suggestion being that the awareness of the working class of its own potential became the most significant factor in electoral politics.

The Labour Party, 1900–14

Judging that it was too small to have a realistic chance of getting into government on its own, the young Labour Party calculated that its best chance of gaining political influence was by co-operating with the Liberals. One outcome of this was the **Lib–Lab pact** of 1903. Some Labour supporters were not very impressed with this compromise and felt that the party had condemned itself to being a weak pressure group.

Key figures

H.M. Hyndman (1842–1921)
A strong advocate of the ideas of the German revolutionary, Karl Marx, who believed the workers should unite to overthrow the capitalist system.

James Keir Hardie (1856–1915)
A staunch Christian who believed that politics should be about the creation of social justice; he was the first chairman of the Labour Party from 1906 to 1908.

Key terms

Co-operative societies
Formed in the nineteenth century to run shops and stores as non-profit-making ventures providing workers with food at affordable prices.

TUC
Trades Union Congress – the body created in 1868 to represent the unions collectively.

Key question
Did the Labour Party make any significant contribution to politics before 1914?

Key term

Affiliated
Formally joined to an organisation.

Table 1.5: LRC and Labour Party membership, 1900–14

	Number of members through trade union affiliation	*Number of individual members*	*Total*
1900	353,000	23,000	376,000
1901	455,000	14,000	469,000
1902	847,000	14,000	861,000
1903	956,000	14,000	970,000
1904	885,000	15,000	900,000
1905	904,000	17,000	921,000
1906	975,000	23,000	998,000
1907	1,050,000	22,000	1,072,000
1908	1,127,000	32,000	1,159,000
1909	1,451,000	35,000	1,486,000
1910	1,394,000	35,000	1,429,000
1911	1,502,000	37,000	1,539,000
1912	1,858,000	37,000	1,895,000
1913	*	*	*
1914	1,572,000	40,000	1,612,000

*The Osborne Judgment (see page 31) made figures unavailable for 1913

Table 1.6: Number of trade union members

1900	1,911,000
1905	1,967,000
1910	2,477,000
1911	2,565,000
1912	3,139,000
1913	3,416,000
1914	4,135,000

What the tables clearly show is how heavily dependent the Labour
Party was on the trade unions for sustaining its membership.
Another interesting indicator is that until 1914 it was very much a
minority of trade unionists who had joined the party. The Labour
Party was in the odd position of being reliant on the trade unions
and yet unable to win the majority of them over to its side.

Yet, despite the pessimism this induced in some supporters, the
Labour Party had made progress. By 1910, it had 42 MPs in the
House of Commons compared with 30 in 1906. The party seemed
to be more than holding its own. In the period before 1914, the
number of trade unions affiliating themselves to the party
continued to grow. This meant an increase both in the number of
party members and in the party's funds. Since one of the unions
that joined was the powerful Miners' Federation, there were firm
grounds for claiming that the party was becoming increasingly
representative of the workers.

Labour also appeared to benefit from the political situation
created by the 1910 election results which had ended the Liberal
government's parliamentary majority (see Table 2.1 on page 39).

Asquith's Liberals now had to keep on working terms with Labour and the Irish Nationalists in case they needed their support in a Commons vote. This did not give Labour an overwhelming influence and it did not mean that it was in any sense a party of government, but it did mean the Liberals had a radical rival in the country.

Labour's difficulties

Yet there was a sense in which Labour suffered from the **hung parliament** produced by the 1910 elections. The Liberal government certainly wanted the support of the Labour MPs but it was not dependent on it. It was the Irish Nationalists, whose 82 MPs outnumbered Labour's by two to one, whom Asquith's government were most concerned to placate. How strong a rival Labour would become nobody could foretell at this stage. In the years 1910–14 the omens were not particularly favourable. In the second election of 1910 Labour's vote slumped and it failed to win a single by-election in the following four years, its failures reducing its number of parliamentary seats by 4 to 38. There were fears that the party would remain merely a fringe movement or wither away altogether.

Hung parliament A situation in which no single party has an overall majority in the House of Commons.

Key term

Divisions within the party

Part of the problem was that, small though it was, the Labour Party, as its origins showed, was an amalgam of interests rather than a party with one clearly defined aim. Its left-wing Marxist element was angered by the party's willingness to support the Liberal government's measures and its reluctance to adopt a revolutionary stance in parliament.

However, the moderates found the Left's talk of revolution tiresomely unrealistic; as they saw it, the actual situation demanded that Labour first establish its credibility as a parliamentary party with the electorate. This could not be achieved by pretending that the party would be swept to power by the electors in a wave of revolutionary fervour. British politics did not work that way. Of course, principles were important, but to turn these into realisable goals a mixture of patience and political opportunism was necessary.

For their part, the trade unionists, in the main hard-bitten working-class men, were often exasperated by the revolutionary socialists in the party, who were strong on ideas but who were invariably middle-class intellectuals who had never done a proper job. The great majority of trade unionists wanted a Labour party that would make its main task the increase of workers' pay and the improvement of conditions. They were not concerned with political theory but with immediate material gains. As one worker put it: 'Party's task is not t'natter on but to put food in ours bellies and clothes on ours backs.'

The gap between the workers and the intellectuals, and the dispute between the moderate centre and the revolutionary Left over the aims and methods to be followed, were to prove defining characteristics of the Labour Party over the next hundred years.

Labour's attitude towards the Liberal reforms

It has often been claimed that Labour had a major input into the Liberals' social and economic reforms of the pre-war period. However, the evidence does not suggest that any of the measures were introduced primarily because of Labour Party influence, or that the Government needed Labour's support to get the legislation through parliament. So strong was the commitment of the Liberals to social reform at this time that the measures would have doubtless been adopted even had there been no Labour MPs in the Commons.

Moreover, there were occasions when Labour showed a deep suspicion of the reforms (see page 25). For example, **Beatrice Webb**, a leading Fabian, opposed the National Insurance Act of 1911 on the grounds that working-class voters were 'too dull witted to understand [it]' and that 'millions of public money will be wastefully collected and wastefully spent [on the] wholesale demoralisation of character through the fraudulent withholding or the fraudulent getting of benefits'.

The most that can be claimed is that the presence in the Commons of a group of Labour MPs indicated the temper of the times. It was in that sense that the Labour Party might be said to have had an influence, not as a promoter of any particular reform, but as a reminder that Britain was moving into the age of welfare with the needs of the deprived classes becoming an issue that no party could afford to ignore. Lloyd George had put this very clearly in 1904 before the Liberals came to power:

> We have a great Labour Party sprung up. Unless we [Liberals] can prove, as I think we can, that there is no necessity for a separate party in order to press forward the legitimate claims of labour, then you will find that the Liberal Party will be practically wiped out.

Labour's record before 1914

In the light of the subsequent replacement of the Liberals by Labour, Lloyd George's warning seems prophetic. But that is only because we know what was to come. In 1914, contemporaries had no reason for regarding the Labour Party as having been especially successful. It may have returned MPs to parliament, but these had achieved little. Its membership may have grown, but this was largely a result of trade union affiliation, not because the party had become popular in the country at large.

Significantly, it had played no meaningful part in the industrial disputes that troubled Britain between 1911 and 1914 (see page 44). This was not so much a lack of will as a failure of confidence. The Labour Party felt hamstrung by the **Osborne Judgment**, which, like the earlier Taff Vale decision, indicated the anti-worker bias that then prevailed in English law. It is true that Asquith's government in 1913 introduced an Act reversing the judgement. However, Labour could claim little direct credit for this even though they were the beneficiaries since the measure entitled the party to resume

Key figure

Beatrice Webb (1858–1943)
Writer and dedicated, if patronising, social reformer who worked with her husband, Sidney Webb, to advance a range of socialist causes.

Key term

Osborne Judgment, 1910
An appeal court ruling that it was illegal for a trade union to use its funds for political purposes, i.e. to support a political party or to pay candidates or MPs.

receiving funds from the unions with the proviso that individual union members could contract out from paying the **'political levy'**.

The inglorious performance of the Labour Party in this period, when it too often appeared a mere bystander in the dramatic conflict between bosses and workers, led a significant number of trade unionists to murmur that, since Labour was so ineffectual, the better option was for the workers to fight for their rights, not through parliamentary representation, but by direct action on the streets and in the factories.

Yet, in spite of its poor pre-1914 performance, historians sympathetic to the Labour Party have tended to regard its rise as logical and natural, if not inevitable. This is an interesting but controversial viewpoint since it largely relies on hindsight and tends to ignore the way people at the time viewed matters. The Labour Party's record in its short history up to 1914 was not impressive. Beatrice Webb commented in 1913:

> The parliamentary Labour Party is in a bad way and has not justified its existence either by character or intelligence, and it is doubtful whether it will hold the Trade Unions. The Labour and Socialist movement is in a state of disruption.
>
> Quoted in P. Adelman, *The Rise of the Labour Party 1880–1945*, 1996

A year later she added, 'if we are honest, we have to admit that the party has failed'. She was referring to Labour's failure to establish itself as a distinct and separate alternative to the Liberals as representative of working-class hopes. There were certainly no clear reasons for thinking that the party was destined for political power. Without hindsight, nobody could foresee the great shift in British politics that would be brought about by the 1914–18 war. It was to be the war that would make it possible for the Labour Party to displace the Liberals as the major radical force in Britain.

Key term

'Political levy'
The portion of a member's union subscription that went to the Labour Party.

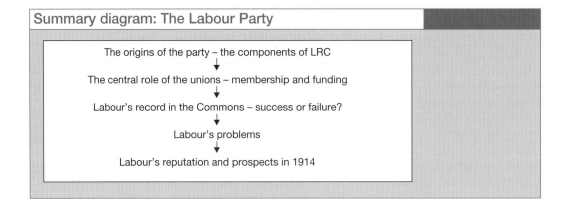

Summary diagram: The Labour Party

The origins of the party – the components of LRC
↓
The central role of the unions – membership and funding
↓
Labour's record in the Commons – success or failure?
↓
Labour's problems
↓
Labour's reputation and prospects in 1914

Study Guide: AS Questions

In the style of AQA

(a) Explain why tariff reform was an important issue in the 1906 election campaign. (12 marks)

(b) How far were the Liberal welfare reforms of 1906–14 inspired by ideological motives? (24 marks)

Exam tips

The cross-references are intended to take you straight to the material that will help you to answer the questions.

(a) Look again at pages 13–15. You will need to explain why Tariff reform was so divisive in 1906 and should consider the views of Chamberlain and the effect of his campaigns on:

- economists/imperialists
- industrialists and manufacturers and those concerned with trade (middle classes)
- working people (explain the link to social welfare/low taxation and cheap foodstuffs as well as provision of jobs)
- the Conservative Party and the opportunity for the Liberals to exploit Conservative weakness.

(b) To answer this question you will need to consider not only ideological motives but also the other motives behind the Liberals' welfare reforms. Your task is to assess whether ideological concerns were of greater importance than other factors. Firstly, you should explain what the ideological concerns were. Look at pages 18–21 and explain the extent to which the ideology of New Liberalism influenced the party after 1906.

Other factors might include:

- the problem of poverty and social surveys by Booth and Rowntree (see page 3)
- national efficiency (see page 3)
- Britain's flagging international position (pages 4–5)
- the influence of the (new) Labour Party (pages 27–30 and 31)
- you might also consider how 'new' the welfare reforms actually were. Look at page 18 and see what had come before.

Consider the reforms individually and in total (pages 21–26 and the assessment on page 26 should help here). Try to arrive at a clear and substantiated conclusion.

In the style of OCR
England in a New Century 1900–24
Study the five sources on tariff reform, taxation and the People's Budget, then answer both sub-questions. It is recommended that you spend two-thirds of your time in answering part (b).

(a) Study Sources B and C.
Compare these sources as evidence for differing views on the advantages of free trade. (30 marks)

(b) Study all the sources.
Use your own knowledge to assess how far the sources support the interpretation that tariff reform offered an acceptable solution to England's economic and social problems during this period. (70 marks)

Tariff reform, taxation and the People's Budget
Source A
Joseph Chamberlain, speech in Glasgow, 1903
The leader of the tariff reform movement argues his case for imperial preference and against free trade:

We have to consolidate the British race. We have to meet the clash of competition. I tell you that all is not well with British industry. The USA and Germany are doing better than us in exports. We are sending less and less of our manufactures to them; and they are sending more and more to us. This means that our Imperial trade is essential to our prosperity; and it is only by a system of Colonial Preference that we can preserve our ties with the Empire. Through Preference, we will retain customers, and provide employment at home. In return, we must tax food. This would add about four pence a week to a worker's expenditure: but only if he should pay the whole of the new duties which I propose. However, I propose no duties on corn coming from the Empire. And, with lower duties on tea and sugar, in practice a working man may be no worse off than before.

Source B
H.H. Asquith, speech in Gloucestershire, 1903
The senior Liberal politician who led the party's opposition to Chamberlain's tariff reform campaign makes the case for keeping the policy of free trade:

You cannot retaliate against your foreign competitors without taxing raw materials and food. Tariff Reform is a proposal to tax British industry, to tax the food of the people, and so lower their wages. It is a scheme based on unproved assumptions. In fact, there is no ground for saying either that British trade is stagnating and in decline, or that the Empire can only be maintained by going back to measures of Protection which were found inadequate in earlier times. Instead of raising the price of bread, let us try to raise the standard of life. Temperance, reform and the taxation of land: these should be the aims of the Liberal Party.

Source C
A policy statement of the Labour Party, 1906
The Labour Party explains its position on economic and social policy:

We are more than Free Traders. We do not regard Free Trade alone as offering a solution to the problem of poverty. As a policy, it is economically sound, and so we support it in the present crisis. It is right as far as it goes. Free Trade has helped us to accumulate national wealth, but the Labour party must now add other policies to Free Trade to enable us to distribute that wealth equally.

Source D
The Labour Party manifesto for the general election, 1906
The Labour Party manifesto outlines the main ambitions of the Labour Party on the eve of the general election:

This election is to decide if Labour is to be fairly represented. The House of Commons is supposed to be the people's House, and yet the people are not there. The elderly poor are neglected, and so are underfed school children. The slums are still everywhere. The unemployed asked for work, but the Conservative government gave them a worthless Act. The government suggests Protection, but that is no remedy for poverty and unemployment. We urge you to forget all differences, and vote Labour.

Source E
David Brooks, The Age of Upheaval, *1995*
A modern historian comments on the position of the political parties on trade and taxation in the general election of January 1910:

By 1910, the Liberals claimed to have shown that Britain could keep Free Trade, and afford expensive social reforms, in a way that Tariff Reformers had been declaring impossible since 1903. However, the recession of 1908–09 allowed the Conservatives to campaign for Tariff Reform as a cure for unemployment. They also emphasised the unfairness of the People's Budget which taxed not only agriculture, but the working man's beer and tobacco. Tariffs would spread the financial burden more evenly than narrow and selective taxation.

Exam tips

(a) You have to show that you have understood the content of the two sources. You do not have to use your own knowledge but you must infer from the evidence contained in the sources. Keep your answer concise and make use of the information concerning the authors of the sources and the intended audience. For example:

- Source B represents the view of the Liberal Party whereas Source C is a typical Labour attitude towards free trade.
- In 1906 the newly formed Labour Party was keen to win as many votes as possible by distancing itself from the Liberal view on free trade but without rejecting the policy completely. Source B, on the other hand, states the case against tariff reform.

(b) You need to balance an analysis of all five sources with your own knowledge to answer the question set. Use your knowledge to demonstrate the strengths and limitations of the sources in terms of their completeness and value as explanations. Offer a judgement based on the general consistency and completeness of the sources as a set. For instance, you might refer to:

- the different and biased attitudes of the political parties evident in Sources A, B, C and D, and comment on the reasons for their respective stances.
- Source E, which sums up the different views but also considers the situation by 1910, four years after the Liberal reforms.

2 Crisis, War and its Consequences – Britain, 1911–18

POINTS TO CONSIDER

Between 1911 and 1914 the Liberal government had to contend with a series of deeply disruptive crises at home. Before these were all fully resolved, Britain found itself at war with Germany from 1914 to 1918, an experience that proved highly formative, politically, socially and economically. In this chapter the pre-war crises and the impact and the consequences of the 1914–18 war are studied in four main sections:

- The pre-war crises, 1911–14
- The politics of Britain at war, 1914–18
- The impact of the war on the political parties
- The Home Front, 1914–18

Key dates

1911–14		Period of acute domestic crises
1911		Parliament Act
1914–18		First World War
1914	August	Britain declared war on Germany
		Parties agreed to a political truce
1915–16		Unsuccessful Gallipoli Campaign
1915	March	Treasury Agreement
	May	Coalition government formed under Asquith
1916	January	Conscription introduced
	July–Nov	Battle of the Somme
	December	Conservatives withdrew support from Asquith
		Lloyd George became PM and formed new Coalition government
		War Cabinet formed
1917	April	U-boat menace threatened Britain's life-line

1918	February	Representation of the People Act Adoption of the Labour Party constitution
	May	Lloyd George survived the Maurice Debate
	November	Armistice on the Western Front
	December	Lloyd George won the 'Coupon Election'

1 | The Pre-War Crises, 1911–14

The Liberals' reforming energy was sustained until 1914, but from 1911 onwards Asquith's government had to contend with a serious set of problems which tended to overshadow its achievements in social welfare provision. A notable feature of government policy from 1911 was its concern with the constitutional and industrial-relations issues that dominated the political scene.

Chief political and constitutional reforms, 1911–14:

Key question
Why did Liberal Britain experience a series of major social and political crises during this period?

- 1911 The introduction of payment for MPs (initially, £400 p.a.). This allowed those without a private income to consider standing for parliament
- 1911 Parliament Act removed the power of the House of Lords to veto Bills passed by the House of Commons
- 1912 Act granting Home Rule for Ireland
- 1913 Trade Union Act allowed union funds to be used for political purposes
- 1914 Act disestablishing the Welsh Church.

A period of acute domestic crises: 1911–14

Key date

Four major crises occupied the Liberals in the period from 1911–14:

a) The conflict between the Lords and Commons
b) The suffragette crisis
c) Industrial strife
d) The Ulster crisis.

These proved so disruptive that they threatened the social and political order itself. The severity of the crises has been interpreted by some observers as evidence of the failure of the Liberals to deal with the problems of their time.

a) The conflict between the Lords and Commons, 1910–11

Arguably, a major struggle between the House of Commons and the House of Lords became unavoidable once the Liberals had won their landslide victory in 1906. Unable to outvote the Government in the Commons, the Conservative opposition had reverted to using its in-built majority in the Lords to block measures to which it objected. Matters came to a head in the controversy over the People's Budget of 1909, in which Lloyd

Key question
How justified were the Lords in resisting the People's Budget and the Parliament Bill?

George had proposed special taxes on rich landowners to pay for old age pensions (see page 23).

The Unionists decided to resist the budget on the grounds that it was an unprecedented attack upon the rights of property. They argued that this entitled them to ignore the long-standing **convention** that the Lords did not interfere with finance bills. Lloyd George, Chancellor of the Exchequer and a strong opponent of aristocratic privilege, thought the whole affair could be turned to the Liberals' advantage. He led the Liberals in denouncing the peers' attempt to maintain their privileges at the expense of the old and the poor of the nation. In a memorable turn of phrase he mocked the Lords for being not, as the peers claimed, 'the watchdog of the constitution' but 'Mr Balfour's poodle'.

In a brilliant speech in 1909, in which he appealed for justice and fairness, Lloyd George savaged the peers for opposing the will of the British people.

> Who made ten thousand people owners of the soil, and the rest of us trespassers in the land of our birth? Who is it who is responsible for the scheme of things whereby one man is engaged through life in grinding labour to win a bare and precarious subsistence for himself, and when, at the end of his days, he claims at the hands of the community he served a poor pension of eight pence a day, he can only get it through a revolution, and another man who does not toil receives every hour of the day, every hour of the night, whilst he slumbers, more than his poor neighbour receives in a whole year of toil?
>
> Lloyd George, a speech in Newcastle, October 1909

Key term

Convention
Since Britain does not have a written constitution, matters are decided by referring to traditional practice or convention.

Victory for the Government

The Lords lost the battle that followed. In 1910, after two general elections had produced a stalemate that left the Liberals still in office, since they could rely on the support of the Irish Nationalist and Labour MPs, the peers reluctantly allowed Lloyd George's budget through. They were promptly presented with a parliament Bill, which set out to limit their powers.

Table 2.1: 1910 election results

January/February	Votes	Seats	% of total votes cast
Conservatives	3,127,887	273	46.9
Liberals	2,880,581	275	43.2
Labour	505,657	40	7.6
Irish Nationalists	124,586	82	1.9
December	Votes	Seats	% of total votes cast
Conservatives	2,420,566	272	46.3
Liberals	2,295,888	272	43.9
Labour	371,772	42	7.1
Irish Nationalists	131,375	84	2.5

Main terms of the Parliament Act, 1911:

Parliament Act: 1911

Key date

- The delaying power of the Lords was to be restricted to two years.
- A Bill sent up by the Commons in three consecutive sessions would become law even though it might be rejected by the Lords.
- General elections were to be held at least once in every five years instead of once in every seven.

For well over a year the Lords resisted, arguing that the 1910 elections had failed to give Asquith's government a clear mandate for such radical change. Added tension was created by the awareness on both sides that were the Lords' veto to be removed, there would be nothing to prevent the Liberals from forcing Irish Home Rule through parliament.

Eventually, in August 1911, in the middle of a heatwave that was so fierce that it melted the peers' starched collars, the Lords gave in. What finally pushed them was the threat of being swamped by 500 new Liberal peers whom the new king, George V, agreed, at Asquith's request, to create if the Lords' resistance continued. Even then, the narrow majority of 17 was achieved only by the decision of 37 Conservative peers to vote for the Bill rather than suffer the 'pollution' of their House.

The Lords' argument

For the sake of balance, the argument of the peers who resisted needs to be understood in its historical setting. The use of the Lords' veto to block the budget was not simply blind reaction on the part of the Conservatives. They asserted that the only way the free-trade Liberals could pay for their ambitious schemes was by resorting to punitive taxation of the landed class. A government, which in two elections had failed to win an overall majority in the Commons, was attempting to bypass the legitimate constitutional rights of the class under attack by improper use of the budget. What the Liberals had done was tantamount to a declaration of class war. Far from defending privilege, the Lords believed they were speaking for the legal and constitutional freedoms of the nation.

Such an argument may sound unconvincing to the modern ear, but in its time it was sincerely held by its proponents. The 'ditchers', as they were called, may have been one of history's losing sides, but their argument still commands the historian's attention.

Interestingly enough, it was at this juncture that the proposition was first heard that the constitution needed a second chamber with equal power in order to prevent the Commons from becoming an **elective tyranny**. There was an accompanying argument that to pay MPs was also a mistake since it would lead to the development of career politicians who would lose all sense of independence and simply become **lobby fodder**. Some observers have since argued that this fear has been borne out by the way in which politics developed in the twentieth century.

'Ditchers'
Those peers in 1911, who were prepared to defend their power of absolute veto to the last ditch.

Elective tyranny
The notion that an all-powerful House of Commons would not mean greater democracy but would simply allow the government of the day to use its majority to do as it wished.

Lobby fodder
MPs going through the division lobbies (i.e. voting) at their party's command regardless of the merits of the case.

Key terms

Key question
Why did the issue of 'votes for women' cause acute problems for the Liberals?

Key term

Suffragists and suffragettes
Both groups agitated for votes for women, but whereas the suffragists were opposed to violent methods, the suffragettes believed that it was only by being prepared to break the law that women could force a male-dominated parliament to respond to their demands.

b) The suffragette crisis

The right of women to vote might be thought to have been a cause that the Liberals would eagerly support. John Stuart Mill (1806–73), the great Liberal philosopher, had regarded it as an essential freedom in a civilised society. However, the fine balance between the two main parties (particularly after the elections of 1910) made many Liberals hesitate. Asquith, in particular, dragged his feet because he feared the political and electoral consequences of what would be a large and irreversible extension of the franchise.

The slowness of parliament to deal with the matter had led to the development of a **suffragist** and a **suffragette** movement. The major suffragette organisation was the Women's Social and Political Union (WSPU), founded in 1903 and led by the dynamic Emmeline Pankhurst, aided by her daughters Sylvia and Christabel. The WSPU undertook a campaign of disruption, which became increasingly violent as the Liberals persisted in their refusal to find parliamentary time to debate the question. Between 1911 and 1914, a series of suffragette outrages, including arson and physical assault, showed the degree of WSPU frustration. One of the most famous incidents occurred when a suffragette, Emily Davison, threw herself under 'Anmer', a horse owned by the King, during the running of the Derby at Epsom race course in 1913. The horse and jockey survived, but Emily died from her injuries four days later.

However, on balance, the violence probably did more harm than good. It tended to alienate moderate supporters. It also provided an excuse for the Government to impose heavy prison sentences on convicted suffragettes. The issue of votes for women was no nearer to being settled when the war intervened in 1914. Mrs Pankhurst immediately called off her campaign and dedicated herself and her followers to the war effort.

A question of prejudice?

'Votes for women' is now viewed as part of the broader campaign for female emancipation that developed in the twentieth century. It is seen as a major step in the overcoming of prejudice. There was certainly prejudice aplenty. Gladstone's wife, Catherine, had suggested that the only way women should be involved in politics was 'to help our husbands'. Marie Corelli, a popular novelist, later supported this view, asking rhetorically, 'Shall we sacrifice our Womanhood to Politics?' Far better, she thought, for women to stay in the background, supporting men in their 'victorious accomplishment of noble purpose'.

'The Cat and Mouse Act' poster of 1913, showing the bitterness with which the Act was regarded by the suffragettes. The Act allowed the authorities, without having to resort to the previous grim practice of force-feeding, to overcome the resistance of the imprisoned suffragettes who went on hunger strike. When their health deteriorated, the women were released on licence, but as soon as they had recovered they were brought back to prison. How effectively does the poster make its point?

The similar sentiments of Alfred Tennyson, England's great poet of the age, struck a chord with many Victorians, male and female: 'Man to command and women to obey; all else confusion'. Lord Salisbury thought politics was too difficult for women 'to worry their pretty little heads about', while a male doctor wrote to *The Times* newspaper in 1912 claiming that the votes for women campaign was a plot by embittered spinsters, 'strangers to joy', to get their own back on the men who would not marry them.

Key question
Why was female suffrage a politically difficult issue for all the parties?

Yet while there were undoubtedly Edwardian MPs who shared what might now be termed gender prejudice, they were not primarily concerned with the rights or wrongs of women's suffrage as a principle. Their worries were party political. For them a female electorate was an unknown quantity. They feared that it would have a harmful impact on their parliamentary strength. This worry applied to all the parties, Conservative, Liberal and Labour. They simply did not know how women would vote.

For the Labour party there was the added complication that if, as was proposed by some in an attempt to lessen tensions, the female franchise were to be phased in by granting it to selected groups of women, this would weaken the case for complete male suffrage which was the party's first priority since forty per cent of men were still without the vote in 1914.

It was also the case that the suffragettes were not always clear in their objectives and there were many disputes within the movement. Even the Pankhursts fell out. Sylvia and Christabel split the WSPU by taking opposed views over suffragette militancy and whether the movement should throw in its lot with the Labour Party. In 1910, their mother, Emmeline, appeared to have compromised her own position when she accepted a **Conciliation Bill**, which meant abandoning the idea of working-class women gaining the vote in return for parliament's granting it to women who owned or occupied property. This was doubtless a tactical move on her part, but it did illustrate how unclear the votes for women issue could be.

Key term

Conciliation Bill, 1910
A cross-party compromise on women's suffrage, which came to nothing.

Lloyd George is an interesting individual example of Liberal Party difficulties. As an MP, he supported the moderate suffragists and consistently voted in favour of the private members' bills promoting women's suffrage. But as a minister, his reactions were governed by political considerations. His worry was that if the extension of the vote was to be made, as with men, on the principle of some form of property qualification, then only middle-class women would be eligible. This he feared would chiefly benefit the Conservatives electorally. For him, it was a question of all or nothing. If women were to gain the vote, it must be all women. As was his way, he negotiated with the various interested groups with a view to reaching a settlement. His motives were not always trusted, however, and he suffered for his pains; in 1912 he was physically assaulted by a group of suffragettes and his house in Surrey was bombed.

Although Lloyd George genuinely tried to find a satisfactory agreement, his leader, Asquith, refused for too long to give ground to the central principle of female suffrage. There is little doubt that the Liberals were damaged by the suffragette issue. They claimed that it was 'a constitutional not a moral question'. But for a party that claimed to be 'the party of principle' their apparent reluctance to treat female suffrage as a matter of fundamental rights weakened their moral standing. In political terms, their failure to resolve the issue proved a major embarrassment.

c) Industrial unrest

Key question
Why did the years 1911–14 witness severe industrial strife?

Despite the Trade Disputes Act of 1906 (see page 21), the years preceding the First World War were a particularly troubled period for the trade unions. By 1912 the cost of living was fourteen per cent higher than in 1906 and unemployment had risen sharply during the same period. Despite the Liberal welfare measures, the gap between rich and poor was widening.

Furthermore, the presence of Labour Party MPs in the Commons did not appear to have brought any clear benefits to the workers. Faced with these failures, many trade unionists began to doubt whether the existing political structure could ever be made to respond to working-class needs. The belief that the legal and parliamentary systems were fundamentally hostile to their interests encouraged a number of unions to consider direct action.

Their views were reinforced by legal decisions such as the Osborne Judgment in 1910 (see page 31), which, in denying the unions the right to use their funds for political purposes, proved that the governing system had an inbuilt hostility to them. The increase in trade union membership from 1.9 million in 1900 to 4.1 million in 1914 was a measure of the growing frustration of the industrial workers. Few British workers were drawn to **syndicalism**, but in the excited atmosphere of pre-war Britain direct action became increasingly attractive to the more militant unions.

Syndicalism
A revolutionary movement calling on workers to smash the industrial–capitalist system by violent action.

Key term

The miners' strike, 1910–11

The miners, traditionally the most combative of the unions, had already in 1908 won the legal recognition of a maximum eight-hour working day. They now struck for the right to a minimum wage. The strike was particularly serious in South Wales where syndicalist influences were at their strongest. In 1910, Winston Churchill as home secretary was accused by the miners of ordering the shooting of strikers. The accusation followed an incident at Tonypandy, where a violent clash between strikers and the local police led the Chief Constable to appeal for troop reinforcements to be sent to help control the situation. Churchill did send an army detachment, as he did to other trouble spots, but this was after the worst of the rioting had occurred; at no time did he issue specific orders that soldiers should use their weapons.

The strike spreads, 1912

For Asquith's government, the most disturbing feature of the striking miners was their call for sympathetic action throughout the whole industrial workforce. The threat grew larger in the summer of 1912, when three major unions – the dockers, the railwaymen and the seamen – went on strike. It was calculated that 40 million working days were lost through stoppages in 1912. Lloyd George, the Chancellor of the Exchequer and the Government's chief negotiator, managed, however, to persuade the railway workers to end their strike in return for a wage increase and the recognition by the employers of their union rights.

The triple alliance, 1914

In a further move to appease the miners, the Government introduced legislation appointing local district wage boards which were responsible for fixing minimum wages in each region. The strike ended, but the tension remained. By 1914 the miners appeared to be coming together with the dockers and railwaymen, to form a 'triple alliance'. The alliance was unofficial and the three unions did not in fact act in unison. It was this lack of co-ordination among the unions, rather than government conciliation, that prevented the threat of a general strike materialising before 1914. Moreover, as with the suffragette and Ulster questions, the coming of the war in 1914 brought a temporary halt to the strife.

The challenge to traditional Liberal values

An interesting aspect of the industrial troubles was the willingness of the Government to intervene directly in relations between employers and workers. It was another example of the extension of state power. It was a development that would soon be hastened by war and which would challenge the thinking of those remaining Liberals who still believed in minimum government and maximum individual liberty.

Key question
Why was Ulster so bitterly opposed to Home Rule?

d) The Ulster crisis

In the nineteenth century there had been a strong movement for Home Rule among Irish Nationalists. However, the demand for independence foundered on the position of Ulster, whose largely Protestant population was not prepared to accept an Irish settlement that gave southern Catholic Ireland a controlling hand (see page 48). Gladstone, the Liberal leader, had introduced Home Rule Bills in 1886 and 1893, but both had failed to pass through parliament. His attempts had split his party and had hardened the resolve of the Unionists to reject Home Rule on the grounds that it undermined the unity of the United Kingdom and betrayed Ulster.

Hard economics also came into it. Ulster was the most industrially advanced region in Ireland. This made Nationalists determined that the area should remain part of the nation should Ireland ever be granted independence. Clearly Ulster Unionism and Irish Nationalism were incompatible.

The period following the failure of Gladstone's Home Rule Bills had been one of relative calm in Ireland, but by 1905 the situation had become dangerous again. In that year a number of radical Nationalist groups in Ireland had come together to form **Sinn Fein**, a political party which claimed that Ireland was a free nation temporarily enslaved by the British. It sought the creation of a **Dail** to rule in the name of the Irish people. According to its chief spokesman, **Arthur Griffith**, Sinn Fein's aim was to break both the political and the economic stranglehold Britain had over Ireland.

Sinn Fein regarded the Irish Nationalist MPs at Westminster as far too moderate in their approach. For Sinn Feiners, Home Rule did not go nearly far enough, since it merely gave Ireland independence in domestic affairs; they wanted complete separation from Britain. This meant there was constant conflict between the Irish Nationalist Party and Sinn Fein. Yet it was the Nationalists who gained a rapid increase in influence in 1910 after the two general elections of that year which left the Liberal government dependent on them for its parliamentary majority (see page 39). Such were the growing tensions in Ireland that Asquith's Liberal government turned again to Home Rule as the only solution.

In 1912, in a Commons evenly split between Liberals and Unionists, the Government relied on the 84 Irish Nationalists, led by **John Redmond**, to force through the Third Home Rule Bill. As was expected, the Lords refused to pass the Bill in 1913, but, since its power to veto measures passed by the Commons had been ended by the Parliament Act in 1911, there was now nothing to stop Home Rule from eventually becoming law.

(see page 39)

Table 2.2: Growing tensions over Ulster

1905	Radical Nationalist groups amalgamated to form Sinn Fein
1910	General elections left Irish MPs holding the balance in Commons
	Edward Carson elected Chairman of the Ulster Unionist Party
1911	Parliament Act ended the Lords' absolute veto
1912	Commons passed the Third Home Rule Bill
1913	Lords rejected the Home Rule Bill
	Ulster Volunteer Force formed by the Unionists
	Irish Volunteers formed by the Nationalists
1914	The Curragh Mutiny
	Britain entered First World War
	Home Rule suspended until the end of the war

Key terms

Sinn Fein
Gaelic for 'Ourselves Alone'.

Dail
Gaelic for 'Parliament'.

Key figures

Arthur Griffith (1871–1922)
An ardently anti-British socialist, who claimed that there could be no Anglo-Irish peace until Ireland was wholly independent.

John Redmond (1856–1918)
MP at Westminster, 1891–1918; led the Irish Nationalist Party from 1900 to 1918. Despite his apparent success over Home Rule in 1912, he was regarded as too conciliatory by many Irish Nationalists.

Edward Carson inspecting Ulster defence volunteers during the Irish dispute in 1914. Why were so many Unionists prepared to join or support the volunteers?

Oglaigh na hEireann.

ENROL UNDER THE GREEN FLAG.

Safeguard your rights and liberties (the few left you).

Secure more.

Help your Country to a place among the nations.

Give her a National Army to keep her there.

Get a gun and do your part.

JOIN THE

IRISH VOLUNTEERS
(President: EOIN MAC NEILL).

The local Company drills at _____

_____

Ireland shall no longer remain disarmed and impotent.

'Enrol under the Green Flag.' A facsimile of a 1914 Nationalist poster, calling on Irish patriots to enlist in the Irish National Volunteers, a counter army to the Ulster Defence Volunteers. How helpful are these two posters in explaining the tensions in Ulster in this period?

The passing of the Home Rule Bill did not fulfil Asquith's hope that it would ease the situation in Ireland. Quite the reverse; the Ulster Protestants reacted to its passing by swearing to the Covenant, a document pledging those who signed it to use 'all means which may be found necessary' to resist Home Rule for Ireland. The Covenanters claimed that the Liberal government had no electoral mandate for Home Rule. Led by **Edward Carson**, they prepared to fight to prevent what they regarded as the subjection of Protestant Ulster to the Catholic south. In 1913 they formed the Ulster Volunteer Force.

The Conservative leader, **Andrew Bonar Law**, added fuel to the flames when he declared, 'I can imagine no length of resistance to which Ulster will go, which I shall not be ready to support'. By the summer of 1914 Ireland had split into two armed camps, the nationalist Irish Volunteers confronting Carson's Ulster Volunteer Force, both engaged in gun-running to build up their stock of weapons. Civil war seemed imminent, a situation made worse by a remarkable development known as the Curragh Mutiny.

The Curragh Mutiny, 1914

In the spring of 1914, 60 British officers stationed at the Curragh army base in southern Ireland, who sympathised with the Ulster Protestants, resigned their commissions to avoid being sent north against the Ulster Volunteers. Technically this was not a mutiny since their resignations meant they were no longer in the army, but in the tense atmosphere the word was seized on by the press to show how dangerous the Irish crisis had become.

The temporary compromise, 1914

Asquith managed to defuse the situation by calling a constitutional conference in June 1914. Reluctantly, both sides agreed to consider a form of compromise. Ireland would be partitioned between:

- the Catholic south, which would be granted Home Rule
- the Protestant north, which would remain part of the United Kingdom.

Conscious of how fragile the compromise was, Asquith persisted in trying to achieve a workable solution. He proposed an Amending Bill which would suspend the operation of Home Rule in Ulster for six years. This made some headway with the moderate Unionists, but it was the coming of the European war in August that made it acceptable as an interim measure. It was agreed that while the Home Rule Bill would technically become law in September, it would be suspended for the duration of the war. This was a respite, not a permanent settlement; Ireland was destined to undergo still greater turmoil (see page 84), but it allowed the Liberals and Conservatives at Westminster to shelve their differences for the time being.

Key question
Why was Ireland on the verge of civil war in 1914?

Key figures

Edward Carson (1854–1935)
MP 1892–1918, Solicitor General 1900–05, Leader of the Ulster Unionist party 1910–21.

Andrew Bonar Law (1858–1923)
MP 1900–23, leader of Conservative Party 1911–21, PM 1922–23; the only Canadian-born British prime minister.

Key question
How great a threat were the crises of the period?

The debate on the crises of 1911–14

There was a theory, once quite fashionable, that what happened in Britain in the years immediately before 1914 was part of a general world crisis that saw political and social upheaval in all the continents. The notion was largely a product of the Marxist hypothesis that the collapse of capitalism would be accompanied by a series of desperate struggles as the ruling classes world-wide tried desperately to cling on to power.

Interesting though the notion remains, the evidence is too imprecise to substantiate it as a working theory. That similar events occur simultaneously does not prove a connection between them. The variation in local circumstances is too wide for a common cause to apply to them all.

Key debate

Did the crises mark 'The Strange Death of Liberal England'?

In 1934 a stimulating and provocative book appeared, entitled *The Strange Death of Liberal England*. Written by George Dangerfield, it argued that the pre-war crises proved that by 1914 the Liberals were incapable of dealing effectively with the social and economic pressures of the early twentieth century. The author concluded that the Liberal Party by 1914 was on the point of extinction. Other historians were keen to develop his thesis. They argued that the fierce confrontations between employers and workers, the violence of the suffragettes, the battle between Lords and Commons, and Ireland being on the verge of civil war were all signs that Britain had entered an era of 'class politics'. It was a new form of political warfare with which the Liberal Party was not equipped to cope.

Contrary views to Dangerfield's

Superficially, the extreme opposition to the Liberal governments does seem to indicate that their policies had failed to satisfy the major demands of the time. However, although Dangerfield's interpretation remains a very helpful starting point, it has been largely superseded by another school of thought which stresses that, difficult though matters were for the Liberals, they were still in office in 1914 after nine years of unbroken government.

- All challenges to their authority had been overcome.
- Contentious measures such as the People's Budget, National Insurance, the Parliament Act and Home Rule had been successfully manoeuvred through parliament.
- Asquith's cabinets had remained united throughout the troubles; no minister resigned office before 1914.
- The Conservatives, despite recovering in the 1910 elections from their landslide defeat four years earlier, had not been able to oust Asquith's government.

- Although the Conservatives made electoral gains in the south of the country, the Liberals maintained their traditional support in the industrial and working-class regions.
- The Labour party had made no serious inroads into the traditional Liberal strongholds.

It is the resurgence of the Liberal Party in this period that has been strongly emphasised by political historians Peter Clarke and Ross McKibbin. It is true that the Labour Party had grown in membership in the country at large, mainly through trade union affiliation. Yet, on its own admission, it had been only a marginal political influence before 1914. Clarke suggests that the Labour Party had begun to see its future role not so much as a separate radical force, but as a part of a Liberal–Labour 'progressive' movement.

All this tends to indicate that the problems of pre-1914 Britain were not proof of the failure of Liberal policies between 1905 and 1914. The decline of the Liberals as a political party had more to do with the impact of the Great War and the political realignment that it caused (see page 63).

Some key books in the debate:
Paul Adelman, *The Decline of the Liberal Party* (Longmans, 1995)
Peter Clarke, *A Question of Leadership: From Gladstone to Thatcher* (Penguin, 1991)
George Dangerfield, *The Strange Death of Liberal England* (Paladin, 1970)
Ross McKibbin, *The Evolution of the Labour Party* (OUP, 1974)
David Powell, *The Edwardian Crisis, Britain 1901–1914* (Macmillan, 1996)
Alan Sykes, *The Rise and Fall of British Liberalism, 1776–1988* (Longmans, 1997)
Trevor Wilson, *The Downfall of the Liberal Party* (Fontana, 1966)

Summary diagram: The pre-war crises, 1911–14

LORDS VERSUS COMMONS

Issues at stake

- Conservative power monopoly
- Irish Home Rule

VOTES FOR WOMEN

Issues at stake

- Liberal values
- The parties' electoral support
- Votes for working men

INDUSTRIAL STRIFE

Issues at stake

- Union rights
- Syndicalist threat to the state
- The political levy

ULSTER

Issues at stake

- Home Rule
- Ulster Volunteers v Irish Volunteers
- Character of island of Ireland

The debate over the crises
↓
The Strange Death of Liberal England

2 | The Politics of Britain at War, 1914–18

Key question
How did the war affect the development of British politics?

Table 2.3: Wartime governments

August 1914–May 1915	Asquith's Liberal government
May 1915–December 1916	Asquith's Coalition government
December 1916–November 1918	Lloyd George's Coalition government

Key dates

Britain declared war on Germany: August 1914

First World War: 1914–18

The 1914–18 war had profound effects on British politics in general and the Liberal Party in particular. So protracted and so draining was the **Allied struggle** against Germany that it became a **total war**, which necessitated an unprecedented extension of State authority. Notions of individual freedom and limited government meant little in the face of the State's claim to direct the lives of its people in the desperate struggle for survival. The demands of total war created a great challenge to Liberal values. The principles of personal freedom, peace and retrenchment were impossible to preserve uncompromised in wartime. The economic free-trade, non-interventionist theories that Liberals had held now seemed largely irrelevant.

Initially, the Liberals had been uncertain about whether to fight Germany but, once they had accepted the necessity of going to war, they had to adjust their political values to it. The powerful anti-war feelings expressed at the time of the Boer War (see page 9) now had to give way to the spirit of patriotism necessary to sustain the war effort. Rationing, conscription and the extension of State authority in many areas of the economy were responses to the needs of waging total war. Survival, not political theorising, was the prime objective.

The Liberal dilemma was expressed in the very first measure necessitated by the war. In August 1914, parliament rushed through the Defence of the Realm Act (DORA), which granted the State and its agencies extensive powers over the lives of ordinary citizens. DORA was regularly re-enacted during the war. Among the powers it granted were:

- government control of arms factories
- censorship of the press and restriction of freedom of information
- duties on imports
- government control of the rail and coal industries
- Ministry of Munitions set up to direct wartime industrial production
- trade unions granted greater recognition and higher wages in return for their agreement to aid the war effort by not striking
- companies required to accept restrictions on their profits and guarantee minimum wages to workers
- measures introduced to improve living standards and control rents in order to lessen social unrest
- conscription introduced, obliging males between 18 and 41 to serve in the armed forces
- food rationing imposed
- restrictions placed on the opening hours of public houses
- passports required for travel abroad
- limitations placed on freedom of movement within Britain.

The pacifist element among the Liberals had hoped that the Chancellor of the Exchequer, Lloyd George, renowned for his vehement denunciation of the Boer War, might lead an anti-war faction in the party or even in the Government. He soon disappointed them. He had had qualms about entering the war, but once Britain was involved, his commitment to it was total. One remarkable feature was that the political truce, which the parties agreed to for the duration of the war, allowed Lloyd George to develop his ideas of **consensus politics**. He was an advocate of

Key terms

Allied struggle
The main Allies were France, Russia and Britain fighting together against the Central Powers – Germany, Austria–Hungary and Turkey.

Total war
A struggle that directly and indirectly involves the whole population.

Consensus politics
Parties suspending their differences and working together on policies they agreed on.

Key date

Parties agreed to a political truce: August 1914

Key terms

Temperance
Opposition to the taking of alcoholic drink.

Shell crisis
Since much of the war on the Western Front took the form of artillery barrages, a constant supply of shells was vital. In 1915 supply was falling short of need.

Gallipoli Campaign
In April 1915 an attempt was made to knock out Germany's ally, Turkey, by an Allied landing in Gallipoli in southern Turkey. The landing proved a bloody failure.

Key question
Why was a coalition formed in 1915?

Key dates

Coalition government formed under Asquith: May 1915

Unsuccessful Gallipoli Campaign: 1915–16

inter-party co-operation and from the beginning of the war strongly urged Asquith to consider broadening the basis of the Government.

Lloyd George as wartime chancellor
The outbreak of war in August 1914 brought no immediate change in the structure of the Government, but, as it became increasingly clear that the war was going to last much longer than originally thought, the pressure for change mounted. Asquith was as patriotic as the next man, but his calm demeanour and refusal to be panicked into rash action (attributes which had proved highly effective during the pre-war domestic crises) now suggested a lack of dynamism.

In contrast, Lloyd George's bustling energy seemed ideally suited to wartime needs. His two wartime budgets in 1914 and 1915 doubled income tax and greatly increased government expenditure. Gone was the restraint he had shown in pre-1914 budgets when he had tried to keep defence expenditure to a minimum. Lloyd George's wartime measures raised income tax from 6d (2½p) to 6s (30p) in the pound and introduced super-tax on annual incomes over £2,500. Alcohol and tobacco were also taxed and Lloyd George aroused widespread unpopularity by his introduction of licensing laws, which severely restricted the opening hours of public houses. He sincerely believed that the drinking habits of the British workers lowered production and weakened the war effort. In a characteristic statement, which recalled the Welsh **temperance** background of his youth, he declared: 'This country is facing three enemies – Germany, Austria and drink – and the deadliest of these is drink!'

The Asquith coalition, 1915–16
The implicit understanding among the political parties who had agreed to a political truce in 1914 was that Asquith's Government would conduct the war in a way that was acceptable to them all. By May 1915, however, serious criticism had begun to be made of Asquith's performance as war leader. As might be expected, the strongest objections came from the Conservatives who, unlike the Labour and Irish parties, had never had any doubts about the rightness of Britain's going to war. The **shell crisis** and the failure of the **Gallipoli Campaign** (1915–16) were the main pretexts for the Conservative demand for a Government shake-up. Asquith gave way before the pressure and accepted that the seriousness of the war situation necessitated the formation of a coalition government. Bonar Law, Balfour and Carson were among the leading Conservatives who received government posts. The Labour Party was represented by Arthur Henderson at the Board of Education.

From Lloyd George's point of view, the formation of the Coalition was welcome in that it provided the opportunity to advance the principle of centre politics. From 1914 he had encouraged Asquith to use the truce agreed between the parties as a means of widening the political base of the Government.

Lloyd George acted as something of a political broker after 1914. It was he rather than Asquith whom Bonar Law approached in 1915 when considering the prospect of coalition. Lloyd George's pre-1914 record helped in this respect. At the time of the impasse over the Lords, he had unofficially discussed the possibility of a coalition with the Conservatives. Although this came to nothing at the time, it did indicate that he took the idea of inter-party dealings seriously.

Benefits for the Conservatives

The prospect of a coalition was especially attractive to Bonar Law. It offered his party a return to government office after ten frustratingly powerless years; this without the necessity of a general election which should have occurred in 1915, but which the Conservatives judged they had little hope of winning. In marked contrast to Conservative elation was the depression that the Coalition created in many Liberals. They felt the party had compromised its principles by allowing the Conservatives back into office, albeit only in minor positions at first. Moreover, as some Liberals saw it, the Coalition was really a face-saving exercise for Asquith, a way of hiding how badly the war effort was going under his uninspiring direction.

Key question
Why were the Conservatives eager for a coalition, but many Liberals opposed to it?

Table 2.4: Party composition of the Coalition Cabinet in May 1915

Liberals	28
Conservatives	10
Labour	1

Lloyd George at the Ministry of Munitions

In the ministerial reshuffle that accompanied the formation of the Coalition, Lloyd George moved from the Exchequer to head the newly created Ministry of Munitions. He was able to make the Ministry a model of what could be achieved when a government department was inspiringly led. His essential aim was to produce more shells, the chief reason for the mounting criticism of Asquith's handling of the war.

Lloyd George, ably served by his departmental officials and by a series of experts he drew from outside politics, had outstanding success in increasing the production of armaments. One particular statistic shows this:

Key question
What was Lloyd George's new contribution to the war effort?

- when the war began the army possessed 1,330 machine guns
- by the time it ended it had 250,000.

Furthermore, by 1918, the supply of shells had begun to exceed demand. Lloyd George ascribed this success to the fact that the Ministry was 'from first to last a business-man organisation'. His use of experts from the areas of industrial production and supply was a step towards his concept of a government of national efficiency, drawing from a pool of the best talents and subordinating party politics to the needs of the nation.

Key date

Conscription
introduced: January
1916

Key term

**Military Service Act,
January 1916**
Imposed compulsory
enlistment on single
males between the
ages of 18 and 41; by
1918, the age limit
had been raised to
50 and the scheme
extended to include
married men.

Key figures

**Edward Grey
(1862–1933)**
MP 1885–1916; one
of the longest
serving Foreign
Secretaries
(1905–16) ever, he
took Britain into the
1914–18 war.

**Reginald McKenna
(1863–1943)**
Home Secretary
1911–1915,
Chancellor of the
Exchequer
1915–1916; a bitter
opponent of
conscription, he left
politics after 1918.

Conscription

As 1915 wore on, it became clear the war was to be a long one, requiring vast resources in manpower. This meant that the existing system of voluntary enlistment would not be able to keep the army up to strength. Something approaching a national campaign, led principally by the Conservatives, had developed by the autumn; it demanded that in the hour of the nation's need able-bodied men should be compulsorily called up for military service.

Knowing how unacceptable this would be to many in his party, Asquith tried to avoid the issue by suggesting various alternatives short of conscription, but eventually he bowed to pressure and supported the **Military Service Act**, introduced in January 1916. A group of 50 Liberals voted against the Bill on the grounds that it was an unprecedented invasion of individual freedom to oblige citizens to engage in warfare. The majority of Liberals shared this view but, nonetheless, voted for the Bill, believing that circumstances made it necessary. It was this acceptance of the argument from necessity that gravely damaged liberalism as a political philosophy.

Conscription caused dissension in the Cabinet. **Edward Grey** and **Reginald McKenna** were among those who were strongly against it. Lloyd George, however, true to his conviction that the war justified extraordinary measures in mobilising the nation, threatened to resign if it were not introduced. He also objected to the concession written into the Act that allowed conscientious objectors exemption from war service. The term referred to those who opposed war on moral and religious grounds; they had to go before an enquiry board to prove they were genuine in their beliefs and could be required to serve in a non-combative role. Some 16,000 men registered on these grounds, contrasting with the three million who had volunteered for service before 1916.

How far Lloyd George's authoritarianism stretched was later shown in 1918 when, against Bonar Law's plea that the Conscription Act should never be used 'as an agent in an industrial dispute', Lloyd George helped Churchill break a strike among munitions workers in Leeds by threatening to send the strikers straight to the war front.

What made the strike particularly notable was that it had begun as a protest by the workers at their being transferred against their wishes from one factory to another. Despite the gains undoubtedly made by the unions during the war in regard to status and the negotiating of better wage deals, there was a strong feeling among the workers that on both the home and war fronts the burden of winning the war was falling disproportionately on them. They were the class having to make the greatest sacrifice, and they doubted that Lloyd George, notwithstanding the many tributes he paid them in his public speeches, was as understanding of this as he should have been.

Lloyd George as war minister, 1916

His success as minister of munitions did not prevent Lloyd George from becoming increasingly depressed during 1916 by the slow progress in the war. He felt that the wrong strategy was being followed. He wanted diversionary campaigns to be mounted that would end the **stalemate** on the Western Front. However, the tragic failure of the Gallipoli venture gave weight to those army chiefs who asserted that the only way to defeat Germany was by the deployment of massive force on the Western Front; hence their demand for ever more manpower and resources to continue their **war of attrition** in Europe.

Lloyd George became so frustrated with the military leaders that he considered resigning from the Government. What stopped him was a turn of fate that dramatically altered his own position and had a profound effect on the eventual outcome of the war. On 5 June 1916, Lord Kitchener, the war secretary, was drowned at sea after the ship on which he was travelling to Russia struck a mine off Scapa Flow. The original plan had been for Lloyd George to accompany Kitchener on a morale-raising visit to Russia, but he had had to withdraw to attend to the crisis that followed the Easter Rising in Ireland (see page 84). This change of plan both saved Lloyd George's life and led to his taking the post that Kitchener had held.

He became war minister only five days after the launching by the British of the **Somme offensive**, the most costly single campaign ever fought by a British army in any war. At first Lloyd George, believing the estimates that the generals gave him, supported the offensive, but when it became evident that the Somme was a deadly strategic miscalculation, he turned bitterly against **General Haig** and **Sir William Robertson**. From the autumn of 1916 he was at loggerheads with the military.

The removal of Asquith, 1916

Lloyd George's success as an organiser increased rather than lessened the tensions between him and the generals. He came to believe that it was their incompetence that was limiting Britain's success in the war. He could not accept that they were planning adequately or using their resources effectively.

Lloyd George's exasperation with the military soon expanded into the belief that what was needed was a much more committed political leadership. He proposed, therefore, the setting up of a three-man war council with himself as its chairman. This was not simple arrogance. He considered that his achievements at munitions and as war minister indicated that he, more than any other civilian politician, both understood and represented the expectations of the nation. He claimed that he knew the people and the people knew him. He seems also to have genuinely believed that Asquith's duties as prime minister were so heavy that it was unreasonable to expect him to be able to dedicate himself solely to the task of running the war.

Unsurprisingly, the Conservatives keenly supported Lloyd George's initiative. They had never been fully content with Asquith

Key question
What circumstances led to Lloyd George's becoming war minister?

Key terms

Stalemate
Since the early weeks of the war in 1914, the war on the Western Front had settled into a confrontation between two massive sets of entrenched armies, neither being able to inflict a decisive defeat on the other.

War of attrition
Wearing the enemy down by sheer persistence and willingness to suffer casualties.

Somme offensive
On the first day of battle, 1 June 1916, Britain suffered 57,000 casualties; by the time the offensive had petered out four months later the figure had risen to 420,000.

Key figures

General Haig (1861–1928)
Commander-in-Chief of the British armies in France, 1915–18.

Sir William Robertson (1860–1933)
Chief of the Imperial General Staff, 1915–18.

Key dates

Battle of the Somme: July–Nov 1916

Conservatives withdrew support from Asquith: Dec 1916

as war leader, even after the formation of the Coalition in May 1915. Bonar Law and Edward Carson let Lloyd George know that they were prepared to back him against Asquith. A series of complicated manoeuvres followed in the autumn of 1916. The key question was whether Asquith would be willing to allow the proposed war council to function without him.

In the end, judging that this would be too great an infringement of his authority as prime minister, Asquith insisted that he must be the head of the council. Lloyd George offered his resignation, whereupon the Conservatives informed Asquith that they were not willing to serve in a Coalition government if Lloyd George was not a member.

What helped tip the balance was that Lloyd George could count all the major national newspapers on his side. He numbered among his friends at least five of the leading editors or proprietors. This proved of obvious political value to him. In 1916, only the *Daily News* supported Asquith unreservedly. It was an article in *The Times*, asserting that the Prime Minister was 'unfit to be fully charged with the supreme direction of the war', that appears to have finally broken Asquith's resistance.

Key question
Why was the overthrow of Asquith such a significant political development?

The leadership crisis in December 1916 showed that Asquith had no natural allies. The willingness of the Labour Party to support him earlier had reflected a commitment to the war effort generally, rather than to Asquith personally, while the Irish MPs had largely lost interest in English domestic politics following the Easter Rising (see page 84).

More significantly for the future of the Liberal Party, 130 of the 272 Liberal MPs declared their readiness to follow Lloyd George. This created a split that would never be fully healed. Although Asquith ceased to be prime minister in 1916, he continued as party leader, refusing to serve in Lloyd George's cabinet; instead he led the parliamentary opposition. This anomaly meant that in effect the Liberals were divided from 1916 onwards between the Asquithians, who claimed to be the official Liberal Party, and the followers of Lloyd George.

It is possible to view this as marking the final great divide between old-style and new Liberalism. Indeed, some historians have interpreted it as part of the class politics of the time, a revolt of the former outsiders in British politics against the existing political establishment. For example, A.J.P. Taylor writes:

> The Liberal leaders associated with Asquith were men of excessive refinement ... Lloyd George's supporters were rougher in origin and in temperament: mostly Radical nonconformists and self-made men ... None was a banker, merchant, or financial magnate; none a Londoner. Theirs was a long-delayed revolt of the provinces against London's political and cultural dominance: a revolt on behalf of the factories and workshops where the war was being won.
>
> A.J.P. Taylor, *England 1914–45*, 1965

Lloyd George's opponents believed that it was a desire for personal power that led him to bring Asquith down. Modern scholarship, however, tends to view this as a myth. The truth is that Lloyd George was never in a strong enough position to plot Asquith's downfall. It was the refusal of the Conservatives to remain loyal to Asquith that made all the difference. By 1916, Lloyd George may well have been dissatisfied with Asquith's leadership, but he could not have removed Asquith simply by his own efforts; it was the Conservatives who were responsible for making it impossible for Asquith to continue.

Asquith must also take some of the blame for his own downfall. Throughout the political crisis he was blind to the larger issues involved. He seems never to have understood the sincerity of those who opposed him, regarding their behaviour as a betrayal of him personally rather than a genuine attempt to improve Britain's war effort.

Key question
What role did the Conservatives play in ousting Asquith from office?

Lloyd George as wartime prime minister, 1916–18

After 1918, Lloyd George was frequently referred to as 'the man who won the war'. No one person, of course, can win a modern war singly, but as a reference to the inspiration he brought to bear as prime minister it is not too much of an exaggeration. His leadership was extraordinary.

At the time he took over as Premier late in 1916, British morale was at its lowest point in the war. The intense German U-boat (submarine) campaign early in 1917, sinking ships and interrupting supplies of food and raw materials, threatened to stretch Britain's resources beyond the limit. Lloyd George privately confided in April 1917 that if shipping losses continued at their current rate Britain would be starving within a month. In some quarters there was talk of a compromise peace, and defeatism was in the air. But Lloyd George's refusal to contemplate anything other than total victory inspired his colleagues, reassured the waverers, and put heart into the nation.

Key question
What special contribution did Lloyd George make to the war effort as PM?

Key dates

Lloyd George became PM and formed new Coalition government: 1916

U-boat menace threatened Britain's life-line: April 1917

Lloyd George's struggle with the military

Given Lloyd George's dynamism and determination, conflict between him and the military could only intensify. The generals objected to an interfering civilian politician deciding war strategy. For his part, Lloyd George would not accept that the generals were entitled to make their demands for huge numbers of men and vast amounts of material without being directly answerable to the Government for the use they made of them.

At the root of the conflict was the question of who was ultimately responsible for running the war. This dispute has sometimes been portrayed as a struggle to decide whether Britain in wartime was to be governed by politicians or generals. There are writers who see Lloyd George as having saved Britain from becoming a military dictatorship, but only at the price of its becoming a political one.

This remains controversial. What is undeniable is that while Lloyd George never wavered in his resolution to carry on the war

Key question
Why were Lloyd George's relations with the military chiefs so strained?

Key terms

The convoy system
Merchant ships
sailing in close
groups, protected
by a ring of
accompanying
warships.

'Garden Suburb'
So called because it
was housed in a
makeshift building
in the gardens of 10
Downing Street.

Key question
In what ways did
Lloyd George
abandon traditional
parliamentary
government?

Key date

War Cabinet formed:
December 1916

Key figure

**Maurice Hankey
(1877–1963)**
Secretary to the
Committee of
Imperial Defence,
1912–38, Secretary
of the War Council
1914–16, Cabinet
Secretary 1916–38.

to complete victory, no matter how long it took, he was appalled
by the scale of the slaughter. He believed that there had to be
alternatives to the mass offensives which seemed the only strategy
the generals were willing to consider. He spent a great deal of his
time as prime minister trying to outwit the generals, without at the
same time weakening the war effort overall.

Part of Lloyd George's technique was to keep the army
deliberately under-resourced while maintaining that his Government
was making every effort to meet the demands of the service chiefs.
His hope was that this would force the generals to reconsider their
unimaginative strategy of mass attack. His success in persuading the
Admiralty in 1917 to adopt the **convoy system** as the main defence
against the deadly U-boat attacks on the merchant ships showed what
could be achieved militarily when new thinking was given a chance.

Lloyd George's methods as PM
In keeping with his idea of consensus politics, one of Lloyd's
George's first moves as prime minister was to increase the number
of Conservatives in the Government.

Table 2.5: Party composition of the Coalition government in
December 1916

Liberals	12
Conservatives	44
Labour	2

Furthermore, Lloyd George chose to run the war by means of a
small inner War Cabinet that operated largely without reference to
either the full Cabinet or parliament. Remarkably, he was the only
Liberal in it.

Table 2.6: Party composition of the inner war cabinet in December 1916

Liberals	1
Conservatives	5
Labour	2

The figures suggest a major decline in Liberal influence. The truth
was that Lloyd George had turned his government into a
predominantly Conservative affair. This was to have very significant
consequences for him and the parties.

Lloyd George's centralising style of government was evident in
other pronounced ways. To retain central direction and control of
the new State agencies, a special cabinet secretariat was set up
under **Maurice Hankey**. Still more significant was the adoption by
Lloyd George of his own private secretariat, directly responsible to
him as head of the War Cabinet. Known as the **'Garden Suburb'**,
this secretariat was made up of a group of advisers and experts
constantly in touch with the Prime Minister. Lloyd George justified
its existence by his need to be in immediate day-to-day contact with
the constantly changing war situation; it made possible the instant
decision-making demanded by the war.

Sceptics detected a more dubious purpose. The workings of the secretariat appeared to them to detach government even further from parliamentary scrutiny. Lloyd George seldom attended parliament between 1916 and 1918. By relying increasingly on outside experts rather than elected politicians, he appeared to be abandoning the traditional methods of parliamentary government. Critics suggested that he was turning the British premiership into an American-style presidency; some even went so far as to accuse him of adopting the methods of a dictator.

Challenge to Lloyd George, 1918

Lloyd George's methods did not go unchallenged. In the summer of 1918, Asquith, in a reversal of what had happened to him two years earlier, led an attack on Lloyd George's handling of the war. In May 1918, General Maurice, a former Director of Military Operations, publicly accused Lloyd George of deliberately distorting the figures of troop strength in order to suggest that the British army in France was stronger that it actually was. Maurice's aim was to prove that it was not the army leaders, but the Government that was responsible for Britain's failure to win a decisive breakthrough on the Western Front.

> **Key question**
> How did Lloyd George overcome the political challenge he faced in 1918?

Taking the side of the generals, Asquith used the accusation to justify introducing a Commons vote of no-confidence in the Coalition. Lloyd George bluffed his way out of the problem by claiming that the figures he had originally quoted had been provided by Maurice himself. This was a distortion but Lloyd George defended himself so confidently that it was Asquith who appeared unconvincing. His performance in the debate fell far short of Lloyd George's. Asquith surrendered the initiative and the Commons voted 293:106 in favour of Lloyd George. The result left Asquith and his supporters looking like a group of disgruntled troublemakers who had irresponsibly sought to embarrass the Government at a time of great national danger.

The importance of the Maurice Debate was that it destroyed the chance of Liberal reunification. Asquith's attack on the Government's policy may not have been personally motivated, but it showed how wide the gap had grown between him and Lloyd George. It deepened the divide between the two factions in the Liberal Party and gave shape to politics for the next four years. Those who opposed Lloyd George in the debate were those who would stand as official Liberal Party candidates against him in the general election held in December 1918.

The Representation of the People Act, 1918

The divisions over the Maurice Debate in May 1918 have tended to overshadow a major piece of legislation that became law a month later. The main terms of the Act were:

- All males over the age of 21 were granted the vote.
- The vote was extended to women over 30.
- Servicemen over the age of 19 were entitled to vote in the next election.

> **Key dates**
>
> Lloyd George survived the Maurice Debate: May 1918
>
> Representation of the People Act became law in June 1918: passed in Feb 1918

Key term

Free vote
Individual MPs allowed to vote without instructions from their party.

Key figure

Constance Markiewicz (1868–1927)
The daughter of an Irish landowner, she married a Polish aristocrat; she became a suffragette and a member of Sinn Fein. Although elected in 1918, she was one of the 73 Sinn Feiners who refused to take up their seats at Westminster.

Key question
What was the political importance of the Coupon Election?

Key dates

Armistice on the Western Front: November 1918

Lloyd George won the 'Coupon Election': December 1918

- Candidates were to deposit £150 in cash, which would be forfeit if they did not gain ⅛ of the total votes cast.
- Constituencies were to be made approximately equal in number of voters (around 70,000).
- The number of seats in the Commons was increased from 670 to 707 to accommodate the enlarged electorate.
- All voting was to take place on a designated single day.
- Conscientious objectors had their right to vote suspended for five years after the war.

To a modern audience, one of the most interesting features of the reform was the extension of the vote to women. The clause in the Bill relating to women's voting rights was overwhelmingly accepted by the Commons on a **free vote**. Nearly all the ministers who had opposed it earlier now voted for it. In explaining his own change of heart, Asquith probably spoke for all those who now believed that the vital role women were playing in the war made the demand for 'votes for women' irresistible. 'Some years ago I ventured to use the expression, "Let the women work out their own salvation." Well, Sir, they have worked it out during this war.'

In 1919, a Sex Disqualification (Removal) Act allowed women to stand for parliament, enter most professions, including the law, and serve on juries. The first woman to be elected as an MP was **Constance Markiewicz**.

The Coupon Election, December 1918

At the end of the war in November 1918, Lloyd George and Bonar Law, the Conservative leader, agreed to continue the Coalition into peacetime. A joint letter carrying both their signatures was sent to all those candidates who were willing to declare themselves supporters of the Coalition. This written endorsement became known as 'the coupon', a wry reference to the ration coupons introduced during the war, and led to the election being referred to as 'the Coupon Election'.

Table 2.7: 1918 election results

	Seats won	Votes	% of total votes cast
Coalition Conservative	335	3,504,198	32.6
Coalition Liberal	133	1,445,640	13.5
Coalition Labour	10	161,521	1.5
(Coalition total)	(478)	(5,121,259)	(47.6)
Labour	63	2,385,472	22.2
Asquith Liberals	28	1,298,808	12.1
Conservatives	23	370,375	3.4
Irish Nationalists	7	238,477	2.2
Sinn Fein	73	486,867	4.5

Judged purely as a piece of opportunism, the election was a remarkable success for Lloyd George and the Coalitionists. However, in the light of later developments, which saw the Liberal Party decline into impotence, it can be argued that Lloyd George's decision to perpetuate the Liberal split by carrying the Coalition into peacetime permanently destroyed any chance the Liberal Party had of reuniting and recovering. A leading modern scholar, Kenneth Morgan, describes the Coupon Election as 'the greatest of disasters for the Liberal Party and the greatest of tragedies for Lloyd George'. This modern estimation reinforces the view expressed nearer the time by Herbert Gladstone, the former Liberal Chief Whip:

> The result of 1918 broke the party not only in the House of Commons but in the country. Local [Liberal] Associations perished or maintained a nominal existence. Masses of our best men passed away to Labour. Others gravitated to Conservatism or independence. Funds were depleted and we were short of workers all over the country. There was an utter lack of enthusiasm or even zeal.
>
> Herbert Gladstone writing in 1919, quoted in Chris Cook,
> *A Short History of the Liberal Party, 1900–76*, 1976

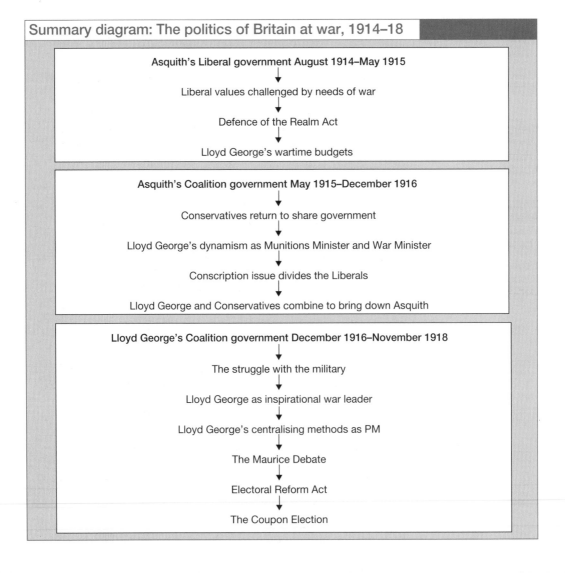

Summary diagram: The politics of Britain at war, 1914–18

Asquith's Liberal government August 1914–May 1915
↓
Liberal values challenged by needs of war
↓
Defence of the Realm Act
↓
Lloyd George's wartime budgets

Asquith's Coalition government May 1915–December 1916
↓
Conservatives return to share government
↓
Lloyd George's dynamism as Munitions Minister and War Minister
↓
Conscription issue divides the Liberals
↓
Lloyd George and Conservatives combine to bring down Asquith

Lloyd George's Coalition government December 1916–November 1918
↓
The struggle with the military
↓
Lloyd George as inspirational war leader
↓
Lloyd George's centralising methods as PM
↓
The Maurice Debate
↓
Electoral Reform Act
↓
The Coupon Election

3 | The Impact of the War on the Political Parties

a) The Liberals

Key question
Was the Liberal Party fundamentally changed by the 1914–18 war?

By the end of the war an increase in State power had occurred that would have been unimaginable, let alone acceptable, in peacetime.

- Large areas of British industry had been brought under central control.
- All public transport had been brought under government control.
- Military conscription had been imposed.
- Food rationing had been introduced.
- Controls had been imposed on profits, wages and working hours.

In 1917 alone, the worst year of the war for Britain, six new ministries came into being:

- Blockade
- Food
- Labour
- National Service
- Pensions
- Shipping.

This growth in government power led to a huge extension of State bureaucracy. The civil service, in terms of personnel and premises, underwent a rapid expansion. In the face of these developments, the traditional Liberal suspicion of bureaucracy was swept aside in the rush to adapt Britain's institutions to the needs of war.

Challenge to Liberal values

The measures were justified by reference to the struggle for national survival, but there were Liberals who protested. They saw the growth of State control as a challenge to the principle of individual liberty. They were usually the same protesters who had opposed the declaration of war; their voice, however, sounded faintly against the general clamour for war and for the reorganisation of society that the war effort demanded. Lloyd George declared: 'a perfectly democratic State has the right to commandeer every resource, every power, life, limb, wealth, and everything else for the interest of the state'.

Even those Liberals who had supported the war from the first were unhappy when faced with the fundamental changes that were being brought about by the war effort. Of necessity, British government during the war became illiberal. DORA, restrictions on free trade and the introduction of conscription were outstanding examples of a whole series of measures and regulations which Asquith's and Lloyd George's governments felt obliged to introduce. The Liberal State at war was very different from the Liberal State at peace.

Irrecoverable lost ground

There is no doubt that the Liberal Party was greatly changed by its experience of war. To put it in negative terms, if the 1914–18 war had not intervened, Asquith might not have resigned, the Liberal social reform programme might have continued with Lloyd George as its main promoter and the challenge to traditional Liberal values would not have become as demanding as it did.

The Liberals lost irrecoverable political ground because of the war. The existence of the **Union of Democratic Control**, representing the Liberals' anti-war tradition, was a constant reproach to the Government. The Irish Nationalists felt betrayed by the Government's policy towards Ireland. Asquith was heavily criticised for the British handling of the Easter Rising, as was Lloyd George for his use of the Black and Tans (see page 86). The Irish Catholic vote in England switched significantly to Labour, while in Ireland the Nationalists moved to Sinn Fein.

Most of the signs indicate that the Conservatives, still wounded after their defeat over the People's Budget and the House of Lords, would not have been able to oust the Liberals in the foreseeable future. Much of this, of course, is speculation. We cannot know what impact the Ulster question would have had on party strength and alignment had the war not led to the shelving of this issue, but it is highly improbable that the traumas and transformations experienced by the Liberals would have occurred without the pressure of the war years.

The impact of Lloyd George's premiership

As prime minister between 1916 and the end of the war, Lloyd George was necessarily preoccupied with ensuring the nation's survival in war. This diverted both him and the Liberals from the progressive policies they had followed before the war. Lloyd George's very success in persuading many of his colleagues to accept increasing State intervention had the effect of diluting his own Liberalism and detaching him from the radical element in his party. Conscious of this, he made a number of important moves towards reconstruction in the last year of the war. His aim was partly political in that he hoped to prevent the radicals from becoming too disgruntled over the slowing down of social reform. It was this that lay behind his 1918 election promise to make Britain 'a land fit for heroes to live in'. The idea took particular shape with the creation of the **Ministry of Reconstruction**.

One of the most notable products of this was the Education Act of 1918, whose main terms were the:

- raising of the school leaving age to fourteen
- abolition of fees for elementary education
- introduction of compulsory medical inspections of secondary school pupils
- authorising of LEAs to set up nursery schools

Union of Democratic Control, 1914–18
A pressure group of Liberal and Labour politicians and journalists set up to protest against the war and urge a negotiated peace.

Ministry of Reconstruction
A body which drew together the various committees that had come into being during the war, its main task being to plan the improvement of social conditions.

Key question
How did Lloyd George's conduct as PM damage the Liberals?

- creation of day release colleges at which young people at work could continue their formal education one day a week
- restriction of the employment of children of school age.

This measure was largely the work of **H.A.L. Fisher**, a university vice-chancellor and one of the outside experts that Lloyd George had invited into government. It was a further step in the provision of state education as a universal, compulsory system.

Liberal reaction to the growth of the State

While a particular measure such as Fisher's Act could be seen as enlightened and progressive, many Liberals were left with the feeling that, overall, four years of war had undermined their most cherished values. By 1918, the principal causes that had characterised pre-war Liberalism had been jettisoned or gravely compromised, namely:

- Britain's entry into the war destroyed the image of the Liberals as a peace party.
- The economic regulation of the State by the wartime governments effectively marked the abandonment of free trade.
- Conscription undermined the concept of the freedom of choice of the individual.

Furthermore, important though the play of politics at parliamentary and government level obviously was, attention must also be drawn to developments in the country at large. Historians have begun to stress the importance of what was happening at constituency level. On balance, the Conservative and Labour parties gained politically from the war, while the Liberals suffered.

The main problem for the Liberal Party was that, although the majority of its members came to accept that the war was justified and, therefore, had to be fought to the utmost, it was hard to accommodate it easily within the Liberal programme as developed since 1906. Having struggled to establish the primacy of welfare issues, the Liberals now found themselves diverted from social reform by the demands of war.

Having overcome the reactionary opposition of the Unionists on a whole range of issues before 1914, the Liberals now had to contemplate the reality of their leaders making common cause with their political opponents. All this tended to take the heart out of party activists at grassroots level. Liberal morale sank. The Conservative Party was always less compromised by the war than either the Liberals or the Labour Party. They had never had any doubts about the correctness of Britain's entry into the conflict. Their traditional claim to be the 'patriotic' party stood them well in wartime and led to a considerable recovery of popularity in the constituencies.

Key figure

H.A.L. Fisher (1865–1940)
Liberal MP, 1916–26, Vice Chancellor of Sheffield University, 1912–18, President of Board of Education, 1916–18.

The impact of electoral reform

An equally important factor accounting for Liberal Party decline was the electoral reform introduced in the last year of the war. The 1918 Representation of the People Act (see page 60) swelled the number of voters from some seven million to around twenty-one million. A number of historians, including Martin Pugh, regard this trebling of the electorate as having had momentous political consequences. Not all the newly enfranchised working class voted Labour in the 1918 election; nonetheless the Labour party's share of the vote rose proportionally with the increase in the electorate from seven per cent to twenty-two per cent and its number of MPs increased from 42 to 60. The trend towards the replacement of the Liberal Party by Labour as the second largest single party had been established.

In a notable book, *The Downfall of the Liberal Party*, written in 1966, Trevor Wilson suggested that the war was the essential reason for the decline in Liberal fortunes. Other historians have queried this and have argued that the war accelerated the decline rather than causing it. More recently, Martin Pugh has suggested that the key factor was not so much that the war undermined the Liberals as that they failed to seize the opportunity that the war offered. Diverted by the demands of war from their progressive policies, the Liberals gave ground to the Labour Party as the new force of reform.

Key question
How did electoral reform in 1918 work to the disadvantage of the Liberals?

The importance of personality

Whatever weight is given to the different interpretations, it is evident that the war was a highly formative experience in the history of the Liberal Party, and indeed in British politics. An issue that commands attention is one of personality. Parties are not only about principles; they are also about people. The roles of Asquith and Lloyd George were critical. Asquith's continuing resentment at what he regarded as Lloyd George's disloyalty and betrayal in 1916 meant that a genuine *rapprochement* between the two was impossible.

The fracturing of the Liberal Party left Lloyd George dependent on the support of Bonar Law and the Conservatives. Whether this amounted to his being the 'prisoner of the Conservatives' is another of the lively debates among historians. It has to be said that many Conservatives at the time did not regard Lloyd George as a prisoner; on the contrary, they saw their party being dragged along behind this maverick and dangerous ex-Liberal leader.

Rapprochement
Resumption of working relations.

Key term

b) The Labour Party in wartime

Although the Labour Party was relatively small in 1914 there were serious divisions within it over the war. The basic question in August 1914 was whether the party should support the war at all. The majority of party members in the Commons and in the country decided to do so out of a genuine sense of patriotic duty. They were also worried on political grounds that if the party went

Key question
What did the Labour Party gain from the war years?

Key figures

Arthur Henderson (1863–1935)
Chairman of the party 1914–17; the first Labour Party member to hold a Cabinet post, Paymaster General 1916.

James Ramsay MacDonald (1866–1937)
Labour Party Chairman 1911–14, Labour Party leader 1922–31, PM 1924 and 1929–35, Leader of National Government 1931–37.

Key terms

No-Conscription Fellowship
A body set up in 1914 devoted to resisting any attempt by the State to introduce a general call-up to oblige citizens to fight.

February Revolution
In February 1917 the tsar, Nicholas II, had abdicated and been replaced by a provisional government.

War indemnities
Reparations paid by the losing side for the cost of the war.

against the tide of public opinion, which was overwhelmingly in favour of war, it might damage itself beyond recovery. **Arthur Henderson**, who became leader of the Labour Party in parliament at the beginning of the war, represented this viewpoint.

The reward for mainline Labour's support of the war came with the inclusion of Labour ministers in the Coalition governments that were formed under Asquith in 1915 and Lloyd George in 1916 (see page 59). However, there were also strong pacifists in the party, such as **James Ramsay MacDonald**, who resigned his position as leader of the Labour MPs in the Commons in August 1914 and remained consistently opposed to the war throughout its duration. In addition, there was a vocal Marxist element on the left of the party who condemned the war as a capitalist conspiracy against the workers. It was this section of the party which became involved in such bodies as the **No-Conscription Fellowship**, and who attempted regularly throughout the war to organise disruptive strikes in the war industries.

The Stockholm Conference, July 1917

A curious incident was to lead to the end of Labour's wartime co-operation with Lloyd George. In July 1917, a meeting was called in Stockholm, the capital of neutral Sweden, by the socialist parties of all the counties still fighting the war. The aim of the gathering was to consider ways of bringing about a negotiated peace. The cue for this had come from the new Russian government, set up after the **February Revolution**, which had proposed that a peace settlement should be considered on the basis of all sides abandoning the demand for **war indemnities**. For obvious reasons all this was regarded by the governments of the combatant countries as undermining the war effort.

Lloyd George had at first agreed that Arthur Henderson, who had earlier gone to Russia on an official government visit, could attend. However, when the French, who were committed to the imposition of heavy post-war penalties on Germany, complained, he backtracked and withdrew his permission. Henderson promptly resigned from the Cabinet.

In the event, this worked to Labour's advantage. Now that Henderson, the Labour Party leader, was no longer a minister, he was able to put his energies into improving the party's organisation and shaping its proposals for both the peace settlement and the domestic policies that Britain should follow after the war was over. This helped to lessen the differences within the Labour Party and give it a more responsible image in the country at large. This contrasted favourably with the divided Liberals and a Conservative Party that appeared willing to subordinate itself to Lloyd George for the sake of being in government. There was a sense in which the Labour Party came out of the war far less damaged politically than either of its two rivals.

The Labour Party constitution

A critical result of Henderson's efforts at restructuring the party was the adoption in February 1918 of a Labour Party constitution. Before then, it had not put its various principles and aims into a clearly stated programme. The constitution was an attempt to define the party for the twentieth century. It was largely the work of Henderson and Ramsay MacDonald, and drew heavily on the ideas of Sidney Webb (see page 31), who prepared the various drafts on which the constitution was finally based. Its key features were:

- the party to be composed of the affiliated: trade unions, socialist societies, co-operative societies, trade councils, local Labour parties
- the party to be managed by a party executive of 23 members elected at the annual party conference
- the annual conference to vote on the policies to be followed
- the means of production, distribution and exchange to be taken into common ownership, i.e. nationalised (Clause IV)
- a commitment to the taxing and redistribution of surplus wealth
- co-operation with the trade unions in the formation of policy
- block voting to be allowed (e.g. affiliated trade union delegates entitled to cast the total votes of all their members).

Key date

Adoption of the Labour Party constitution: February 1918

Throughout the following decades there would be continued debate and disagreement among party members about the constitution's strengths and limitations, but at the time it helped give the Labour party a sense of stability. It emboldened the Labour members in Lloyd George's Coalition to break free of him; as soon as the armistice had been announced in November 1918, all the leading Labour ministers resigned, thus reclaiming their political independence. It was a remarkable move for a parliamentary party barely a decade old and hinted at the confidence Labour's brief experience of government had brought it.

c) Conservative gains from the war period

The Coalition governments which Asquith and then Lloyd George formed involved a governmental restructuring that resulted in Conservatives taking key executive posts in the inner Cabinet. Thus, without winning an election victory, the Conservatives found themselves in positions of authority for the first time since 1905.

In addition to becoming the majority in Lloyd George's Coalition, the Conservatives derived a number of other unplanned gains from the war period. The marked increase in the size of the electorate that followed the 1918 Representation of the People Act certainly helped the Labour Party, but not exclusively so. Not all working class voters supported the Labour Party. Indeed, it is

Key question
How had the war years worked to the benefit of the Conservative Party?

calculated that in all the elections from 1918 onwards approximately a third of working-class voters in practice opted for a party other than Labour. A similar proportion of trade unionists did the same. One reason for this in 1918 was the Conservatives' wholehearted and consistent support for the war. It is reckoned that their record on this won them substantial support among servicemen and their families in the 1918 Coupon Election.

There was the further factor that, as the electorate grew in size, constituencies had to be reshaped to accommodate this. How the Conservatives benefited from this is neatly summed up by Stuart Ball, a modern expert on the history of the Conservative Party: 'Conservative seats in the Home Counties with expanding populations were sub-divided to form several new constituencies, whilst many Liberal seats with small electorates in the West, the North and in Scotland disappeared.'

These electoral benefits were in a sense accidents; the luck had fallen to the Conservatives. But there were other advances that they could be said to have earned for themselves. They gained, for example, from their willingness to learn the social lessons that the war had provided. This applied particularly to the Conservative officer class who by tradition came from a privileged background. Their experience in mixing with the men they led and lived with in the hazardous conditions of war often had the effect of breaking down their prejudices. Young Conservatives like **Harold Macmillan** came back from the trenches with a respect for the serving men that easily transformed into a wish to make the world a better place for them and their families in peacetime. Such an attitude was to help modernise the Conservative Party in its thinking and make it adaptable to the democratic politics of the twentieth century.

The newfound confidence among the Conservatives showed itself in the eagerness with which the party went about reorganising itself as an electoral force. In marked contrast to the depression and faintheartedness with which the Liberals approached the 1918 election (see page 62), the Conservatives began to streamline their local constituency branches with a view to getting their supporters out in strength at elections. It was a sign that the Conservatives were coming to the realisation that politics was no longer a matter of relying on its traditional block support. The task now was to win over the new electorate.

Key figure

Harold Macmillan (1894–1986)
An MP for 38 years, served as an officer in both world wars, Foreign Secretary 1955, Chancellor of the Exchequer 1955–57, Leader of the Conservative Party and PM 1957–63.

Summary diagram: The impact of the war on the political parties

The Liberals

Damaged by:
↓
The extension of state power an affront to Liberal values
↓
The impact of Lloyd George's premiership
↓
Effects of electoral reform
↓
Loss of active support at grassroots level
↓
Personal dispute between leaders

Labour

Initial divisions between pro-war and peace elements in the party
↓
But party gains from inclusion in Asquith and Lloyd George Coalitions
↓
Breach with Lloyd George strengthens the party's moral status
↓
Adoption of a constitution adds to party's political stability and acceptability
↓
1918 electoral reform helps treble its popular support

Conservatives

Gain from:
↓
Inclusion in Asquith and Lloyd George governments
↓
Consistent support for the war wins the patriotic vote
↓
1918 electoral reform benefits the party
↓
War experience of young Conservative candidates broadens the party's understanding of society
↓
Attention paid to party organisation and fund raising

4 | The Home Front, 1914–18

So vital was the part played by the civilian population in the war effort that it is arguable that the outcome of the First World War was decided as much on the domestic front as on the military one. The efforts of the armies on the Western Front would have counted for little had they not been backed by a working population capable of sustaining the industrial output that the war demanded. This was an aspect of total war; everybody was a participant.

Key question
What impact did the war have on British society?

There was another sense in which ordinary people were directly involved in the struggle: the huge number of volunteers and conscripts who entered the armed forces meant there was hardly a family in Britain not directly affected by the war. Deaths and casualties at the Front brought bereavement and grief into all but a few British homes. As John Keegan, a leading military historian, movingly puts it:

> The telegraph boy on his bicycle became for parents and wives during both world wars literally an omen of terror – for it was by telegram that the awful flimsy form beginning 'We regret to inform you that' was brought to front doors, a trigger for the articulation of the constant unspoken prayer, 'Let him pass by, let him stop at another house, let it not be for us.' In Britain during the First World War that prayer was not answered several million times; on seven hundred thousand occasions the telegraph boy brought the ultimate bad news of the death of a son, husband or brother.
>
> John Keegan, *War and Our World: The Reith Lectures 1998*, 1999

Table 2.8: UK troop casualty figures, 1914–18

Total number of troops	Killed	Wounded
5,700,000	702,000	1,670,000

When the results of the war are examined it is natural that the death and casualty lists overshadow all other considerations. One in every eight soldiers died and one in four was injured. Yet there were aspects which historians now see as positive. When the war first broke out in 1914 there was a fear that the disruption it would bring would cause severe distress to the mass of the working population. In the event, however, the war brought a number of advantages to the working class. This was largely because the war created a huge demand for extra industrial workers. The trade unions gained greatly from this since it increased their bargaining power; so essential were industrial workers to the war effort that their co-operation was vital.

The Treasury Agreement, March 1915

Key date

Treasury Agreement: March 1915

The most striking example of this was the Treasury Agreement of 1915. Lloyd George, as Chancellor of the Exchequer, used his great negotiating skills to thrash out with the TUC what proved to be one of the most important social contracts of the war. This was a settlement that enlisted the trade unions as an essential component in the war effort. In return for accepting non-strike agreements and **'dilution'**, the unions were guaranteed improved wages and conditions.

Key term

'Dilution'
The employment of unskilled workers in jobs previously restricted to skilled workers.

The real significance of the Treasury Agreement lay not in its details but in its recognition of the trade unions as essential partners in the war effort. They were now participants in the running of the State; they could no longer be regarded as outsiders. Lloyd George aptly referred to the Treasury Agreement as 'the great charter for labour'.

Conscription

One of the unexpected consequences of the introduction of conscription in 1916 (see page 55) was the boost in status it gave to many industrial workers. There had been estimates that some 650,000 'slackers' would be netted by conscription. But in fact the imposition of compulsory military service initially saw a drop in the number of men enlisted. This was because of the need to exempt workers in reserved occupations. Men working in jobs that were considered vital to the war effort, mining and munitions being key examples, were not to be called up. The result was that 748,587 exemptions were added to the million-and-a-half already **starred workers**. In the early months following the start of conscription the average weekly enlistment fell to 10,000 – only half the figure it had been under the voluntary system.

The shortfall in enlistments was eventually made up by raising the upper age limit from 41 to 50 and by including married men. Quite aside from the military considerations, what the exemption from conscription highlighted was how dependent Britain was on its workers for survival. The nation's heroes were not confined to the battlefield. Nor were its heroines.

Starred workers
After 1914, volunteers who were thought to be already doing vital war work had a star put against their name and were exempted from military service.

Key term

The role of women

Key question
How was the position of women affected by the war?

The banners carried down London's Whitehall, in July 1915, in the last suffragette demonstration did not demand votes for women. Instead, they read: 'We demand the right to serve.' In many respects their wish was granted. A huge number of women entered the workforce during the course of the war. The following figures suggest the scale.

Direct war work:

- 100,000 women joined auxiliary (non-combative) units of the armed services
- 100,000 became military nurses in such units as the First Aid Nursing Yeomanry (the FANYs).

Other work:

- 200,000 women worked in government departments
- 500,000 did clerical work in the private sector
- 250,000 became land workers
- 50,000 women worked in public transport as tram and bus conductors
- 800,000 females were employed in engineering workshops.

To these figures should be added the many thousands who worked on a voluntary, unpaid basis in hospitals, canteens and welfare centres.

Members of the First Aid Nursing Yeomanry in France in 1917. How did the work of the FANYs help to advance the status of women?

Calculations suggest that over 4.9 million industrial workers left their jobs to join the armed services between 1914 and 1918. The gap this created in the workforce was filled in the following ways:

• natural increase in population of young people of working age – 650,000
• delayed retirement of existing workers – 290,000
• foreign workers – 100,000
• wounded men who did not return to active service – 700,000
• through overtime and longer hours the equivalent of – 1,000,000
• women workers taken on – 1,700,000.

Women's response to the call to enter the factories to replace the workers who had gone to the Front made them an indispensable part of British industry. Without them, the output of the munitions factories, on which the war effort depended, could not have been sustained. Yet the large influx of women into the factories created a particular problem for the trade unions. Few of the female workers were members of a union. Not unnaturally, the women felt entitled to the same level of pay as had been received by the men they replaced. However, the unions were not ready to press for this. Since most women were classed as unskilled, union officials worried that if their claims were pushed it would weaken the claims of men for higher wages. The broad result was that although workers' pay certainly rose during the war, women did not share proportionally in this. The principle of equal pay was still many decades away.

It is clear that women made an unprecedented contribution as workers to the war effort and that their status and reputation were greatly enhanced in consequence. However, historians are wary of seeing this as a permanent social advance since, once the war was over, the great majority of women gave up their jobs to the returning male workers. It is true that female shorthand typists had come to stay; they largely took over from the ink-stained male clerks who had been such a feature of nineteenth-century offices. However, it was a different story in the factories. The rush of women into the factories in wartime proved a blip on the graph. As Table 2.9 shows, by 1920 the proportion of women in the industrial workforce was little higher than it had been before the war.

Table 2.9: Percentage of women in the workforce

	Industry %	Transport %	Agriculture %	Commerce %	All workers %
July, 1914	26	2	9	27	24
July, 1918	35	12	14	53	37
July, 1920	27	4	10	40	28

Yet in more subtle ways women had made advances that they were not subsequently to give up. Their clothing and hairstyles became more practical. It was not so much that hemlines were raised (that would not happen until the 1920s) as that dresses became lighter and more adapted to the needs of regular physical movement that work demanded. The need for women to travel between home and work on a daily basis, or live away from home altogether, produced a sense of independence. This was sometimes expressed by women going into public houses on their own, something which only those regarded as floozies had dared do before.

The trade unions

Between 1914 and 1918 trade union membership rose from four million to six million. The stronger position of the unions resulted in higher wages and improved working conditions for workers. Yet this did not mean peace on the industrial front. Having declined during the first two years of the war, strike action increased during the last two. This was evidence of a powerful feeling among the workers that on both the home and war fronts the burden of winning the war was falling disproportionately on them. They were the class that was having to make the greatest sacrifice, and they doubted that the Government, despite the many public tributes it paid them, fully understood this. Such feeling was intensified when the returning troops observed how well many of those who had stayed behind in Britain had done out of the war.

Key question
How did the war affect the workers in Britain?

Table 2.10: Industrial strikes, 1913–19

	Working days lost	Number of strikes	Number of strikers
1913	9,804,000	1,459	664,000
1914	9,878,000	972	447,000
1915	2,953,000	672	448,000
1916	2,446,000	532	276,000
1917	5,647,000	730	872,000
1918	5,875,000	1,165	1,116,000
1919	34,969,000	1,352	2,591,000

Key question
Did the 1914–18 war create a new economic situation or simply accelerate existing trends?

Key terms

Gross National Product (GNP)
The annual total value of goods produced and services provided by Britain at home and in trade with other countries.

National Debt
The total amount owed by a government to its domestic and international creditors. At the end of the 1914–18 war Britain owed so much that a quarter of the revenue raised by the Government had to be spent on paying the interest charges (£325 million) on the National Debt.

Staple industries
The enterprises on which Britain's industrial strength had traditionally been based, e.g. textiles, coal mining, iron and steel production and ship building.

The economic impact of the First World War
Government spending

By 1917, spending by the Government amounted to sixty per cent of **Gross National Product** (GNP). (The remarkable change this represented can be understood by noting that in 1813 at the height of the Napoleonic wars, British government spending amounted to only seven per cent of GNP.) The Government raised the capital needed by borrowing from banks at home and in North America. About two-thirds came from such loans. The remaining third was raised from increased taxation. This resulted in income tax being quadrupled between 1914 and 1918. Overall, government borrowing increased the **National Debt** from £650 million to £8,000 million.

Measured by output, the war years were a period of growth for British industry as production expanded to meet the huge demand for goods and materials. But it was an unnatural growth that hid an underlying downward trend. The fact was that Britain's **staple industries** were in long-term decline. For many decades British industry had been seriously weakened by foreign competition, notably from Germany and the USA (see page 5). It had been handicapped by its own inability to adapt to new trends. It had also failed to re-invest or attract new investment. This meant that it lacked the capital to buy new machinery or develop modern production techniques.

For Britain, the war created a damaging trend in the countries which before 1914 had been major purchasers of British goods. Wartime blockade had obliged many of these countries to produce for themselves since they could no longer import supplies. They developed their own manufacturing industries and simply stopped buying from Britain. Having been forced to become self-sufficient, after 1918 these countries protected their gains by tariffs and trade embargoes.

Britain's dated basic industries were not able to adjust sufficiently to meet this change in the economic world order. Old-fashioned production methods left British manufacturers with high overheads. This made them reluctant to drop their prices since this would cut their profits. The consequence was a lack of competitiveness and a fall in demand for British-made goods. The rest of the world no longer wanted the products of Britain's traditional manufacturing industries at the prices British manufacturers were now forced to set.

What the First World War did, therefore, was to hasten a decline that had already begun. Equally significant was the move away from free trade. The pressure of war led the Government to impose restrictions and import duties on foreign imports. A critical aspect of all this was the increasing role played by the Government in economic matters. Although the free trade argument had not been finally defeated, a process had begun of government involvement in the running of the economy that was to be a marked and controversial feature of Britain in the twentieth century.

Summary diagram: The Home Front, 1914–18

The impact of war casualties on ordinary families

↓

The Treasury Agreement, 1915, gives status to unions

↓

Conscription results in gains for the industrial workers

Status of women

↓

Indispensable to the war effort

↓

Failure to achieve equal pay

↓

Majority of women factory workers give up their jobs at war's end

↓

Lift in social status, steps towards fuller emancipation

↓

Enfranchised in 1918

The trade unions not entirely co-operative – strikes continue in wartime

Economic impact of the First World War

Rise in government spending

60% of GDP spent on war

Large increase in National Debt

War distorts international economy – weakens Britain's already declining staple industries

Study Guide: AS Questions

In the style of AQA

(a) Explain why the Liberals carried out a reform of the powers of the House of Lords in 1911. (12 marks)

(b) How important was the impact of the First World War on the collapse of the Liberal Party by 1922? (24 marks)

Exam tips

The cross-references are intended to take you straight to the material that will help you to answer the questions.

(a) As well as looking at pages 38–40 of this chapter you should re-read page 6 (the position of the House of Lords) and pages 23–24 on the Peoples' Budget in Chapter 1. Remember you will need to compile a list of reasons for the 1911 Parliament Act and these might include:

- the behaviour of the House of Lords before 1909 and the Conservative domination
- issues concerning finance, taxation and social welfare
- Lloyd George's determination to pass the Peoples' Budget of 1909
- the general elections of 1910 and the influence of the Irish Nationalists.

Remember that your answer should show how these factors were inter-linked and you should try to distinguish between the short and long term, and more and less important, showing some personal judgement.

(b) To answer this question you will need to identify the ways in which the First World War undermined the Liberal Party's values (pages 51–53 and 63) and how the actions of Lloyd George and the formation of a coalition in the war years, weakened the Liberals' position. Page 53 will be helpful here, as will material on the Labour Party (beginning on page 66) and on the Conservatives (beginning on page 68). Other factors affecting Liberal decline would involve the long-term elements such as Liberal weakness after the 1910 elections (see Chapter 1), the impact of electoral reform (page 66) and the leadership of Lloyd George, before and after (in addition to during) the war (page 94). The decline of the Liberal Party has been the subject of extensive historiography and it would be helpful to refer to this, although your answer should demonstrate your own understanding and convey a personal judgement.

In the style of OCR
England in a new century, 1900–24
Study the five sources on the issue of women's suffrage, 1906–14 and then answer both sub-questions. It is recommended that you spend two-thirds of your time in answering part **(b)**.

(a) Study Sources B and D.
  Compare these sources as evidence for attitudes towards militancy. (30 marks)

(b) Study all the sources.
  Use your own knowledge to assess how far the sources support the interpretation that militancy did more harm than good to the cause of women's suffrage during the period from 1906 to 1914. (70 marks)

The issue of women's suffrage, 1906–14
Source A
W.L. Blease, The Emancipation of English Women, *1910*
The views of a male supporter of women's suffrage are explained in a published article

It is useless to talk about the equal worth of women, as long as men exercise their power to exclude them from any activity they may wish to enter. It is useless to declare they are willing to admit women into everything except politics. In England, where politics is so important, disfranchisement brands the disfranchised with a permanent mark of inferiority. An adult who is unfit to take part in politics will inevitably be made to feel inferior in education, in professional and industrial employments, and in social relations.

Source B
Millicent Fawcett, a private letter, November 1910
A leading suffragist, writing to a friend, criticises the militant actions of the WSPU

I do think these personal assaults of the past five years are extraordinarily silly. The Prime Minister's statement on the possibility of a Bill for women's suffrage was not exactly all we wanted. But it was better than anything offered before. It made *The Times* say the next day that it put the women's suffrage question definitely before the country at the coming general election, and that if there is a Liberal majority it will be a mandate to the government to grant women the vote. And then these idiots go out smashing windows and bashing ministers' hats over their eyes.

Source C
The Clarion, *June 1913*
A pro-suffragette Labour newspaper comments on the Liberal government's actions

The women are winning again. Morale is high. What they have lost by window-smashing has been restored to them by the Government's new Cat and Mouse Act rushed through Parliament. Consider what it means. The Spanish Inquisition never invented anything so cruel! 'Wait-and-See Asquith' has tried both force and trickery against them. But the fact is undeniable that the bravery of the women has beaten him.

Source D
Emmeline Pankhurst, My Own Story, *1914*
A suffragette leader defends the growing militancy of the WSPU

In the year 1906 there was an immensely large public opinion in favour of women's suffrage. But what good did that do the cause? We called upon the public for more than sympathy. We called upon it to give women votes. We have tried every means, including processions and meetings, which were not successful. We have tried demonstrations, and now at last we have to break windows. I wish I had broken more. I am not in the least sorry.

Source E
Viscount Ullswater, A Speaker's Commentaries, *1925*
James Lowther (later Viscount Ullswater) comments on the effects of suffragette violence on Parliament's attitude to the women's cause. Lowther was the Speaker of the House of Commons during the period of suffragette militancy. He had been a Conservative MP and was personally opposed to women's suffrage.

By 1913, the activities of the militant suffragettes had reached a stage at which nothing was safe from their attacks. The feeling in the House of Commons, caused by these lawless actions, hardened the opposition to the demands of the suffragettes. As a result, on 6 May the private member's bill that would have given women the vote, for which the Government had promised parliamentary time so that it could become law, was rejected by the House of Commons by a majority of forty-seven.

Exam tips

The cross-references are intended to take you straight to the material that will help you to answer the questions.

(a) You have to show that you have understood the content of the two sources. You do not have to use your own knowledge but you must infer from the evidence contained in the sources. Keep your answer concise and make use of the information concerning the authors of the sources and the intended audience. For example:

- Both Sources B and D represent the views of leading suffragettes, but at different stages of the movement's history, i.e. 1910 and 1914.
- Source B was stated in private and not intended for publication as this sentiment was not widely shared by suffragists at this time. Four years later, Source D reflects on the lack of progress since 1910 in spite of Liberal promises and victory in the general election.

(b) You need to balance an analysis of all five sources with your own knowledge to answer the question set. Use your knowledge to demonstrate the strengths and limitations of the sources in terms of their completeness and value as explanations. Offer a judgement based on the general consistency and completeness of the sources as a set. For instance, you might suggest that:

- Sources B and E support the interpretation, but for different reasons: Source B is anxious not to harm the suffragettes' chances of getting the vote, whereas Source E, which represents the view of the establishment, openly opposes women's suffrage.
- In contrast, Sources A and C hold the Liberal government responsible for impeding women's suffrage rather than the militancy of the movement itself.
- Source D on the other hand argues that women had to become militant because all other avenues of advancing their cause had proved fruitless.

You might conclude that MPs were adversely affected by the violent behaviour of some of the women down to 1914 and that, though some MPs believed they should be given the vote, most condemned their methods (see pages 41, 43–44).

3 Post-War Britain, 1918–29

POINTS TO CONSIDER

When the War ended in 1918 there were great hopes that Britain would reap the rewards of victory. But the post-war years proved troubled times. Lloyd George's Coalition was defeated in 1922, having been judged by the electorate to have failed to meet the challenges facing Britain. There followed a two-year period of Conservative government which proved equally undistinguished. In 1924, in a remarkable turn of events, a minority Labour Party under Ramsay MacDonald found itself in government. But it was a short-lived administration; after less than a year, the Conservatives were back in office, a position they held until 1929. These developments are examined under the following headings:

- The post-war coalition, 1918–22
- The Conservative government, 1922–24
- The first Labour government, 1924
- Baldwin's government, 1924–29

Key dates

1913		Marconi Scandal
1916	April	The Easter Rising
1917	October	The Russian Revolution
1919	January	First Dail Eireann elected
	June	The Versailles Treaty
	September	Dail prohibited; increasing violence by IRA
1920		Treaty of Sevres
1920	June	Government recruited 'Black and Tans' to suppress the IRA
1921	March	Anglo-Russian trade agreement
	December	Anglo-Irish Treaty
1922	September	Chanak crisis
	October	Carlton Club meeting Lloyd George resigned
	November	Conservatives took office under Bonar Law
	November	Election returned Conservatives with a majority of 87 seats

1923	May	Baldwin replaced Bonar Law as PM
	November	Lloyd George rejoined Liberal Party
	December	Election saw Labour become the larger opposition party
1924	January	Labour government formed under Ramsay MacDonald
	September	The Campbell case
	October	Zinoviev Letter crisis
		Election returned Conservatives to power
1924–29		Baldwin's Conservative government
1925	April	UK returned to gold standard
	July	Red Friday
1926	May	General Strike
	March	Samuel Commission report
1927	May	Trade Disputes Act
1928	April	Reform Act granted vote to women on same terms as men
1929	May	Election returned Labour as largest single party

1 | The Post-War Coalition, 1918–22

Reconstruction, which had begun during the war, was continued into the post-war period. A massive demobilisation programme, involving the return of over one million men to civilian life, was set in motion under Winston Churchill's direction as war secretary. Ambitious proposals were drawn up for improved health facilities, unemployment pay and pensions. However, the grim economic circumstances in post-war Britain, caused by high inflation and declining orders for British goods, largely thwarted these schemes, though there was apparent success in regard to housing.

A particular feature of Lloyd George's 1918 election campaign had been his repeated promise to provide homes fit for heroes. He was sincere in his desire to improve living conditions for ordinary people and entrusted the task to **Christopher Addison**, the minister of health. Addison was responsible for introducing in 1919 the first Housing and Town Planning Act. The aim of the measure was to encourage local governments to clear slums and to construct low-rent homes (referred to as council houses) specifically for the working class. In one respect the Act was a major success; by 1922, over 200,000 such houses had been built.

Yet while there was no doubting Addison's enthusiasm, he had a limited understanding of the economics involved. Unlike the situation in wartime, when, as Lloyd George's successor as minister of munitions, he had had the power to direct the relevant industries, he had no control over the building industry. He was

Key question
What problems stood in the way of post-war reconstruction?

Christopher Addison (1869–1951)
Trained as a doctor, Liberal Minister of Munitions 1916–17, President of Local Government Board 1919, Minister of Health 1919–21; joined the Labour Party in 1922.

Key figure

given the run-around. His response was to spend as much government money as possible. This worked insofar as houses were built, but the cost was excessive. His ministry paid for houses at the rate of £910 per unit, whereas the true building cost was only £385. The Government was using public money to pay a huge subsidy to the building industry.

Faced with an outcry, Lloyd George had no option but to remove Addison and apologise in the Commons for the mess that his sacked minister had made. By 1922, government grants for new housing were withdrawn altogether. The scandal was that by that time the increase in population meant there was a shortage of over 800,000 homes among the poorer sections of the community. Yet despite the embarrassment for the Coalition over its housing policy, an important social principle had been established. What Addison's Act had laid down was that housing was now, like education, considered a necessary public service which the local authorities were responsible for providing. Later measures illustrated that this was now a working principle of government (see pages 98 and 101).

National Insurance

A development for which Lloyd George was personally responsible was the extension of National Insurance. The Liberals' measure of 1911 had covered only three million workers (see page 24). During the war another million munitions workers had been added to this number. Between 1920 and 1921 Lloyd George extended the provisions to cover eight million more workers, twelve million in total. The aim was to protect workers against short-term unemployment which, at a time of high demand for labour, seemed the only cover that was likely to be necessary.

What neither Lloyd George nor anybody else could know at this time was that in a few years the problem would not be casual short-term unemployment but persistent long-term joblessness. It was this development that has tended to divert attention from the post-war Coalition's considerable achievement in the area of social service advance.

Post-war industrial problems

Throughout the Coalition years from 1918 to 1922, Lloyd George continued with his aim of improving industrial relations. He maintained links with both employers and trade unions and encouraged them to think in terms of conciliation rather than confrontation. Unfortunately, these successes were overshadowed by the larger drama of the post-war breakdown in industrial relations. It was coal mining that attracted the greatest attention. Coal, once one of Britain's staple exports and the basis of her nineteenth-century industrial strength, was becoming increasingly difficult to mine profitably. The **wartime blockade** of Britain had greatly reduced foreign orders, which were not renewed after 1918. In addition, even their most sympathetic supporters found it difficult to deny that the mine owners were obstinate and out of touch with the real economic world. The mining unions demanded that the industry, which had been

Key term

Wartime blockade
Between 1914 and 1918, in an attempt to inflict economic damage on each other, Britain and Germany had imposed blockades to prevent supplies being imported or exported.

Key question
What problems confronted the post-war Coalition on the industrial front?

brought under government control during the war, should not be returned to the owners: mining should be **re-nationalised**.

Lloyd George was unable to satisfy them on this; nor could he sanction government interference in order to meet the miners' wage demands. He was able, however, to use his negotiating skills to defuse the situation in 1921 when it appeared likely that the railwaymen and transport workers would join the miners in a general strike. However, the embers of syndicalism had been fanned in the South Wales coal fields and the Coalition had to face continuing unrest and disorder there and in the industrial areas of Britain that were suffering from the post-war **recession**.

It was Britain's inability to cope with the effects of the worldwide industrial slump that undermined Lloyd George's promise that the workers of Britain would be well rewarded for their heroic wartime efforts. By 1922, unemployment had risen to over one million, inflation had leapt ahead of wage levels, and the existing social services were stretched beyond their capacity. Worse still, by 1922 the economic recession had become so bad that the Government, rather than expand social welfare provision, had to cut back. The withdrawal of resources, known as the **'Geddes Axe'**, applied to education, hospitals and housing.

All governments tend to be judged primarily on their economic record. The evident failure of the social and economic policies of the Coalition tended to dwarf its successes in other spheres. The mistakes seemed too many, suggesting that the problems of post-war Britain had proved too great for Lloyd George's Government to cope with effectively. Even an apparent social policy success, such as the Addison Act which resulted in 200,000 new homes, brought it little public approval since the measure was thought not to go far enough and any real improvements were attributed to the Labour-controlled local councils, which were largely responsible for implementing the policy.

The Anglo-Irish question

In 1914, the Act granting Home Rule to Ireland had been suspended for the duration of the war (see page 48). It was, therefore, an issue with which Lloyd George's post-war Coalition had to deal when peace came. But things had not stood still in Ireland after 1914. Another dramatic twist in the story had occurred in the form of the Easter Rising.

The Easter Rising, 1916

The suspension of the Home Rule Act at the start of the war had only shelved the Irish problem; it had not solved it. This became very apparent in April 1916 when a breakaway group of Irish Nationalists seized the General Post Office in Dublin and posted up a signed proclamation announcing the establishment of the Irish Republic. The rebels, as they were immediately dubbed by the British authorities, had hoped for two things: an invasion of Ireland by German forces, and a nationwide rising by the Irish people. Neither took place.

Key terms

Re-nationalised
Brought back into public ownership (i.e. government control).

Recession
A slowing down of economic growth, usually caused by a falling off of demand for manufactures, which is then followed by falling profits, lowered wages and the laying off of workers; particularly severe recessions become depressions.

'Geddes Axe'
Named after Sir Eric Campbell-Geddes, Chairman of the special government committee that recommended the spending cuts.

Key question
What difficulties faced the post-war Coalition over Ireland?

Key question
Why had a crisis arisen in Ireland in 1916?

The Easter Rising:
April 1916

Key date

Key term

'Terrible beauty'
The Irish poet, W.B. Yeats, used this haunting oxymoron to describe the 'terrible' nature of violence and the uplifting 'beauty' of sacrifice.

After four days of desperate fighting, the republicans were overwhelmed by a British force and their ringleaders rounded up. Yet what had begun as an ill-organised, poorly supported and failed rising soon took on the proportions of a great modern Irish legend. It became a **'terrible beauty'**. This had less to do with the romantic self-sacrifice of the republicans than with the severity, as the Irish people perceived it, with which they were then treated by the British. The seven individuals who had signed the proclamation, plus eight others, were all tried and shot. In the bitter reaction among many Irish people to such reprisals, it tended to be overlooked that the death sentence on 75 others was commuted to life imprisonment.

Rebel prisoners being marched out of Dublin by British soldiers, May 1916. How did the British treatment of the defeated Republican rebels intensify Irish nationalism?

Anxious not to allow the abortive Rising to create further problems in Ireland, Asquith turned to Lloyd George to contain the situation. Lloyd George immediately entered into discussions with Redmond, the Irish Nationalist leader, and Carson, leader of the Ulster Unionists. His main object was to prevent the Irish problem from undermining the British war effort. He confided to Carson:

> In six months the war will be lost ... The Irish-American vote will go over to the German side. They will break our blockade and force an ignominious peace on us, unless something is done, even provisionally, to satisfy America.
> Quoted in Martin Gilbert (ed.), *Lloyd George,* 1968

In his urgency to reach a temporary settlement Lloyd George was not above giving contradictory promises to both Redmond and Carson, which persuaded them to accept a compromise, referred to as the 'Heads of Agreement'. This granted immediate Home Rule for the 26 counties of southern Ireland, while the Six Counties of Ulster remained part of the United Kingdom until after the war when their permanent constitutional status would be decided by an imperial conference.

Lloyd George gave Redmond the impression that the separation of Ulster from the rest of Ireland was purely temporary; at the same time he reassured Carson that it would be permanent. However, Lloyd George's manoeuvring came to nothing, for when the Heads of Agreement were put to the Coalition Cabinet, the Unionist members refused to ratify it. They claimed Lloyd George had gone too far to appease the Irish Nationalists. The most stubborn opponent was **Lord Lansdowne**, who insisted that the Agreement be modified so as to satisfy Unionist objections. When Redmond learned of this he broke off negotiations and the Agreement became a dead letter.

Sinn Fein and the IRA

The failure of Redmond's moderate Irish MPs at Westminster to reach a settlement in their 1916 negotiations with the Unionists had put a powerful propaganda weapon into the hands of the extremists who argued that force was the only way to achieve Irish independence. The parliamentary party began to lose ground to the more extreme Sinn Fein party which had come to prominence in 1914. In 1917, led by **Eamon de Valera**, who had played a major role in the Easter Rising, Sinn Fein won two by-elections.

Matters became even more strained in 1918 when Lloyd George's Coalition attempted to extend conscription to Ireland. Sinn Fein, despite being outlawed, won 73 seats in the Coupon Election, seats which it pointedly refused to take up at Westminster. Instead, in September 1919 it defiantly set up its own **Dail Eireann** in Dublin. In the same year Sinn Fein's military wing, the Irish Volunteers, reformed itself as the Irish Republican Army (IRA), dedicated to guerrilla war against the British forces.

IRA activists became so disruptive that in June 1920 Lloyd George sanctioned the recruitment of a special irregular force, known as the **'Black and Tans'**, to deal with the situation. The tough methods used by this force soon led to their being hated by Irish Nationalists, who accused Lloyd George of employing them deliberately to terrorise the civilian population of Ireland. Indeed, Lloyd George was accused of applying the same methods in Ireland that twenty years earlier he had denounced as barbarous when used against the Boers (see page 9).

Moves towards a political settlement

When it became apparent that military force was not bringing peace to Ireland, Lloyd George's thoughts turned again to the idea of a constitutional settlement acceptable to both Nationalists and Unionists. After decades of bitterness over Home Rule, this would not be easy, but the atmosphere of the times encouraged change. The Versailles Treaty, the major post-war peace settlement, had enshrined the principle of national **self-determination**. Indeed, Britain had been one the nations that had pressed for the principle to be accepted at Versailles. It made no sense, therefore, for Britain to continue to deny that principle to Ireland. There was also the undeniable fact that

Key figures

Lord Lansdowne (1845–1927)
Foreign Secretary 1900–05, Conservative leader in the House of Lords 1903–16.

Eamon de Valera (1882–1975)
Leader of Sinn Fein 1917–26, President of the Dail 1919–21, President of Ireland 1959–73; saved from execution after the Easter Rising by the fact that he had been born in the USA and so could claim American citizenship.

Key terms

Dail Eireann
Irish parliament.

'Black and Tans'
So called from the colour of their outfits which were made up from a job lot of police and military uniforms. It was said that this force was recruited from violent prisoners in British military gaols.

Self-determination
The right of peoples to form a nation and government of their own choice.

Key dates

Government recruited 'Black and Tans': June 1920

First Dail Eireann elected: Jan 1919

Versailles Treaty: June 1919

Dail prohibited;
increasing violence by
IRA: September 1919

Anglo-Irish Treaty:
December 1921

Key figures

**Austen Chamberlain
(1863–1937)**
MP 1892–1937,
Chancellor of
Exchequer 1919–21,
Foreign Secretary
1924–29; son of
Joseph Chamberlain
and half-brother of
Neville
Chamberlain.

**Lord Birkenhead
(1872–1930)**
MP 1906–19,
Attorney General
1915–19, Lord
Chancellor 1919–22.

Key question
How close did the
Treaty come to
solving the Anglo-Irish
question?

Home Rule had been on the Statute Book since 1914; it was law, even though it had yet to be implemented.

There were also signs that the Conservatives were ceasing to be as rigidly attached to the Unionist cause as they had been before 1914. They had grown weary of the strife in Ireland. Accordingly, in 1921, Lloyd George gathered together a team of negotiators that included the new Conservative Leader, **Austen Chamberlain**, as well as **Lord Birkenhead**, previously one of the staunchest opponents of Home Rule. He then offered de Valera a truce and invited him and the other Irish leaders to London to discuss the drafting of a treaty of settlement.

When they arrived, Lloyd George shrewdly played upon the idea that he represented the last hope of a just settlement for Ireland. He suggested that if they could not reach an acceptable agreement under his sympathetic leadership it might well be that he would have to resign, to be replaced by Bonar Law whose unyielding resistance over Home Rule would destroy any chance of settlement. His argument was persuasive enough to induce them to accept the appointment of a boundary commission, charged with the task of detaching Ulster from the rest of Ireland. What this acceptance meant was that Irish Nationalists had given ground on the critical issue; they had dropped their previous insistence that Ulster must be part of an independent Ireland.

With this as a bargaining factor, Lloyd George was able to convince the Unionists that the rights and independence of Ulster had been safeguarded. It was essentially the same position as had been reached in the 1916 negotiations, but on this occasion the Unionists did not scupper the talks. As Lloyd George had perceived in 1916, a settlement depended ultimately on Unionist acceptance. In December 1921, after a long, complicated series of discussions, in which all Lloyd George's arts of diplomacy, if not duplicity, were exercised, the parties finally signed the Anglo-Irish Treaty.

The Anglo-Irish Treaty, 1921
The essential feature of the Treaty was partition:

- Southern Ireland was granted independence as the Irish Free State.
- Most of Ulster remained part of the United Kingdom.

In the event, the Treaty split the Irish parties and a savage civil war broke out in Ireland, fought between the pro-Treaty Nationalists, led by Michael Collins, and the anti-Treaty Republicans, led by de Valera.

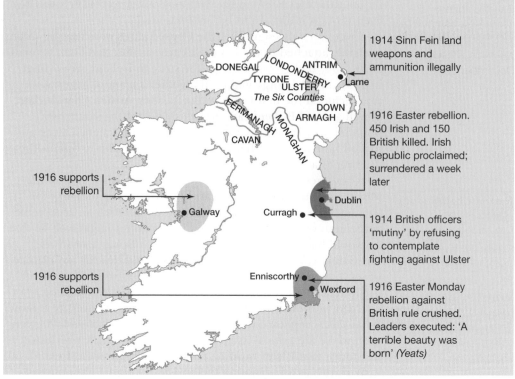

Figure 3.1: The 1921 Treaty settlement partitioned the island of Ireland into the Irish Free State and Northern Ireland (comprising the Six Counties). Northern Ireland is sometimes loosely referred to as Ulster, although historically Ulster had been made up of nine counties – the six shown, plus Donegal, Cavan and Monaghan. The fact that Northern Ireland did not include these last three was of immense importance, since it left the Protestants in a majority in the North. Why did the Treaty not provide a permanent settlement of the Ulster question?

In retrospect, the settlement of 1921 can be seen as both a remarkable historical achievement and a contemporary political failure. A British politician had had the vision, the skill and the luck to undertake successfully something which, since the 1801 Act of Union, had evaded all other statesmen who had approached it – a workable solution to the Anglo-Irish question. Subsequent events were to show it was far from being a perfect solution; nevertheless, judged against the scale of the problem confronting him, Lloyd George's achievement was immense.

The political failure lay in the fact that the treaty was necessarily a compromise. The Unionists were left feeling betrayed by Lloyd George's willingness to give in to what they regarded as republican terrorism. The Nationalists could not forget his use of the Black and Tans; neither could they regard the Treaty as anything other than a concession reluctantly and belatedly extracted from a British government who granted it only when all other means of maintaining the Union had failed.

> **Key dates**
>
> Conservatives took office under Bonar Law: November 1922
>
> Lloyd George resigned: October 1922

Key question
Why did the Coalition break up in 1922?

The end of Lloyd George's post-war Coalition, 1922

One of the repercussions of Lloyd George's Irish policy was that it finally killed off the idea of a permanent coalition or centre party. To be workable this would have had to include Labour as well as Conservative and Liberal members. Labour had found the methods that Lloyd George sanctioned in Ireland deeply distasteful and, therefore, unsupportable.

Conservative and Labour doubts

It is doubtful in any case that a genuine fusion of Liberals and Conservatives was possible. At Lloyd George's suggestion, talks had been held between the **Chief Whips** of the parties in 1920, but these had broken up with nothing substantial agreed. The fact was that Conservative support for Lloyd George was a matter of expediency, not principle; it did not imply any real desire to make that support indefinite. The chances of a genuine coalition were always slim. Lloyd George did not really have enough to offer either the Conservative or Labour parties for them to consider a permanent coalition. They entertained thoughts of union only as a means of having a say in affairs until they felt sufficiently secure to strike out on their own.

The Coalition's declining reputation

After four years, the commonly held view of the Coalition was of a tired, ineffectual administration, led by an individual who was past his best and was sustained in office by a combination of his own love of power and a Conservative Party which would continue to support him only as long as it served its own interests. Commentators and newspapers began to express distaste for the low tone of the Coalition, a reference to the unattractive mixture of economic shortcomings, political expediency and financial corruption that had come to characterise it.

Lloyd George and corruption

The charge of corruption took particular strength from the so-called 'Lloyd George Fund', which provided an easy target for those wanting to blacken his name. Unashamedly, Lloyd George had used his power of patronage as prime minister to employ agents to organise the sale of honours and titles on a commission basis. **Maundy Gregory** was the most notorious of these salesmen. It was said that the asking rate during the Coalition years was between £10,000 and £12,000 for a knighthood, and between £35,000 and £40,000 for a baronetcy.

During this period, some 90 peerages and 20,000 **OBEs** were purchased by well-heeled, if not always well-born, social climbers. Lloyd George justified the practice by referring to the long tradition of patronage in Britain; the sale of titles, he suggested, was not new to British history. He argued that it was a justifiable means of raising political funds, given that he did not have access

Key terms

Chief Whips
The MPs who perform the vital function of organising the party in parliament.

OBE
Order of the British Empire.

Key figure

Maundy Gregory (1877–1941)
A highly colourful character who always sported a monocle; son of a clergyman, he was variously a teacher, an actor, a theatrical producer, a spy and a political fixer.

to the donations that the Conservatives regularly received from the business world or the Labour Party from the trade unions.

Whatever the validity of this claim, it did not prevent opponents from likening the honours sale system to the pre-war **Marconi scandal** as yet another example of Lloyd George's dishonesty. It provided a powerful additional argument for those Conservatives who had begun to question their party's continued support for Lloyd George. They pointed out that that support had always been conditional and suggested that the corruption of the Coalition, added to its policy failures, was now beginning to taint the Conservative Party itself.

Foreign problems

More damaging for Lloyd George was a particular crisis abroad: the Chanak affair. The trouble arose from the resentment of the defeated Turks at the dismemberment of their country under the terms of the 1920 Treaty of Sevres, the agreement that formally ended the war between the Allies and defeated Turkey. Under their new leader, **Mustapha Kemal**, the Turks threatened to take back by force the territories they had lost to their old enemy, Greece. Lloyd George, in the tradition of Gladstone, sided with the Greeks against their former oppressors. In September 1922, he ordered British reinforcements to be sent to Chanak on the Dardanelles, a likely area of confrontation. War threatened, but diplomacy eventually prevailed and the Turks withdrew. At home, Lloyd George's action was condemned by many Conservatives as an unnecessary and irresponsible piece of sabre-rattling that might well have led to a major war.

The Conservatives abandon Lloyd George

The Conservatives' chance to undermine Lloyd George came shortly afterwards, when Lloyd George announced his intention of calling a general election. This posed a critical question for the Conservatives. Should they, in the light of the obvious unpopularity of the Coalition, continue to support Lloyd George?

This demanding issue was discussed at a decisive meeting of the Conservative Party, held at the Carlton Club in October 1922. **Stanley Baldwin**, soon to be the leader of the party, joined Bonar Law in urging their colleagues to disassociate themselves from a prime minister who was no longer worthy of their trust. In his influential speech at the meeting, Baldwin spoke of Lloyd George as 'a dynamic force which had already shattered the Liberal Party and which was well on its way to doing the same thing for the Conservative Party'. Baldwin's words helped swing the conclusive vote: the Conservative MPs voted by 187 to 87 to abandon Lloyd George and the Coalition by standing for election as a party in their own right.

The political wisdom of leaving a tired and unpopular Coalition was shown in the results of the general election held a month later. The Liberals, who went into the election as a party divided between the respective supporters of Lloyd George and Asquith, suffered a heavy defeat. They were never again to be in

Key dates

Marconi Scandal: 1913

Treaty of Sevres: 1920

Chanak crisis: September 1922

Carlton Club meeting: October 1922

Key term

Marconi scandal, 1913
In 1913, there had been suggestions that Lloyd George had used his inside knowledge as Chancellor of the Exchequer to buy and sell shares in the Marconi Company for a large profit.

Key figures

Mustapha Kemal (1881–1938)
Known later as Kemal Ataturk, he distinguished himself as a miltary leader in the First World War and later became an international statesman and the founder of modern Turkey.

Stanley Baldwin (1867–1947)
Born into a prosperous iron-manufacturing family. MP 1908–37, Leader of the Conservative Party 1923–37, Chancellor of the Exchequer 1922–23, PM 1923–24, 1924–29, 1935–37.

government as a party. The defeat of the Coalition ended Lloyd George's ministerial career and also destroyed the possibility of his building an effective centre party in British politics.

Table 3.1: November 1922 election results

	Votes	Seats	% of total votes cast
Conservatives	5,500,382	345	38.2
Labour	4,241,383	142	29.5
National Liberal (Lloyd Georgians)	1,673,240	62	11.6
Liberals (Asquithians)	2,516,287	54	17.5

Key question
In what sense were the Liberals the victims of the electoral system?

The parties and the 1922 election

The Liberals lost a large number of seats, dropping from a combined figure of 161 for the two sections of the party in 1918 to a combined figure of 116 in 1922. This contrasted sharply with the Conservatives holding their own with 345 seats in 1922 compared with 358 in 1918. The most impressive feature was Labour's achievement in doubling its seats from 73 to 142.

Key date

Election returned Conservatives with a majority of 87: November 1922

Yet, as was noted in regard to the 1906 election (see page 17), the number of seats won and lost can blind one to the actual figures relating to the popular support for the parties. In an electorate that had been more than doubled by the 1918 Representation Act, the Conservatives increased their vote by 1.6 million and Labour by 1.8 million. What is often overlooked is that the combined Liberal vote also rose significantly – by 1.4 million. This could hardly be described as a massive rejection of the Liberals. The critical factor was not loss of popular support, but votes unevenly distributed in the constituencies. Although Labour had won 26 more seats than the Liberals it had done so with only 0.4 per cent more of the popular vote. In proportional terms it had taken:

- 15,943 votes to elect each Conservative MP
- 29,868 votes to elect each Labour MP
- 36,116 votes to elect each Liberal MP.

Obviously the divisions within the Liberal Party had seriously weakened it politically, but it was the imbalance in the electoral system that made a recovery by the Liberals after 1922 an impossibility. The Liberals were destroyed as a party of government not by the will of the people but by the workings of the system. They were the victim of the undemocratic nature of British elections. Of course, this was not the result of some malign plan by the Liberal Party's opponents. It just happened that way. It was the unplanned outcome of the strange way in which the electoral pattern evolved.

Judging the Coalition

The Coalition of 1918–22 has not had a good press. Lloyd George has often been criticised for running a cross-party government that did not conform to the normal pattern of party politics and, therefore, could not survive. The suggestion is that by governing in peacetime without a genuine party majority, Lloyd George made himself 'the prisoner of the Tories'. He could carry on only as long as the Conservatives backed him. His final defeat in 1922, following the withdrawal of Conservative support, is thus interpreted as in some way marking a return to normal two-party politics which had been disrupted by the war and Lloyd George's wish to stay in power.

The objection to this line of argument is that it assumes that the two-party system is normal and necessary to British politics. What brought Lloyd George down was not his defiance of two-party politics, but the decision of the Conservatives to abandon him. Had it served their purpose to continue supporting him, they would have done so. They were looking after their own interests, not defending some abstract principle of party politics. Moreover, the notion of Lloyd George as 'prisoner' was the interpretation of later observers. Few contemporaries saw it that way. Indeed, Martin Pugh has suggested that after 1922 it suited the Conservatives to portray Lloyd George as having been not their prisoner, but a dictator over them. In this way they were able to absolve themselves from the mistakes of the Coalition years.

Lloyd George

David Lloyd George was the dominant British politician of the first quarter of the twentieth century and ranks with Churchill as one of the greatest figures of the age. Such was the range of his activities that in studying him one is studying all the major events of his time.

Profile: David Lloyd George (1863–1945)

1863	– Born in Manchester
1864–77	– Brought up in Wales
1884	– Qualified as a lawyer
1888	– Married Margaret Owen
1890	– Became Liberal MP for Caernarvon (remained MP for this constituency for the next 55 unbroken years)
1923	– Rejoined Liberal Party
1926	– Became Liberal Party leader
1936	– Visited Germany and met Hitler
1937–39	– Attacked Neville Chamberlain's appeasement policy
1940	– Declined invitation to join Churchill's Coalition
1945	– Created Earl Lloyd George of Dwyfor
	– Died

Lloyd George's career can be broken down into a number of identifiable periods:

1890–1905

These were his early years as a young Liberal MP, espousing Welsh causes and making a name for himself as a radical. He became a nationally known figure with his withering onslaughts on the

---

Unionist government for its mishandling of the Anglo-Boer War (1899–1902). He added to his reputation by vigorously defending free trade against the protectionist policies advanced after 1903 by Joseph Chamberlain and the Conservatives.

1905–14

This was his great period as a social reformer. As a dynamic member of Asquith's pre-war cabinet, first as President of the Board of Trade and then as Chancellor of the Exchequer, he was responsible for promoting a whole range of measures that marked the first step towards the welfare state. His 1908 introduction of old age pensions was followed a year later by the so-called 'People's Budget', which threatened to undermine the landed class by the introduction of a tax on the land. The dispute that this started reached its climax with the bitter clash between the Lords and Commons over the Parliament Bill in 1911, the same year in which his National Insurance Act was introduced.

1914–16

Holding in turn the offices of chancellor of the Exchequer, minister of munitions and war secretary, Lloyd George made a major and dramatic contribution to the organisation of Britain's war effort.

1916–18

In a highly controversial episode Lloyd George took over from Asquith as prime minister in December 1916. During the next two years he committed his inexhaustible energies to the defeat of Germany. In leading the nation to victory he fought a series of running battles with the politicians and the generals. He made enemies but his immense personal contribution was an undeniable factor in Britain's survival and success. He was widely accepted in Britain as 'the man who won the war'.

1918–22

Lloyd George continued as prime minister at the head of a peacetime Coalition government, a decision which widened the growing split in the Liberal Party. He added to his renown as an international statesman by personally leading the British delegation at the Versailles Peace Conference in 1919. Another outstanding achievement in this period was his presiding over the negotiations that led to the signing of the Irish Treaty of 1921, the nearest that any single politician had come to solving the Anglo-Irish question. However, his attempts to fulfil his wartime promise to make Britain 'a land fit for heroes' made little headway. Growing domestic problems and increasing disenchantment with Lloyd George led the Conservatives, the main prop of the Coalition, to withdraw their support from him in 1922. This effectively ended his premiership. Lloyd George was never again to hold office.

The importance of Lloyd George in British domestic politics, 1905–23

The only PM not to have spoken English as his first language, Lloyd George was characterised by his Welsh fire and oratory. He loved political battle, but he could also be disarmingly courteous and conciliatory. Although he remained a Liberal throughout his life, he was a keen advocate of coalition politics, believing that a pooling of the finest minds and talents from all the parties would serve Britain best.

Lloyd George was what would now be called colloquially a hustler, a wheeler-dealer. It was frequently suggested that he loved politics for its own sake, for the excitement it brought, rather than because it offered a means of improving the public good. It was further argued that he was essentially power-hungry and that he used the Liberal Party merely as a vehicle for furthering his own ambitions.

His impact on the Liberal Party

Whatever the truth of those charges, it is certainly the case that his career fundamentally altered the character of the Liberal Party. He appreciated that 'party' was an unavoidable feature of the political structure, but he tried to move towards a position in which consensus politics would replace strict party alignments.

It was said in his time, and has been repeated since, that Lloyd George's natural home was the Labour not the Liberal Party. He always rejected this notion. Yet, judged purely in terms of the policies he followed, it is sometimes difficult to see where he differed from the Labour Party. His work as a social reformer in the pre-1914 period was very much in tune with the programme of the Labour Party of that time. Furthermore, his widening of central government authority during the war extended the powers of the State to an unprecedented degree that took him way beyond anything the old Liberal Party would have contemplated.

This connects with the central dilemma created by the Liberal Party's attempt to modify its policies. Precisely because it was a halfway stage, the progressive, but still limited, social service programme that the New Liberalism advanced between 1906 and 1914 was bound to be superseded by the full-blown welfare state socialism of the Labour Party. Some historians have seen this as the basic explanation for the decline of Liberalism in the twentieth century. They have argued that the Liberal Party fell between two stools: in trying to be socially progressive it forfeited its claim to represent traditional values; yet, despite its apparent radicalism, it did not go far enough along the road of State control.

It was thus unable to provide an effective challenge to either the Conservatives, representing the force of tradition, or the Labour Party, standing for nationalisation and state direction of the economy.

Key question
In what sense can Lloyd George be said to have damaged his party?

Contemporaries and later critics condemned Lloyd George for treating his party in so cavalier a way as to destroy it as a political force. Since it was during the most active period of his career that the Liberal Party declined in importance, some of the blame must fall on him. His challenge to Asquith in 1916 led to a permanent split in the party.

Lloyd George – a dictator?

It was often said of Lloyd George that he was the man who won the war. This referred not merely to his ability to inspire the nation, but also to his success in preventing the generals from turning Britain into a military dictatorship. To speak of the power of the generals in such a way may appear exaggerated, but it is equally exaggerated to suggest, as some commentators have, that Lloyd George became a political dictator.

The charge of dictatorship rests on Lloyd George's neglect of parliament and his use of a personal secretariat to bypass the normal political channels. The fact is, however, that the electoral structure in Britain prevented dictatorship. No matter how strong Lloyd George's authority may have appeared to be, he was always dependent on the support of the Conservatives in parliament. This was amply demonstrated in 1922 when his governmental power-base ceased to exist once the Conservatives chose to withdraw their support from him.

His contribution to improved industrial relations

A persistent and disruptive influence in British industrial relations has been the notion of rivalry between capital and labour, employer and employee, as natural and therefore unavoidable. Lloyd George devoted much of his time to negotiating with bosses and workers, endeavouring to achieve settlements that were not simply compromises, but recognitions that employers, employees and government had a common interest.

There are strong grounds for saying that it was Lloyd George who made the trade unions an integral part of British politics. His direct appeal to them in 1915 to suspend their agitation for the duration of the war and to enter into partnership with the Government was a recognition of their indispensability to the national war effort and gave the unions a consciousness of their status and responsibility.

Key question
Did Lloyd George have any political principles?

Lloyd George's political ideas

An essential point to grasp about Lloyd George is that he did not have a political philosophy. He certainly had strong dislikes and firm opinions, but these did not constitute an ideology in the sense of a structured programme founded on consistent attitudes. His Liberalism sat lightly upon him. He made politics a matter of personality.

There is a vital distinction to be made between Liberalism as a political party and liberalism as a political philosophy. In many respects it can be shown that small 'l' liberalism, far from disappearing, survived to become the common outlook in Britain. Its biggest victory was in its impact upon the Conservative Party and the Labour Party. Each of these incorporated liberal values into their respective conservative and socialist platforms, and indeed into their political practice. It would be too much to suggest that this was exclusively the result of the career of Lloyd George. Nonetheless, it is possible to argue that his attempt at consensus politics and his achievements in coalition government, whatever their short-term failures or deficiencies, created a powerful precedent.

It is difficult to deny that Lloyd George weakened the Liberal Party to the point of political impotence. At the same time, it is also arguable that he proved the most creative British politician of the twentieth century. He, more than any other single individual in British public life, laid down the basic political agenda for much of the rest of the twentieth century:

- the State as economic planner
- the redistribution of wealth through taxation
- social reform and the welfare state
- the acceptance of trade unions as part of the political and industrial framework.

These were the basic features of British domestic politics in the twentieth century. In his House of Commons tribute in 1945, Winston Churchill, his great colleague of the pre-1914 period, emphasised that it was Lloyd George's work as a social reformer that ranked as his greatest achievement:

> There was no man so gifted, so eloquent, so forceful, who knew the life of the people so well. Much of his work abides, some of it will grow greatly in the future, and those who come after us will find the pillars of his life's toil upstanding, massive and indestructible.
>
> Quoted in Martin Gilbert (ed.), *Lloyd George*, 1968

Summary diagram: The post-war Coalition, 1918–22

The problems of post-war reconstruction

Demobilisation
Health facilities
Unemployment
National Insurance and pensions
Housing
↓
Set against grim economic circumstances
– high inflation and falling demand for British goods

The Anglo-Irish issue

Legacy of the Easter rising
IRA v Black and Tans
The Treaty, 1921
↓
A major achievement but essentially a compromise
Mutual bitterness remained
Civil war in the new Ireland
↓

End of the 1918–22 Coalition

Its fall the result of:
↓
Policy failures – economic, social, foreign affairs
Lloyd George's tarnished reputation
Corruption
Abandonment of Lloyd George by the Conservatives
Continued split in Liberal ranks meant certain defeat in 1922 election
↓

Lloyd George's political significance 1905–22 assessed

Key question
Why were the
Conservatives in
office for such a short
period?

2 | The Conservative Government, 1922–24

Despite the Conservatives' decisive break with Lloyd George and the reassertion of their separate identity as a party, their period in office between 1922 and 1924 was disappointingly short of achievement. The poor economic situation and growing unemployment stifled any major initiatives. The Government's attempts to reduce **British debts** to the USA resulted in an agreement that verged on humiliation for Britain. One of the few bright notes was Chamberlain's Housing Act.

Chamberlain's Housing Act, 1923

This measure, introduced by **Neville Chamberlain**, the minister of health, laid down the following:

- Housing subsidies would take the form of a central government grant.
- This was to be paid annually to local authorities over a twenty-year period.
- The amount of the subsidy was £6 for each property erected for council housing by private builders.

The 1923 election

Seriously unwell with throat cancer when he became PM, Bonar Law had to retire in May 1923 after only eight months in office. His place as prime minister was taken by Stanley Baldwin, who judged that the best way to reverse the recession and tackle unemployment was to return to a policy of protection. He called a general election, hoping to gain a mandate for his plans.

Since his attempts to create a third force in British politics had come to nothing, Lloyd George took the only course remaining to him. He decided to rejoin the official, though much reduced, Liberal Party. In preparation for the1923 election, he and Asquith agreed to ignore their differences and reunite their supporters in a single party with free trade as their rallying cry.

Table 3.2: December 1923 election results

	Votes	Seats	% of total votes cast
Conservatives	5,538,824	258	38.1
Labour	4,438,508	191	30.5
Liberals	4,311,147	159	29.6

Although the Conservatives emerged from that election as singly the largest party, their decline from an overall majority of 75 to a minority of 100 represented a serious electoral rebuff and could be read as a rejection of Tariff Reform. Following a defeat on a confidence vote in the Commons, Baldwin resigned in January 1924.

Since the Liberal and Conservative parties had fought the election on opposite sides over protection, a coalition between them was out of the question. Despite increasing their strength from 116 to 159 seats between the 1922 and 1923 elections, the Liberals were now only the third-largest party and obviously could not form a government on their own. As the larger opposition party, Labour was entitled to take office even though it lacked an overall majority. So it was that after less than twenty years as a parliamentary party Labour found itself forming a government.

By 1923 Labour had pushed the Liberals into third place in British party politics. Why this had occurred can be conveniently summarised by comparing the reasons for the decline of the Liberals with those for the rise of Labour.

Key term

British debts Britain had borrowed heavily from the USA during the war. At the end of his negotiations with the Americans in 1923, Baldwin, the Chancellor of the Exchequer, had committed Britain to repaying £46 million annually for 62 years.

Key dates

Baldwin replaced Bonar Law as PM: May 1923

Election saw Labour become the larger opposition party: December 1923

Lloyd George rejoined Liberal Party: November 1923

Key figure

Neville Chamberlain (1869–1940) MP 1918–40, Chancellor of Exchequer 1923–24, 31–37, Minister of Health 1924–29, PM 1937–1940; son of Joseph Chamberlain and half-brother of Austen Chamberlain.

Liberal decline

- The split between Asquith and Lloyd George during the 1914–18 War created a breach in the Liberal Party that was never properly healed.
- The Liberals did formally reunite in 1923, but it was an unconvincing affair. Lloyd George kept his own party premises and staff and he and Asquith remained suspicious, if respectful, of each other. The result of the disunity was that the Liberals never again held office in their own right.
- Liberal values, such as the freedom of the individual, had been compromised by restrictive government measures during the war, particularly the introduction of military conscription. Liberalism could be said to have lost its moral authority.
- The Liberals had in a sense legislated themselves out of existence. Impressive though their pre-1914 reform record was, it marked the limit to how far they were prepared to go in changing the roots of society. They may have been radical but they were not revolutionary.
- Party politics in the twentieth century was an increasingly expensive affair. The Liberal Party was strapped for cash. As Lloyd George was fond of pointing out, his party had neither the donations from the business world that the Conservatives had, nor the funds from the trade unions that Labour had.
- Before 1914 the party had always been able to rely on the parliamentary support of the Irish Nationalists. This was no longer available after Sinn Fein boycotted the House of Commons in 1918 and Home Rule for southern Ireland was implemented in 1922.
- Despite, or perhaps because of, its long period in office since 1905, there was a distinct decline in enthusiasm among the party's grassroots workers in the constituencies.
- The 'first past the post' electoral system proved a killer of Liberal hopes of recovery. The party was unable to spread its popular support in such a way as to win key marginal seats. Knowing that the Liberals were unlikely to win an election, the party's supporters began to ebb away.

Labour's rise

Key question
How by 1923 had Labour come to replace the Liberals as the second-largest party?

- Working-class voters defected from the Liberal Party to the more radical Labour Party.
- Labour's strong trade union links provided it with a sound financial base.
- The Labour Party had a good war record. After initial misgivings, it played a major role in the patriotic war effort. This did much to dispel fears that it would be an unreliable defender of British interests.
- Its senior politicians had gained experience as cabinet ministers in the Coalition governments, thereby showing that the party was as capable of government as any of the other parties.
- It improved its constituency organisation during the war and in 1918 adopted a formal constitution setting out its programme.

• As a young party, there was a freshness and enthusiasm about its constituency workers that the established parties found hard to match.

It should be stressed that none of the reasons and explanations in these two lists should be taken to mean that the rise of the Labour Party was an inevitable process. Without the war there is no reason to suppose that the Liberal Party would have been irrevocably divided, or that the State would have moved so far towards controlling society, a development that undermined the Liberal Party's traditional defence of the liberty of the individual.

Summary diagram: The Conservative government, 1922–24

• A government burdened by debt
• Chamberlain's Housing Act (1923) was the only major measure
• Baldwin fought election on protection ticket
• 1923 election left Labour as larger opposition party

Why had the Liberals declined? – Why had Labour risen?

---

3 | The First Labour Government, 1924

Labour's taking office under Ramsay MacDonald in January 1924 was a truly remarkable turn of events, yet in a sense it was on sufferance. Asquith was prepared to commit his Liberals to conditional support of the Labour Party for two reasons:

• It was a way of ousting the Conservatives from power.
• He calculated that since Labour would be dependent on Liberal support he would be able to exercise effective control over the new Government, limiting it to those measures of which the Liberals approved, and capable of bringing it down altogether should he choose.

Asquith also reckoned, as did the Conservatives, that the inexperience of Labour would lead it to fail in office and thus discredit itself as a party of government. Indeed, it remained true throughout Labour's nine months of office in 1924 that its minority position denied it the opportunity of introducing radical or socialist measures.

As a realist, Ramsay MacDonald was well aware of how tightly he was restricted. The composition of his cabinet, which contained few left-wingers and a number of non-Labour Party personnel, was an indication that he appreciated the limitations that political circumstances placed upon him. It was for this very reason that some of his party colleagues had advised against taking office.

MacDonald's decision to press on was based on his belief that to decline office would look like cowardice and that the very act of assuming power, even if only for a limited time and with little chance of following radical policies, would, nonetheless, make the vital point that Labour had arrived as a party that respected the

Key question
Why were the other parties willing to accept the formation of a Labour government in 1924?

Key date
Labour government formed under Ramsay MacDonald: January 1924

Key question
Why was Ramsay MacDonald willing to form a minority government?

constitution and could govern responsibly. In this regard, MacDonald's was a notable achievement.

Labour's record

During its nine months of office in 1924 Labour introduced only three main measures and those were non-controversial:

- Restrictions on unemployment benefit were eased.
- More public funds were directed to educational provision.
- Wheatley's Housing Act (1924) was passed.

John Wheatley, the minister of health in the first Labour government, developed Chamberlain's scheme (see page 98) in the following ways:

- The subsidy paid per property unit was raised to £9.
- The annual payment to local councils was extended to 40 years.

Wheatley impressed upon the local authority officials, responsible for implementing the policy, that the council housing subsidised in this way was to be rented not sold. His fear was that if the properties became available for purchase they would be bought by the relatively prosperous, whereas the whole point of the scheme was to provide homes for the poorest at affordable rents. The success of this Act was clear in the statistic that showed that by 1933 half a million council houses had been built.

The Campbell case, September 1924

The Government's short life came to a premature end as a direct consequence of the Campbell case in September 1924. The Government ran into trouble when it appeared to interfere improperly in the justice system. It was accused of using its influence to have a prosecution withdrawn against a left-wing journalist, J.R. Campbell, for encouraging troops to mutiny. Campbell had urged soldiers to disobey orders if ever they were called upon to fire on striking workers.

Although the Conservatives roundly attacked the Government over this they were not out for blood. Nor were the Liberals; Asquith was quite willing for a committee of inquiry to consider the matter, which in the course of things would have meant many months passing before any report would appear. However, for some reason best known to himself, Ramsay MacDonald chose not to use the time he had been offered. Instead, he made the vote on the setting up of the inquiry a matter of confidence in the Government. He announced that if the Commons voted in a majority for the inquiry, he would resign. When the House duly did so, the Prime Minister kept his promise and thus brought about the end of the first Labour government over a legal trifle.

It was an extraordinary move on Ramsay MacDonald's part. Yet, while he had made a strange tactical error, he showed shrewdness on a broader political front. He judged that the Liberals were a spent force. He believed that, although his own party was not yet strong enough in the Commons to sustain itself

---

Key figure

John Wheatley (1868–1930)
Born in Ireland, raised in Scotland, worked as a miner and became a strongly left-wing MP for a Glasgow constituency, Minister of Health 1924.

Key question
How did this case help bring about the Labour government's downfall?

Key date
The Campbell case: September 1924

for a long period in office, the very fact that it had come into government showed that Labour had replaced the Liberals as the only realistic alternative party to the Conservatives. The soundness of his analysis was borne out by subsequent events. Although the Labour government had gone out of office after only nine months, largely because of the Campbell case, popular support for the Labour Party actually increased in the election that followed in October 1924. It is true that it lost 40 seats while the Conservatives gained 151, but it was the Liberals who came off by far the worst, losing 119 seats and nearly 1.4 million votes. This was the clearest sign yet that Labour had superseded the Liberals as the second main party in Britain.

Table 3.3: October 1924 election results

	Votes	Seats	% of total votes cast
Conservatives	8,039,598	419	48.3
Labour	5,489,077	151	33.0
Liberals	2,928,747	40	17.6
Communist	55,346	1	0.3

Labour's success in increasing its support was even more remarkable when set against the remarkable crisis which confronted it at the time of the election.

The Zinoviev Letter crisis

On 25 October 1924, four days before the election, the *Daily Mail* carried the following headline: SOVIET PLOT: RED PROPAGANDA IN BRITAIN: REVOLUTION URGED IN BRITAIN. Beneath the headline it printed a letter purportedly from Grigor Zinoviev, chief of the **Comintern**. It was addressed to the **British Communist Party**, urging its members to infiltrate the Labour Party and use it to bring down the British State. The letter is believed by historians to have been a forgery, concocted by **White Russian** émigrés to suggest that the Labour Party was a front for Soviet subversion.

To understand why the letter created such excitement it has to be pointed out that Ramsay MacDonald's government had negotiated trade and diplomatic agreements with the Soviet Union. An Anglo-Russian treaty had been drawn up containing the following main terms:

- Britain agreed to advance a £30 million loan to the Soviet Union.
- In return, the Soviet Union would pay compensation for the British financial assets and investments the Communists had seized after taking power in the Russian Revolution of 1917.

Key dates

Election returned Conservatives to power: October 1924

The Zinoviev Letter crisis: October 1924

Russian Revolution: October 1917

Key terms

Comintern
The Communist International, the Soviet agency for fomenting revolution in other countries.

British Communist Party
Set up in 1920, it was always subservient to the Comintern, which provided the bulk of its funds.

Key question
How did the Zinoviev Letter affect the fortunes of the Labour Party?

Key term

White Russians
The Communists' (Reds') main opponents, largely made up of émigrés who had fled Russia after defeat in the civil war of 1918–20.

Key date

Anglo-Russian trade agreement: March 1921

ON THE LOAN TRAIL.

Key terms

Revolutionary Russia
In October 1917, the Russian Communist revolutionaries had taken power under Lenin and then called on workers everywhere to do the same and overthrow their governments.

USSR
Union of Soviet Socialist Republics (often shortened to Soviet Union), the formal title of revolutionary Russia.

A cartoon of October 1924 ironically sums up the attitude of large sections of the press towards the affair of the Zinoviev Letter. The caption reads:

'In a document just disclosed by the British Foreign Office (apparently after considerable delay), MZINOVIEFF, a member of the Bolshevik dictatorship, urges the British Communist Party to use "the greatest possible urgency" in securing the ratification of Mr. MacDONALD's Anglo-Russian Treaty, in order to facilitate a scheme for "an armed insurrection" of the British proletariat.' Why might many people in Britain at this time have been willing to accept the Zinoviev Letter as authentic?

While the treaty was never put into operation since the Government went out of office before it could be ratified, it provided ammunition for those in Britain who believed that relations between MacDonald's government and **revolutionary Russia** were far too close for Britain's good. Yet, in answer, Ramsay MacDonald could refer to his far from negligible record in foreign affairs where he had been concerned with promoting more than just better relations with the **USSR**.

Ramsay MacDonald and foreign affairs

During Labour's brief period of office, Ramsay MacDonald made a considerable contribution to the improvement of international relations generally, and those between France and Germany in particular. He was the first and only British prime minister to attend the **League of Nations** in Geneva. While there he was instrumental in the drafting of the Geneva Protocol, whose main proposals were as follows:

- Nations were to agree to accept that disputes would be settled by collective decisions.
- Nations would actively consider ways of achieving disarmament.
- Nations would act together to prevent or deal with unprovoked aggression.

The Protocol was not formally accepted by the League, but it was an interesting restatement of the principle of **collective security** and one which was particularly pleasing to the pacifists who were still an important part of the Labour movement. In more practical terms it encouraged France and Germany to lessen their animosity. At a conference in London, which he chaired, Ramsay MacDonald persuaded both countries to move towards a settlement of the **reparations** issue. Up to this point France had consistently demanded that Germany pay the full amount originally laid down in the Treaty of Versailles; Gemany had equally consistently argued that the reparations were unrealistically heavy and so could not be paid.

The readiness of France and Germany to reconsider their positions led to international agreement over the **Dawes Plan**, whose main terms were:

- France agreed to lower the reparations figure to a level which would not cripple Germany.
- Germany was to be allowed to pay the lower rate for five years, which would give its industry the chance to recover.
- Germany would be entitled to raise international loans to help it recover economically.
- Britain was to act as go-between, collecting the sums paid and passing them on to the USA to help pay off Britain's war debts.

Since the Dawes Plan was not agreed upon until 1925, nearly a year after Labour lost office, Ramsay MacDonald was not accorded as much credit as he deserved. Nevertheless, it may justifiably be claimed as one of the major achievements of the first Labour government.

Key question
What impact did Ramsay MacDonald have on foreign policy?

Key terms

League of Nations
The body, to which all nations were entitled to belong, set up in 1919, with the aim of settling all future international disputes by referring them to the collective judgement of the League's members.

Collective security
The concept of all nations of good will acting together to stop an aggressor nation.

Reparations
Payment required of Germany to compensate for the war damage the Allies claimed it had caused.

Dawes Plan, August 1925
A scheme devised by General Dawes, an American banker, based essentially on Ramsay MacDonald's earlier proposals.

Summary diagram: The first Labour government, 1924

Reasons why a minority Labour Party formed a government:

↓

Liberals and Conservatives hoped that Labour would prove
incapable of effective government

↓

Ramsay MacDonald eager to prove
Labour was ready for office

↓

Labour had become an acceptable political force

Reasons for Labour's loss of office:

- Always vulnerable to combined Lib–Con attacks
- Ramsay MacDonald's poor handling of Campbell case

1924 election saw increase in Labour vote despite Zinoviev Letter

---

Labour's record:

- Improved unemployment benefit
- Educational provision
- Wheatley's Housing Act
- Foreign policy achievements

---

4 | Baldwin's Government, 1924–29

Key question
How successful was
Baldwin's government
during this period?

Back in office in November 1924, after Labour's resignation,
Stanley Baldwin formed a government that over the next five years
introduced a number of important measures. His Chancellor of
the Exchequer was Winston Churchill, who, after twenty years as a
Liberal, had now returned to the Conservative Party. Baldwin
accepted that tariff reform was no longer a viable policy and he
quietly shelved it. Instead he adopted a broad policy aimed at
improving British trade and finances; he also gave attention to a
number of social reforms. However, one underlying problem – the
sluggish economy, and one particular event – the General Strike,
have tended to overshadow his administration.

Key dates
Baldwin's
Conservative
government: 1924–29

Red Friday: July 1925

Industrial troubles – the path to the General Strike

a) Red Friday, July 1925

One of the few direct moves of the Labour Government in favour
of the workers in 1924 had been its backing for an agreement that
protected the wages of the miners. However, the mine owners,
who had originally accepted the agreement, soon went back on
their word. In June 1925 they declared that they were obliged to

cut wages, citing as justification the desperate state into which the British coal industry was sliding; orders were falling and production costs were increasing. Not surprisingly, the miners' union (the Miners' Federation) resisted bitterly. When the TUC supported them, a general strike was planned for 31 July (nicknamed Red Friday).

However, Baldwin's government bought itself time by offering a temporary subsidy to maintain wage levels and by setting up the **Samuel Commission**. The move prevented a strike but the basic problem had not been solved. Much would hang on the Commission's report, which was scheduled to be delivered by the spring of the following year, 1926. In the intervening months, British industry began to experience the harmful consequences of a fateful financial decision made by Winston Churchill at the Treasury.

b) The return to the gold standard

Before 1914 Britain's currency had been on the **gold standard**. This had given it a strength that led foreign investors to buy sterling and use it as a common form of exchange. Nearly all major trading nations had followed Britain and adopted their own gold standard, which gave stability to international commerce. It was the economic disruption caused by the First World War that made it impossible for countries to keep to this. In 1919 Britain suspended the operation of the gold standard for a period of six years.

1925 was, therefore, the year in which it would begin to operate again. The big consideration for Churchill was at what rate to value the pound sterling when it returned to the gold standard. He decided to strengthen the pound by restoring it to its pre-war parity with the **US dollar**. This meant raising the pound's exchange rate from $3.40 to $4.86.

While this bold step helped British financiers, it deepened the plight of British exporters, who found it even harder to sell their goods abroad at the newly inflated prices required by the increased value of the pound. This was because the real gold value of sterling raised its exchange rate against all other currencies as well as the dollar. Foreign traders had to pay larger amounts of their own currency when purchasing British goods. This was an obvious disincentive to buy British. The return to the gold standard in April 1925 thus added to the growing tendency for British goods to be priced out of the market.

The General Strike, 1926

It was in this depressed atmosphere of falling sales that the Samuel Commission presented its report in March 1926. Its main recommendation was that the coal industry be totally restructured, but it urged that in the meantime the miners should accept a cut in wages. The Miners' Federation angrily rejected this and again called on the TUC to support them by organising a **general strike**, to begin on 30 April. Many of the mine owners responded by imposing **lock-outs**.

Key term

Samuel Commission
Under the Chairmanship of Herbert Samuel, its remit was to examine the problems of the mining industry and put forward solutions.

Key question
What part did the gold standard play in increasing Britain's economic difficulties?

Key terms

Gold standard
The term refers to the position in which a nation's currency is kept at a high value by tying it to the price of gold.

US dollar
As the world's strongest currency, the dollar was taken as the financial benchmark. All other currencies were measured in terms of their exchange value against the dollar.

Key question
Was the General Strike an 'avoidable folly'?

Key dates

UK returned to gold standard: April 1925

Samuel Commision report: March 1926

Key terms

General Strike
The idea was that all the unions affiliated to the TUC would call their members out on strike in sympathy with the miners.

Lock-outs
Literally locking out the workers by closing the gates of the collieries.

From the beginning, there was poor liaison between the TUC and the miners. Moreover, none of the TUC leaders genuinely wanted a strike on this scale; they hoped that, as had happened a year earlier, the Government would back down rather than risk conflict. However, unlike 1925, the Government was now prepared to call the TUC's bluff. Indeed, many in the Cabinet, most notably Churchill, wanted a show-down with the labour movement. Nonetheless, talks in Downing Street between Government officials and TUC leaders seemed, by Saturday 1 May, to be on the verge of success. A compromise, by which the employers would withdraw their lock-out notices and the workers would lift their strike threats, was close to being agreed.

But then there occurred an episode that destroyed the negotiations and made a strike unavoidable. On the evening of 2 May, news broke that the printers at the *Daily Mail* had refused to typeset a provocative editorial by the paper's editor. The key passage to which the printers objected read:

Key date

General strike: May 1926

> We do not wish to say anything hard about the miners themselves. As to their leaders, all we need say at this moment is that some of them are (and have openly declared themselves) under the influence of people who mean no good to this country.
>
> The general strike is not an industrial dispute; it is a revolutionary movement, intended to inflict suffering upon the great mass of innocent persons in the community and thereby put forcible constraint upon the Government.

This was just what the government hawks, such as Winston Churchill and Lord Birkenhead, had been waiting for. When he heard of the printers' action, Birkenhead declared delightedly, 'Bloody good job!' Baldwin and his cabinet were pressed into delivering an ultimatum to the TUC, stating that no further talks could take place unless the 'overt action' of the printers was condemned by the TUC and all strike notices withdrawn. The TUC protested they had not been consulted by the printers at the *Mail* and that they were still willing to negotiate. But, by declining to wait for the TUC's reply, the Government closed the door to a settlement. The next day, 3 May, the Government declared a state of emergency and the TUC began its long-threatened strike.

The failure of the General Strike

Key question
Why did the strike never become an effective challenge to the Government?

Despite its apparent militancy, the TUC's threats were largely rhetoric; it did not want a strike. As a consequence, the workers' side had made few preparations. It was never, in fact, a general strike. Only selected unions were called out, the main ones being:

- transport and railway workers
- printers
- workers in heavy industry
- gas and electricity workers.

While these would have made up a formidable industrial force if they had acted resolutely together, from the beginning there was a crippling lack of cohesion. Some workers in the unions and regions selected simply carried on working.

In marked contrast, the Government was fully ready. Indeed, the reason for the Government's climb-down, in July 1925, had been to give itself time to prepare for a confrontation. It was greatly aided here by the **Emergency Powers Act** of 1920. Under the terms of this six-year-old measure, the Government had set up the Organisation for the Maintenance of Supplies (OMS), which created a national network of voluntary workers to maintain vital services should a strike occur. One of the key initiatives of the OMS was to do a deal with the road hauliers to keep food supplies moving.

Compared with the Government's preparations, the organisation of the strike by the TUC was rudimentary and ineffectual. It was only on the eve of the strike, when the leaders of the **TGWU** obliged their TUC colleagues to recognise what they had let themselves in for, that detailed plans were belatedly and hurriedly drawn up.

There was little active support for the strikers from the general public. Many ordinary people sympathised, but did little to help. Those who did become involved tended to be on the Government's side. Ex-officers from the armed services enrolled as special constables, while university students, in keeping with their tradition of engaging in things they never quite understand, volunteered as bus and train drivers. It was all a bit of a lark for these **'bright young things'**. The **BBC**, which was officially neutral in its news bulletins, was careful to say nothing critical of the Government or supportive of the strikers. Such activities have been described as 'class war in polite form'.

Ironically, it was a class war only for one side. Certainly there were some hotheads and left-wing extremists among the strikers who wanted to turn the affair into a blow against the capitalist system, but these were very much a minority. The aim and behaviour of the mass of the strikers were peaceful and responsible. This has been neatly put by A.J.P. Taylor:

> The voluntary recruitment of the First World War and the strike of 1926 were acts of spontaneous generosity, without parallel in any other country ... The strikers asked nothing for themselves. They did not seek to challenge the government, still less to overthrow the constitution. They merely wanted the miners to have a living wage.
>
> A.J.P. Taylor, *English History, 1914–45*, 1965

Given the Government's readiness, the TUC's reluctance and the general public's indifference, the strike stood no chance of success. There were violent clashes here and there between police and strikers but few unions were willing to support the miners in a fight to the finish. On 12 May, after ten days, the TUC called off the strike without winning any concessions from the employers or the Government. The miners themselves carried on for another seven months before they, too, gave in unconditionally.

Key terms

Emergency Powers Act, 1920
Introduced during the days of the Lloyd George Coalition, this measure granted the Executive wide authority and extraordinary powers in the event of a major disruption of essential services.

TGWU
The Transport and General Workers Union.

'Bright young things'
The young people of the privileged classes who, in reaction to the horrors of the Great War, chose in the 1920s and 1930s to live irresponsible, carefree lives.

BBC
Began in 1922 as the private British Broadcasting Company; in 1926 it became the British Broadcasting Corporation funded by a compulsory licence fee paid by listeners.

Key dates

Trade Disputes Act: May 1927

Reform Act granted women vote on same terms as men: April 1928

Election returned Labour as largest single party: May 1929

Trade Disputes Act, May 1927

In the aftermath of the General Strike, the Government introduced a Trade Disputes Act aimed at making another general strike impossible. It:

- outlawed general and sympathetic strikes
- restricted strike action to specific disputes
- forbade trade union funds being used for political purposes unless the individual member chose to contribute by 'contracting in'.

To the opponents of the strike this seemed an appropriate way of forestalling further industrial troubles; to the strikers it appeared deliberately punitive.

Key question
What social and economic reforms of note had Baldwin's government introduced?

Chief measures of Baldwin's government

As the following list of measures shows, there was more to Baldwin's 1924–29 government than the General Strike.

1925   A Pensions Act enabled contributors to draw their pension at 65.
Britain's currency was returned to the gold standard (see page 106).

1926   An Electricity Act set up the National Grid to provide power throughout Britain.

1927   The BBC established a national radio broadcasting system.
A Trade Disputes Act restricted trade union freedoms.

1928   A Parliamentary Reform Act granted the vote to women on the same terms as men, i.e. all citizens over the age of 21.

1929   In an effort to stimulate production and commerce, a Local Government Act exempted all farms and twenty-five per cent of factories from local rates. The Act also effectively ended the old Poor Law (see page 3) by abolishing the Boards of Guardians and phasing out the workhouses.

Nevertheless, the Conservative Party's 1929 election slogan 'safety first' was hardly an inspiring one after five years in office, and its failure to control rising unemployment counted against it. In the election its share of the vote dropped by ten per cent compared with 1924. The Liberal Party staged a recovery by nearly doubling its aggregate vote. But its share of the vote was too widely and thinly spread. The most impressive feature of the election was the increase in the Labour vote, sufficient to return it as the largest single party. It was time for a second Labour government.

Table 3.4: May 1929 election results

	Votes	Seats	% of total votes cast
Labour	8,389,512	288	37.1
Conservatives	8,656,473	260	38.2
Liberals	5,308,520	59	23.4

Summary diagram: Baldwin's government 1924–29

The path to the General Strike

	Development	TUC action	Government action
July 1925	Mine owners reduced wages. Miners agreed to await Samuel Report.	Backed miners' strike threat.	Offered miners a wage subsidy. Set up Samuel Commission. Made preparations to meet a strike.
Mar 1926	Samuel Commission urged miners to accept wage cuts. Miners' Federation called strike' for 30 April.	Gave Federation uncertain backing.	
April–May 1926		Joined Government in talks which seemed on verge of success.	Hawks press for showdown.
2 May	Printers at *Daily Mail* refused to set editorial.	Denied knowledge of printers' action.	Delivered ultimatum to TUC.
3 May		TUC declared a general strike.	Declared a state of emergency.

Government's chief measures, 1925–29:

1925	Pensions Act
	Gold standard restored
1926	National Grid established
1927	BBC established a national radio broadcasting system
	Trade Disputes Act
1928	Granted the vote to women on same terms as men
1929	Local Government Act.

Study Guide: AS Questions

In the style of AQA

(a) Explain why a Labour government came to power in 1924.

(12 marks)

(b) How successful was Baldwin in dealing with the General Strike of 1926? (24 marks)

Exam tips

The cross-references are intended to take you straight to the material that will help you to answer the questions.

(a) Re-read pages 99–101. There are many factors involved here, including: why the 1923 election was called, the weaknesses of the Conservatives and Liberals and the strengths of Labour. You would also have to explain why MacDonald was prepared to form a minority government and why the other parties were prepared to accept this. There is not time to write extensively on all these factors but you would need to pick out and justify what you consider to be the most important factors and separate the long- and short-term reasons in order to show some judgement.

(b) Re-read pages 105–109. Baldwin's success may seem obvious, given the failure of the General Strike, and there is plenty to write about the way the Government prepared for and countered the strike through the Emergency Powers Act, securing 'success' in the 1927 Trade Disputes Act. However, Baldwin's 'success' needs to be evaluated against the other factors that caused the strike to collapse, for example, its own aims and organisation as well as public attitudes.

In the style of OCR

Domestic issues, 1918–1951

Assess the most important problems that led to the fall of Lloyd George's government in 1922.   (50 marks)

Exam tips

The cross-references are intended to take you straight to the material that will help you to answer the question.

You need to show that you have understood the focus of the question and that you can select an appropriate range and depth of evidence to support your argument. Organise the problems that led to Lloyd George's fall from power according to the most difficult and/or damaging. It will not be enough to list problems or evaluate them, you must link the problems to his fall and make a judgement on their relative importance. Some of the problems you are likely to assess are:

- the difficulty of keeping the support of the Coalition government (page 89)
- the opposition of the Conservatives to Lloyd George, his policies and presidential-style leadership (pages 90, 95)
- economic problems and Lloyd George's solutions (pages 82–84)
- the role of the Carlton Club and opposition from Austen Chamberlain (page 90).

Ensure that you conclude with a judgement on the most important problems.

---

4 From Labour to the National Government, 1929–39

POINTS TO CONSIDER:
Throughout its two years in office, Ramsay MacDonald's second government was troubled and eventually overwhelmed by mounting economic problems. Setting himself the task of leading Britain through the financial crisis that struck it in 1931, the Prime Minister 'betrayed' his party by abandoning it to form a National Government, composed largely of Conservatives. This proved popular with the electorate and the National Government stayed in power until 1940. The great issue of the time remained the economy and it was against the background of the Depression of the 'hungry thirties' that the new government operated in its early years. It also had to face growing threats on the foreign front; this was the era of communist and fascist regimes. These developments are studied under the following headings:

- The second Labour government, 1929–31
- The financial and political crises of 1931
- The National Government – Domestic affairs, 1931–37
- The National Government – Foreign affairs, 1935–39

Key dates

1929–31	The Second Labour Government
1929–35	The Depression
1929 August	The Young Plan
1929 October	The Wall Street Crash
1930	Coal Mines Act
	Housing Act
	Gandhi's 'salt protest'
1931	Education Bill
	London Transport Bill
	The May Committee
	Agricultural Marketing Act
	End of Labour government

1931		Ramsay MacDonald formed National Government
		Ramsay MacDonald expelled from Labour Party
		Election confirmed National Government in power
	September	The Invergordon Mutiny
		Gold standard abandoned
1933		The Nazis took power in Germany
		Oxford Union 'King and Country' debate
1933		Housing Act
1934–35		Peace ballot
		Baldwin as PM
1935		Housing Act
1936		German occupation of the Rhineland
		Abdication Crisis
1936–39		Spanish Civil War
1937		Chamberlain became PM
1938		Munich agreement
1939		German occupation of Czechoslovakia
		British guarantees to Poland
		Britain declared war on Germany

1 | The Second Labour Government, 1929–31

Key question
What economic and political constraints did MacDonald's second government work under?

It was with apparent reluctance that Ramsay MacDonald took office in June 1929. Despite its impressive showing in the election, Labour still did not have an overall majority and there was a fear in the party that, as in 1924, this would prevent its following genuinely radical policies. The Prime Minister seemed aware of this when he appointed a cabinet that was predominantly right wing and moderate. However it was not a concern over being defeated by a combined Conservative–Liberal vote that inhibited the Labour government most. The truth was that Labour's second period of office coincided with the onset of a severe international economic depression. Whatever its reforming intentions may have been, the Labour government was eventually overwhelmed by the economic problems that this created. Yet, despite the restrictive atmosphere in which it had to operate, Ramsay MacDonald's second government was not without its achievements.

The Second Labour Government: 1929–31

Coal Mines Act: 1930

Key dates

Coal Mines Act, 1930

This measure attempted to alleviate the bitterness within the mining industry in the aftermath of the General Strike four years earlier. Its main terms were:

Key figures

Arthur Greenwood (1880–1954)
Son of a painter and decorator in Leeds; MP 1922–31, 1932–54, Minister of Health 1929–31, in Churchill's War Cabinet 1940–42, Deputy Leader of Labour Party, 1935–45.

Charles Trevelyan (1870–1958)
A Northumberland landowner who moved from the Liberals to Labour; MP 1899–1918, 1922–31, Parliamentary Secretary to the Board of Education 1908–1914, President of the Board of Education 1924, 1929–31.

Herbert Morrison (1888–1965)
A police constable's son; MP 1923–24, 1929–31, 1935–59, leader of the London County Council 1933–40, Minister of Transport 1929–31, Home Secretary 1940–45, Foreign Secretary 1951, disappointed never to have been PM or Labour Party leader.

Key dates

Agricultural Marketing Act:1931

Housing Act: 1930

Education Bill: 1930

London Transport Bill: 1931

- miners' working hours were reduced from 8 to 7½ hour shifts
- employers were entitled to fix minimum wages and production quotas
- a commission was set up to consider how unprofitable mines could be phased out with least damage to miners' livelihoods.

Agricultural Marketing Act, 1931

In an attempt to provide an overarching authority that could improve the supply of food to the public, the Act set up boards of food producers with the power to fix prices and arrange supplies more efficiently.

Housing Act, 1930

Introduced by **Arthur Greenwood**, the minister of health, the Act extended the earlier work of John Wheatley (see page 101) by re-introducing government subsidies for council housing and granting greater powers to local authorities to enforce slum clearance. As a result of this measure, there were more slums cleared between 1934 and 1939 than in the whole of the previous half century.

Education Bill, 1930

Charles Trevelyan, as president of the Board of Education, tried to build on the work he had begun while holding the same post in the first Labour government. He introduced a bill that would have raised the school leaving age to fifteen. But even before the House of Lords rejected his bill, it had met with resistance from a seemingly strange quarter. Catholic MPs on the Labour back benches complained that insufficient attention had been paid in the Bill to the particular needs of Catholic schools. Their objection was that Catholic parents who paid taxes that went towards the general provision of state education still had to provide out of their own pocket for the upkeep of Catholic schools. The debate over faith schools and how far they should be financed by the State would still be an unresolved question in the twenty-first century.

London Transport Bill, 1931

This measure, introduced by **Herbert Morrison**, did not become law until 1933. It created a public corporation responsible for providing cheap and efficient bus and underground transport for London's population.

Where Ramsay MacDonald's second government proved especially disappointing to the left wing of the Labour Party was in its failure to reverse the Trade Disputes Act passed in 1927 in the wake of the General Strike (see page 109). The original Act had been seen by many as a vindictive move against the unions and it was hoped that, with Labour in office again, steps would be taken to undo its main terms. However, when the Liberals let it be known that they would not support such an adjustment, the Government did not press ahead with it.

Foreign affairs

On balance the Government's record in foreign affairs was more impressive than its domestic performance. Ramsay MacDonald regarded foreign policy as his special forte. In 1924 he had combined the offices of prime minister and foreign secretary. He would have liked to have done the same in 1929 but he allowed himself to be persuaded to make Arthur Henderson foreign secretary, though he reserved the right as PM to involve himself in foreign policy when he thought fit.

Henderson, who had insisted that he was the man for the job and would not consider any government post other than foreign secretary, was justified in his self-confidence. After only two months in office he played a key role as negotiator in a conference at the Hague which ended with the European nations agreeing to the **Young Plan**, which saw Germany accepted as an equal nation in Europe again.

Henderson also made a considerable impression at the League of Nations in Geneva. Both the French and the Germans found him amenable and dependable and he helped bring the representatives of those two peoples closer together than at any point since 1918. Such was the sense of trust he engendered among his foreign counterparts that he was able to rejuvenate the disarmament talks that had stalled. In recognition of his achievement he was made president of the disarmament conference in 1932. It was no fault of Henderson that the economic depression and the descent of Germany into **Nazism** would soon wipe out the advances he had made.

Ramsay MacDonald also worked for international conciliation. In October 1929 he visited the United States, with which Britain's relations had not always been warm in the 1920s, largely because the Conservative governments had feared that America's strong anti-imperialist stance was an implied threat to Britain's own empire. The main issue Ramsay MacDonald discussed during his visit was the relative strength of national navies. It was this question that had stymied talks on disarmament. The powerful maritime nations – the USA, Japan and Britain – were reluctant to risk reducing their armed fleets.

Early in 1930, as a result of MacDonald's American talks, Britain hosted a tri-nation conference specially convened to seek a compromise on naval matters. The key agreement reached at the conference was **the ratio principle**. The USA, Britain and Japan agreed in their warship building programmes to abide by a ratio of 5:5:3. As with Henderson's work, subsequent events were to diminish MacDonald's achievement. Japan was unhappy with the agreement and soon ceased to abide by it as it prepared for war. However, the closer contacts Britain made with the USA were to have important consequences when the Second World War came in 1939.

Anglo–Soviet relations

There had been an understandable hope among the left-wing members of the party that with Labour in office there would be a major improvement in Britain's relations with the USSR, which had nose-dived at the time of the Zinoviev Letter in 1924 (see page 102). It was believed that 'left could speak unto left', the notion being that socialist Britain was well fitted to understand Socialist Russia.

Yet Ramsay MacDonald's government never showed any inclination to follow an international socialist path. The Prime Minister believed sincerely in the need to pursue international co-operation as a principle, but at no time was he willing to risk national interests by aligning Britain with Soviet ideas of revolution. Indeed, a major part of Ramsay MacDonald's achievement as a political leader was that he made his party electable by showing the voters that, no matter what a few hotheads on the fringe might say, the Labour Party was a responsible and committed upholder of the British parliamentary system.

This did not prevent diplomatic progress being made. In October 1929, the Government formally resumed full relations with the USSR; ambassadors were exchanged and embassies established, but beyond the formalities little else was done. The proposals put forward at the time of the 1924 Labour government for an Anglo-Soviet treaty covering loans and trade were not resurrected.

India

Ramsay MacDonald could also justifiably claim that it was during his second Labour administration that the first tentative steps were taken towards the independence of India. This had been a stated aim of the Labour Party since its earliest days. In December 1929 the **Indian Congress Party**, not waiting for the outcome of talks on dominion status, made a declaration of Indian independence.

Knowing that the British would not recognise this, **Mohandas Gandhi**, regarded as the father of modern India, organised a 'salt protest'. In 1930, collecting thousands of followers along the way, he led a 250-mile march to the coastal town of Dandi. There he picked up a lump of salt from the beach and crushed it in his hands. It was a simple but hugely symbolic gesture. Gandhi was protesting against the way the people were not allowed to gather natural sea salt but were forced to buy the heavily taxed government-owned variety. For this he was arrested and imprisoned.

This was an embarrassment for Ramsay MacDonald's Government. Dedicated to Indian independence, it now found itself in a situation where it was the ultimate authority suppressing the independence movement. Striving for a way out, Ramsay MacDonald called a Round Table conference in London in November 1930. At first the Congress Party refused to attend. But after a series of complex manoeuvres, which included Gandhi's being released from prison and invited to the conference, they accepted. However, by the time Gandhi arrived for the talks the Labour Government had resigned from office.

Key date

Gandhi's 'salt protest': 1930

Key term

Indian Congress Party
The main nationalist party in India, dedicated between 1858 and 1947 to ending British rule, which had formally operated since the Government of India Act of 1858.

Key figure

Mohandas Gandhi (1869–1948)
Known popularly as Mahatma (great soul), Gandhi was a devout Hindu who believed, nevertheless, in the equality of all religions; arguably the most influential revolutionary of the twentieth century; his philosophy of non-violent protest became the model for civil rights movements everywhere.

It was the brevity of the Labour government's term of office and its sudden end that prevented it from achieving a settlement of the Indian question at this stage. Nevertheless, the Government's contribution was far from negligible. It had shown a willingness to accept that any lasting settlement would have to be on Indian terms. India would have to be granted its freedom. The question was when and how that would come.

2 | The Financial and Political Crises of 1931

By 1931 Britain had begun to suffer severely from the effects of the worldwide depression which had begun two years earlier in the USA (see page 123). Unemployment had risen to nearly three million. To meet the hardship suffered by the victims the Government raised unemployment benefit. However, the decline in industrial production in Britain had caused a sharp fall in revenue from taxation and the Government simply began to run out of money. **Philip Snowden** as Chancellor of the Exchequer had no new ideas; there was nothing especially socialist about his budgets. On the contrary, his approach to finance was a very conventional one. He was not prepared to take risks. He believed in **balanced budgets**, which entailed restricting public expenditure to essentials.

It was this conservative attitude that so frustrated younger members of the Labour Party such as Oswald Mosley (see page 131), who believed that there were alternative economic and financial strategies that a Labour government ought to be trying.

The May Committee

Still seeking a solution along traditional lines, Snowden, in February 1931, appointed a special committee under Sir George May as Chairman to consider ways out of the financial crisis. Making no attempt to consider a new economic approach, the May Committee had nothing to suggest in the report that it presented in July other than cuts in public expenditure. It recommended a wide range of reductions in pay for teachers, civil servants and those in the armed services. The report's lack of originality led to its being described by John Maynard Keynes (see page 164) as 'the most foolish document I have ever had the misfortune to read'.

The May Committee's proposal that aroused the most dissension within the Government was the suggestion that unemployment pay be cut by ten per cent (the initial proposal was twenty per cent). Many in the Cabinet believed that if this were to be done it would destroy the very principle for which the Labour Party had been created – the protection of the working class. But Ramsay MacDonald was also under pressure from the international bankers, who were unwilling to advance further loans to Britain unless it reduced its welfare expenditure. He told his colleagues that there was no alternative but to make the cuts. When this proposal was put to a cabinet vote, ten of the 21 members rejected it.

Key question
Why was was the Labour government brought down by the financial crisis of 1931?

Philip Snowden (1864–1937)
A Methodist, teetotaller, pacifist and supporter of the suffragettes; MP 1906–18, 1922–31; Chancellor of the Exchequer 1924, 1929–31.

Key figure

Balanced budgets
Keeping a balance between the revenue received by a Government and the amount it spends (public expenditure).

Key term

The May Committee: 1931

Key date

Key question
What form did Ramsay MacDonald's 'betrayal' of his party in 1931 take?

Key dates

End of Labour government: 1931

Ramsay McDonald expelled from Labour Party: 1931

The end of the Labour government – Ramsay MacDonald's act of 'betrayal'

The Cabinet split was the prelude to what became known in Labour Party history as 'the great betrayal'. Unable to carry a united cabinet with him, Ramsay MacDonald declared his intention of resigning on his and the Government's behalf. After consultations with the leaders of the two opposition parties, Herbert Samuel of the Liberals and Stanley Baldwin of the Conservatives, he went formally to see the King, George V.

Since what is said in an audience between monarch and prime minister is never revealed, it is not known precisely what passed between the King and Ramsay MacDonald. All we can know for sure is that Ramsay MacDonald did not resign. Instead, he came back to tell his bemused colleagues in the last Labour cabinet meeting that he had agreed to stay on as prime minister in a new Coalition or 'National Government'.

'Country before party'

His explanation was that he was putting 'country before party'. He claimed that the economic crisis facing Britain was so serious that it could be met only by forming a cross-party government of national unity. This did not satisfy the Labour ranks; it enraged them. They protested that it had all been a plot on his part to retain personal power and that the National Government was already decided on long before he told the cabinet. He had gone behind the backs of his colleagues and done a deal with the opposition leaders. Ramsay MacDonald was immediately expelled from his party and his name became reviled among succeeding generations of Labour supporters.

Hugh Dalton, a Labour junior minister at the time, was present at the critical cabinet meetings. He wrote of Ramsay MacDonald's sitting alone on one side of a long table facing his accusers on the other. It was, said Dalton, 'as though a martyr was speaking, just before a cruel death'. Dalton described how those Government members unwilling to accept the slashing of unemployment pay blamed the whole crisis of 1931 on the bankers who had tried to hold the Labour government to ransom.

The Prime Minister defended the bankers; he claimed that, far from acting improperly, they had offered the Government 'the most valuable help'. It was the desperate financial circumstances, not malicious design that had created the need to reduce welfare expenditure. Britain could not cope without an international loan. 'Otherwise,' said Ramsay MacDonald, 'sterling would have collapsed. There would have been a run on the banks, and then a run on the Post Office.'

The impact on the Labour Party

Since only three ministers and a handful of Labour backbenchers switched their loyalties to the National Government, there was a sense in which the Labour Party had undergone a purification. True, it took a pummelling at the polls in 1931, losing 236 seats and seeing its popular support drop by 1.7 million votes, but it was now free in opposition to redevelop its ideas and policies.

Yet, interestingly enough, despite the condemnation of Ramsay MacDonald's behaviour in 1931, the younger brand of Labour politicians, including Dalton, Morrison, Bevin and Attlee, who in the 1930s were to work for the recovery and growth of the Labour Party, did so along the lines that MacDonald had laid down. This centre-right orientation of the Labour leadership would create many bitter quarrels within the parliamentary Labour Party and in the movement as a whole, but it would also determine the essential structure and electoral politics of the Party. Notwithstanding his 'betrayal' in 1931, MacDonald's legacy endured.

George Lansbury became Labour Party leader following the general election of 1931, taking over from Arthur Henderson who had filled the gap after Ramsay MacDonald's expulsion. Although he was a revered figure in the party, his advancing years meant that Lansbury had little to offer in terms of new ideas; his anti-war views inhibited him from adopting a strong stand on the rise of fascism and Nazism (see page 139).

He was succeeded in 1935 by Clement Attlee, known at this time by his military title, Major Attlee. In his characteristically quiet but authoritative way, Attlee skilfully maintained the balance between the competing wings of the party and provided a leadership that helped the party revive during a difficult period when the National Government remained electorally dominant.

The 'popular front'

A complication with which Labour had to contend was the effect of a turnabout in Soviet policy. During the 1920s and 1930s the Soviet Union had taken a consistently contemptuous line towards the non-Marxist socialist parties of Europe, such as the Labour Party, dismissing them as 'social fascists' whose leaders had supinely co-operated with the corrupt governments of the day in keeping the workers down. But, after 1935 Stalin, fearful at the rise of an aggressive Nazi Germany, tried to gain some sort of security by reversing his policy of non-alignment with the Left. Through the Comintern (see page 102) he now appealed to the parties of the left in Europe to unite in a **'popular front'** against the evils of fascism.

Stalin's change of heart came too late. The European socialists were unwilling to switch direction simply to suit their previous abuser, the Soviet Union. Although the Communist sympathisers within left-wing parties threw themselves energetically into promoting the popular front, the mainstream parties, including the Labour Party in Britain, were understandably reluctant to respond to what they regarded as mere Soviet expediency in the face of German aggression. This led to a series of struggles within the Labour Party between the advocates of the popular front and the party centre, which remained suspicious of Soviet intentions. The suspicions were borne out when Stalin made nonsense of the whole 'popular front' campaign by performing a still more extraordinary turnabout by entering into the **Nazi–Soviet Pact** in August 1939.

Key figure

George Lansbury (1859–1940)
Pacifist, very active in local politics, Minister for Works 1929–31, Labour leader 1932–35.

Key question
What was at issue in the dispute over joining the popular front?

Key terms

'Popular front'
An alliance of all communist, socialist and progressive parties.

Nazi–Soviet Pact
A non-aggression agreement between Germany and the USSR, signed in August 1939.

Summary diagram: The second Labour government, 1929–31

PRINCIPAL MEASURES
- Coal Mines Act, 1930
- Housing Acts, 1930, 1933, 1935
- Education Bill, 1930
- Agricultural Marketing Act, 1931
- London Transport Bill, 1931

1931 CRISIS
- Snowden's budgets
- The May Committee
- Ramsay MacDonald's betrayal

FOREIGN AFFAIRS
- India
- Young Plan
- League of Nations
- Anglo-Soviet relations

Key question
Was the National Government simply Conservative rule by another name?

Key dates

Ramsay McDonald formed National Government: 1931

The Invergordon Mutiny: September 1931

Key term

Invergordon Mutiny, September 1931
In protest against scheduled cuts in service pay the 12,000 sailors from the fifteen ships of the Atlantic fleet, moored at Invergordon in Scotland, declared that they would not obey orders.

3 | The National Government – Domestic Affairs, 1931–37

a) The formation of the National Government

Knowing that they would fill the majority of the cabinet posts and that Ramsay MacDonald would be dependent on them, the Conservatives as a party fully backed the National Government. Although Lloyd George did not personally join the Government, he did commit the official Liberal Party to the support of what was now a heavily Conservative-dominated coalition led by Ramsay MacDonald.

Notwithstanding the political bitterness it created, the formation of a new government did ease the financial crisis in the short term. A loan of £80 million (roughly equivalent to £1.5 billion in today's money) was immediately advanced by American bankers. The price for this was that Britain had to continue with the programme of cuts that had brought about the end of the Labour government. But, in the face of strong opposition from those most directly affected by the tax hikes and pay reductions, expressed most disturbingly in the **Invergordon Mutiny**, the Government limited the cuts to around half the original figures proposed.

The hostile reaction to the cuts, and the knowledge that the £80 million was fast being used up, increased the pressure on the Government to abandon the gold standard. This was duly done on 19 September, five days after the Invergordon Mutiny. The devaluation that this entailed did not have the disastrous effects that had been widely feared. The pound fell by a quarter of its value, from $4.86 to $3.40, but this did not cause any major disruptions in the money markets and had the consequence over the longer term of making British exports cheaper and therefore more competitive.

Cartoon by A.W. Lloyd published in the *News of the World* on the 11th October 1931. Premier (to his companions): 'Now then, altogether, boys, and good luck!' A cartoon showing MacDonald, Baldwin and Herbert Samuel (National Liberal leader) taking the plunge by calling an election to confirm the National Government in office; on the edge of the pool, Henderson and Lloyd George prepare to enter the water. How well does the cartoonist capture the attitudes of the various parties towards the National Government?

Despite the extraordinary way it had come into being and its early shocks, the National Government proved popular at the polls. In the 1931 election it gained over two-thirds of the aggregate vote, a figure unequalled in modern times. Clearly the majority of the voters did not regard Ramsay MacDonald's action as betrayal. They broadly accepted that the exceptional crisis justified the creation of a new form of government whose first concern was, as MacDonald put it, not party politics but national recovery.

Key dates

Election confirmed National Government in power: 1931

Gold standard abandoned: 1931

Table 4.1: October 1931 election results

	Votes	Seats	% of total votes cast
Conservative	11,978,745	473	55.2
Liberal National	809,30	35	3.7
National Labour	341,370	13	1.6
Liberals	1,403,102	33	6.5
National Government (total)	(14,532,519)	(554)	(67.0)
Labour	6,649,630	52	30.6
Independent Liberal	106,106	4	0.5
Communist	74,824	0	0.3
New Party	36,377	0	0.2

Notably, neither Oswald Mosley's New Party (see page 131), nor the Communist Party won any seats. Equally notable, as an example of electoral imbalance, was the statistic showing that it took the Conservatives just 25,325 votes to return an MP, whereas it took Labour 127,877.

The performance of the National Government in the 1930s tends to be judged by historians in relation to its handling of two major problem areas: the economy and foreign affairs (see page 135). The new Government that Ramsay MacDonald now led had to contend with the financial and economic problems that had helped bring down his previous Labour government. These are best understood by reference to the Depression, the term that is still useful as a description of what Britain experienced for much of the 1930s.

b) The Depression

1929 was a critical date in international history. It marked the beginning of an economic depression that was to last for a decade and affect nearly every country in the world, Britain included. It was in the October of 1929 that the United States, the world's most powerful economy, underwent the **'great crash'**. This financial disaster was followed by a severe industrial decline between 1929 and 1932. In a desperate effort to limit the damage, the USA immediately introduced restrictive measures. It erected prohibitive trade barriers to keep out foreign goods and it recalled its foreign loans. Britain was one of the first countries to be harmed by these policies. Since the American market was now largely closed, the British manufacturing industries could not sell their goods in what had been their biggest outlet.

Britain's staple industries, which were already in decline (see page 75), were particularly badly hit. There was the added problem for Britain that its trade with the USA had previously been the major means by which it had raised the capital to pay off its loans. Unable now to trade with America, Britain found itself in an impossible position. It was saddled with debts and could not raise the capital to meet them. It is true that Britain was itself owed large amounts by France, Italy and other allies from the wartime. However, since these countries were also victims of the international depression there was little prospect of their being able to pay what they owed to Britain.

Key question
How did Britain become caught up in America's economic depression?

Key term

The 'great crash'
The collapse of the American stock market, which destroyed share values and investments.

Key dates

The Depression: 1929–35

The Wall Street Crash: Oct 1929

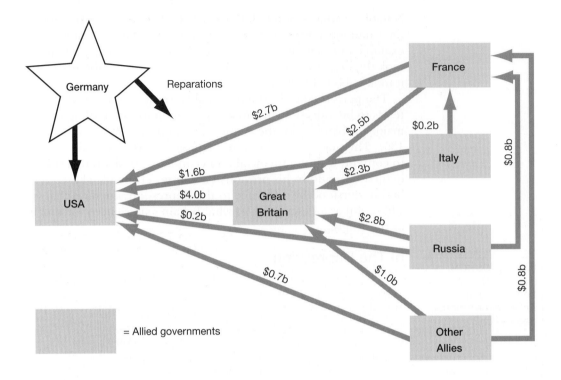

Figure 4.1: The diagram illustrates the links created by the loans and borrowings among the Allies during the First World War. The arrows point from the debtor to the creditor countries, showing how much was owed. In theory, Germany was committed to paying large reparations to the Allies. But the relatively small amounts it did pay came from loans advanced by the USA which stood at the centre of the whole interlocking system. This was why the health or otherwise of the United States' economy was of such vital concern to Europe. How does the diagram support the notion that 'If the USA sneezes, Europe catches a cold'?

The following tables help provide a picture of how the industrial depression, at its worst between 1930 and 1936, affected Britain.

Table 4.2: Unemployment in Britain, 1921–40

1921	1.58 million	1931	2.64 million
1922	1.50 million	1932	2.64 million
1923	1.28 million	1933	2.40 million
1924	1.12 million	1934	2.10 million
1925	1.22 million	1935	2.00 million
1926	1.28 million	1936	1.90 million
1927	1.12 million	1937	1.49 million
1928	1.20 million	1938	1.70 million
1929	1.28 million	1939	1.60 million
1930	1.98 million	1940	1.10 million

Table 4.3: Percentage of unemployed in certain trades in 1936

All trades	12.5
Shipbuilding	30.6
Coal mining	25.0
Shipping	22.3
All textile trades	13.2
Commerce and finance	3.8
Printing and paper	6.2
Skilled building craft	6.3
Chemical trades	7.9
Engineering	8.3

Key question
Did the 1930s witness an economic decline or a boom?

Tables 4.2 and 4.3 illustrate the blight affecting the staple industries in Britain. In 1936 the overall unemployment figure for all British trades was 12.5 per cent. However, shipbuilding, mining, shipping and textiles all showed much higher figures. In contrast, the **service industries** all had single figure rates of unemployment.

The service industries were those enterprises developed after the First World War to meet the growing demand for modern convenience and leisure goods such as radios, refrigerators, vacuum cleaners, newspapers and magazines. The building, electrical engineering, printing and chemical trades rapidly expanded to provide these commodities, which were directly aimed at stimulating consumer demand.

Key term

Service industries
Those enterprises that catered directly for consumer demand.

The discrepancy between the decline of the staple industries and the boom in the consumer industries is striking. It indicates that there was no single trend that could be observed. Whether one saw growth or decline depended on where one looked. This is clearly evident in the statistics in Table 4.4. Low in the relatively prosperous London and the South-East, unemployment was noticeably higher in the areas where the staple industries were concentrated, principally:

- the manufacturing centres of Birmingham and the Black Country
- coal and steel in Yorkshire and Wales
- textiles in Lancashire
- shipping and shipbuilding on the Tyne and in Scotland and Northern Ireland.

Key question
Was the Depression of the 1930s a national or a regional problem?

Revisionist historians suggest it is inaccurate to speak of the 'hungry thirties', as if the 'Depression' or 'Slump' had been a universal experience in Britain. They regard it not as a single phenomenon but as several. What observers see depends on where they stand. Table 4.4 indicates that the Depression was very much a regional affair. In those areas of Britain dependent on the old industries for their livelihood, the Depression was severe and enduring. If, however, the focus of attention is shifted to such regions as the Thames Valley or the Home Counties, the picture becomes one of remarkable growth. The increase in house-building and in the purchasing of cars and domestic commodities could be taken as both cause and effect of the good times prevailing in these areas.

Table 4.4: Percentage of unemployed according to region in 1936

SE England	5.6
London	6.5
SW England	7.8
Midlands	9.4
NW England	16.2
NE England	16.6
Scotland	18.0
Northern Ireland	23.0
Wales	28.5

Living standards between the wars

As the previous section noted, the Depression was a patchy affair. It did not affect the whole of Britain equally. Unemployment and industrial decline were not universal. Indeed, in a number of areas there was spectacular growth. However, that was of little comfort to those in the depressed regions. They complained that a southern-dominated parliament and government did not fully appreciate the sufferings of their countrymen in the north. It was part of a north-west/south-east divide often described as the '**two nations**'. It was little consolation to the victims of the slump to be told that things were better elsewhere in the country.

Yet, after acknowledging the poverty that so many in the regions experienced, the fact remains that for many of the population the inter-war years were a time of genuine economic advance. Figure 4.2 is instructive here. It shows that at no time did **retail prices** move ahead of wages; the lines of the graph remain parallel throughout the 'twenties and 'thirties, indicating that purchasing power was maintained even when wages appeared to fall. This meant that **real wages** increased. For those in work, times were better, not worse, during the Depression.

Key question
Did living standards rise or fall during the Depression?

Two nations
The term was first used in the nineteenth century to define the division of Britain between the rich and the poor, and between the areas of Britain which were flourishing and those which were in decline.

Retail prices
The price paid for goods by the purchaser in the shops.

Real wages
The purchasing power of earnings when set against prices. When prices are high money will buy less; when prices are low the same amount of money will buy more.

Key terms

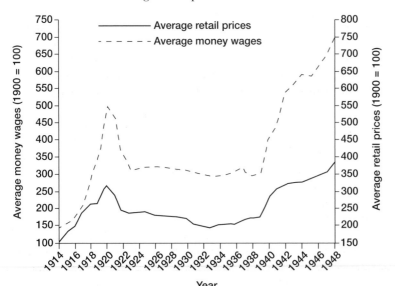

Figure 4.2: A graph comparing prices and wages in Britain, 1914–48.

Key question
In what respects did conditions improve for part of the population?

Growth in consumerism

The grimness of the conditions of the laid-off workers in the staple industries was only too real, but it was far from being the whole story. Between 1924 and 1935 real wages rose as a national average by seventeen per cent. This gave the majority of people in Britain greater purchasing power, a fact proved by the expanding sales of consumer goods, known popularly as **'mod cons'**. The women's cosmetics industry also experienced a very rapid growth as working-class women began to use the lipsticks, powders and perfumes that had previously been exclusive to their richer sisters. Access to popular entertainment became widespread. Reading tabloid newspapers and magazines, listening to the radio, going to the cinema and watching professional sport became the main leisure activities of the British people. One measure of this is that between 1924 and 1935 cinema audiences grew from 36,000 a year to eight million.

A housing revolution

In this same period over one million houses, many having indoor lavatories and hot running water, were provided at low rent by the local authorities (see page 115). In addition to these council houses, two-and-a-half million homes were provided by the building industry for private sale. A major factor enabling people of fairly modest incomes to buy houses was the increase in the 1930s of the number of **building societies**.

Key measures in the provision of homes for ordinary people were the National Government's Housing Acts of 1933 and 1935, which were a development of the measures introduced by Greenwood in 1930 during Ramsay MacDonald's second Labour Government (see page 115). Each of the National Government's pieces of housing legislation granted increased government subsidies to those local councils who were prepared to tackle the problems of slum clearance and overcrowding. The subsidies were put to effective use. In 1936 the average weekly rent paid by council house tenants in Britain was an affordable 11 shillings (55 pence).

Housing was one of the success stories of the National Government. By 1939 a third of the four million houses in Britain had been constructed in the twenty years since 1918, many of those during the 1930s. The developments in the provision of both private and council house building in the inter-war years began a housing revolution, which was to be a notable aspect of social advance in the twentieth century. In 1914, only ten per cent of the population owned their own homes. Fifty years later, this proportion had grown to sixty per cent.

An impressive feature of these new homes was their use of electricity as the chief source of power. By 1939, the spread of **the National Grid** was providing electricity to nearly all of urban Britain, a development that largely explains the rapid rise in living standards that occurred across the nation. This was of particular significance for women. By tradition they were the workers in the

Key terms

'Mod cons'
Short for modern conveniences, i.e. household accessories such as vacuum cleaners, refrigerators and radios.

Building societies
Finance companies that advanced mortgages (loans) over long periods of time (e.g. 20 or 25 years), which made it possible for those on regular incomes to buy houses, knowing that they would be able to pay back the capital and interest.

The National Grid
A nationwide network of high-voltage lines carrying electricity from generating stations to homes and factories.

Key date

Housing Acts: 1933, 1935

home. The drudgery that so many of them had experienced was not ended by electricity, but their burdens were lessened.

c) The National Government's economic policies

As its reaction to the 1931 crisis had shown, the National Government had no genuine answer to the economic problems of the day. Its only response was to return to protective tariffs in an attempt to stimulate industrial recovery. This was unimaginative; protection itself would not have ended the Depression. It can be said of the National Government, as of all the inter-war governments, that they did not have economic policies that were informed or realistic enough for the problems they faced.

This was most obviously the case in regard to unemployment. Apart from a set of largely ineffectual **deflationary gestures**, the National Government did not really have a strategy for dealing with unemployment. It shied away from the intervention advocated by Keynes and Oswald Mosley (see pages 164 and 131). The strongest criticism of the Government's failures tended to come from outside parliament. Memorable examples were the hunger marches, invariably peaceful, not to say poignant, protests by the unemployed, who felt they had no other way of drawing attention to their desperate condition than by taking to the streets. The most famous of these was the Jarrow March of 1936, which involved two hundred unemployed Tyneside shipyard workers walking from Jarrow to London.

What ultimately helped the National Government was not its own policies, such as they were, but the recovery in world trade that occurred towards the mid-1930s and which was sustained by large-scale re-armament in the late 1930s. Although unemployment remained high for peacetime and was the outstanding domestic issue of the time, it did fall from its peak of 2.6 million in 1932 to 1.7 million in 1938.

The 1935 election result showed that, despite the inability of the National Government to deal with unemployment, it had largely maintained its support. The Liberals were clearly no longer a political force, and although the Labour party had increased its popular support under Attlee's leadership, it was not yet able to convert that into seats in the Commons.

Key question
Did the National Government have any real economic policies?

Deflationary gestures
The cutting of public expenditure in the hope that this would limit inflation and so encourage manufacturers to continue producing and, therefore, employing workers.

Key term

Table 4.5: 1935 election results

	Votes	Seats	% of total votes cast
Conservatives (including National Labour and National Liberal)	11,810,158	432	53.7
Labour	8,325,491	154	37.9
Liberals	1,422,116	20	6.4
Communists	27,117	1	0.1

An interesting statistic is that this was the last election in Britain in which the winning party polled more than fifty per cent of the vote. All governments since then have been minority governments. In no genuine sense has a party been voted into office by popular will. Elections are won or lost by the results in the marginal constituencies. In electoral terms Britain is not a democracy since individual votes are not equal; it depends where they are cast.

Another fascinating detail is that for most of the century most female voters supported the Conservatives. It has been calculated that had women not been enfranchised there would have been no Conservative governments between the 1930s and 1990s. An equally remarkable reading of the figures is that it was only Labour's strength in Scotland that at any time gave it a majority in the House of Commons. Without the Scottish vote, the Conservative Party would have been continuously returned to office.

d) Ramsay MacDonald's record as prime minister

Key question
How significant were Ramsay MacDonald's periods of office as prime minister?

Age and declining health led to Ramsay MacDonald's retirement in 1935. He had already gone on too long; in his last years he often became rambling and incoherent. Friends hid their embarrassment, and critics their contempt, behind their hands. Yet it would be unfair to let this last image dominate his reputation. It is true that he had split the Labour Party, and that he had no genuine answer to the economic problems that dogged all three of his administrations, 1924, 1929–31 and 1931–35. Yet his constructive contribution to political life far outweighed his failings. The development of the Labour Party as an electable and acceptable part of the political system was largely his work and his attempts to create harmony in international relations won him the admiration of many in Britain and abroad.

Ramsay MacDonald's record as prime minister:

- His decision to lead his minority parliamentary party into office showed Labour had arrived as a party of government.
- His pursuit of moderate policies freed Labour of the accusation that it was a front for Marxist extremists.
- He broke the party over his decision in 1931 to stay in office and form a coalition, which resulted in Labour's being out of office for the next fifteen years.
- In putting 'country before party' and leading the National Government he was advancing the notion of consensus politics.
- In none of his three administrations was he prepared to abandon traditional orthodox financial and economic policies.
- He earned a deserved reputation as a peacemaker in international affairs.

e) Baldwin as prime minister, 1935–37

Key question
What strengths did Stanley Baldwin's personal qualities bring to the National Government?

In 1935 Ramsay MacDonald was followed as prime minister by the Conservative leader, Stanley Baldwin, who formed his third government. Much to the annoyance of his political opponents, Baldwin's policy of 'masterly inactivity' appeared to suit the situation. He continued to present the image he had developed as prime minister in the 1920s of the pipe-smoking Englishman who loved his country and its people and who could be relied upon in a crisis. This had been evident in his handling of the General Strike in 1926, where his calmness had prevented his government colleagues from going to extremes (see page 106).

The Abdication Crisis, 1936

This was also apparent in his handling of the Abdication Crisis in 1936, a situation created by the wish of Edward VIII to marry Mrs Wallis Simpson, an American divorcée. Baldwin took a consistently constitutional approach, refusing to be drawn into the moral issues that many others thought were at stake. He advised the King that for him to take a divorced woman as his marriage partner would be incompatible with his position as head of the Church of England, which did not recognise divorce. He informed Edward that the Government would have to consider resigning if he pressed on with his marriage plan.

Although a group of Conservatives formed an unofficial **'King's Party'**, the majority of MPs, the whole of the Labour Party, and, as far as can be judged, public opinion, supported the Prime Minister's principled, some said high-minded, stand. Baldwin's view prevailed. In December 1936, after just 325 days as uncrowned king, Edward VIII put his personal desires before his sense of duty and announced his abdication. Six months later he married the woman without whom, as he told the nation in his abdication broadcast, he could not live.

Baldwin's record as PM

Baldwin was a great parliamentarian and was admired for his lack of pettiness and his generosity of spirit towards his political opponents. Indeed, it has been suggested that his calm leadership and lack of vindictiveness played no small part in Britain's avoiding the political extremism that marred so many European countries between the wars (see pages 131, 137). Like Ramsay MacDonald, he appears genuinely to have believed in putting country before party when Britain's interests were at stake. It is doubtful that the National Government could have worked at all had Baldwin not backed it from the beginning with his special brand of moderation and absence of political rancour. Such were the political uncertainties after 1931 that traditional politics might have fractured had he not been there to hold things together. Even while Ramsay MacDonald was prime minister, it was Baldwin who was the chief stabilising influence.

Baldwin wanted class divisions to be eradicated from politics and society. It was for that reason that some of the right-wing Conservatives sometimes disapproved of him. They complained that his notions were 'half-way to socialism'. At times he also received strong criticism from the press whose proprietors found his 'safety-first' approach unattractive. It is an interesting reflection of the less-than-clear political divisions between the parties that Baldwin should have been regarded as too socialist in his approach, while Ramsay MacDonald was considered not socialist enough.

Key dates

Baldwin as Prime Minister: 1934–35

Abdication Crisis: 1936

Key term

'King's Party' An unofficial grouping of some 60 MPs, including Winston Churchill, who argued that Edward VIII should be allowed to make his own decision, free from political pressure.

His strengths:

- His calm but firm leadership was of great value in Britain at a time of political extremism elsewhere in Europe.
- His lack of small-mindedness and respect for opponents made him a figure around whom compromise and conciliation could develop.
- He rode major domestic crises ably, e.g. General Strike (1926) and the Abdication Crisis.
- He made the National Government work when there was a risk of politics fracturing.

His weaknesses:

- His lack of insight in economic matters meant he made no significant contribution to resolving unemployment.
- His detachment from foreign affairs limited his understanding of the character of developments in Nazi Germany and fascist Italy.

Key question
How did Oswald Mosley influence British politics in this period?

Key figure

Oswald Mosley (1896–1980)
Was variously a Conservative, an Independent, a Labour MP, and a Fabian, but he found none of the parties satisfied his particular political notions. That was why in the end he turned to a form of politics outside the mainstream.

f) Oswald Mosley and the BUF

One of Ramsay MacDonald's interesting ministerial appointments in 1929 was an able and ambitious young man, **Oswald Mosley**, who was made Chancellor of the Duchy of Lancaster. Although this was a non-cabinet post, Mosley was one of a group entrusted with the task of examining ways of tackling unemployment. He found, however, that when he presented his own formal set of proposals on the matter they were turned down by the Cabinet on the grounds that they were either too impractical or too expensive. Among Mosley's suggestions were:

- greater use of tariffs to raise revenue
- the money raised through tariffs to fund pensions and unemployment cover
- funded early retirement schemes in industry to free up jobs for younger workers
- government control of the banks to prevent financial problems arising.

The 'New Party'

Frustrated by his rejection, and in spite of being very well received at the 1930 Labour Conference, Mosley decided to go it alone. He resigned from the Labour party and founded his own 'New Party' based on the proposals he had put to the Cabinet. The New Party fielded 24 candidates in the 1931 election, on a programme of tackling joblessness. It failed to attract public support, each of the 24 who stood gaining an average of only 1,500 votes.

The BUF

This dismal performance intensified Mosley's despair of parliamentary politics, which, he claimed, were no longer capable of answering Britain's needs. In 1932 he founded the British Union of Fascists (BUF). While the BUF was prepared to contest elections, its ultimate aim was the establishment of a **corporate state** in which parliament would cease to exist or have only a minor role to play.

Mosley took as his model Benito Mussolini and his Italian fascists. Mussolini (1883–1945) was a former socialist who became embittered by what he regarded as the effete character of the Italian political system. He led his followers, the fascists, to power in 1922 and ruled as Il Duce (the leader) until 1943. Mosley was impressed by Mussolini's intense nationalism and his hatred of communism. He was also taken with Mussolini's re-organisation of the Italian state along corporatist lines, which, he believed, had rid Italy of the type of economic problems that still threatened Britain.

As with all the fascist parties in Europe at this time, there was a very strong racist element in Mosley's BUF. It viciously denounced the Jews, asserting that it was their worldwide influence and grasping methods in banking and trade that were principally responsible for the economic depression.

Although Mosley himself was an interesting character with many striking ideas, his fascist movement never gained truly popular support. That is not to deny that it was not capable of frightening the authorities by causing serious disorder, as witnessed in the Battle of Cable Street in October 1936. Declaring its hatred of immigrants, the BUF planned a provocative march through London's East End, an area that was home to many Jews and Irish. This was met with barricades and fierce and violent resistance from locals who forced the march to be diverted away from the area.

While creating disturbance was relatively easy, becoming a credible party was altogether more difficult and the BUF never advanced beyond being a lunatic fringe. Although his ideas on economics attracted people as diverse as **Aneurin Bevan** and Harold Macmillan, Mosley's political notions appealed only to social misfits and those with personality disorders. The only people with any sort of social standing who joined the BUF were a few second-rate writers and minor aristocrats. It is true that the *Daily Mirror* and the *Daily Mail* showed some initial sympathy for Mosley's plans to lessen unemployment, but, as soon as the latent racism of his movement became overt, the newspapers dropped him.

The BUF had some success in local politics but it is highly doubtful that it would ever have been an electoral force nationally. This was never actually put to the test as there were no general elections between 1935 and 1945, but since the highest recorded number of BUF members in the 1930s was 50,000, the party's chances of winning any seats appear negligible.

Reasons for the failure of the BUF to progress in 1930s Britain:

- It was dependent on Oswald Mosley and never had a separate identity as a credible political movement.
- Able though Mosley undoubtedly was, he was surrounded in the BUF by mediocrities.

Corporate state
Power concentrated at the centre, entitling the Government to direct the running of society and the economy.

Key term

Aneurin Bevan (1897–1960)
Labour MP 1929–60, Minister of Health 1945–51, Minister of Labour 1951; of Welsh coal-mining stock, he became the outstanding voice of the left wing of the Labour Party.

Key figure

Key date

The Nazis took power in Germany: 1933

- Mosley's style of leadership, based on Mussolini in Italy and Hitler in Germany, was alien to British politics and won him few admirers outside his own fascist ranks.
- Apart from its ideas on unemployment, the BUF had no real plan of action. It relied too greatly on stirring up hatred and emotion without ever knowing how to use these in a sophisticated political form.
- It was only in the grim economic atmosphere of the early 1930s that the BUF had any attraction. Once the economy began to pick up, British fascism began to wither.
- Unlike Italy and Germany, Britain had a long-established and stable political system which, despite the Depression of the 1930s, never came under serious threat from extreme movements like the BUF.
- Notwithstanding the personal wealth which Mosley and some of his aristocratic associates put into the BUF, the movement never raised enough funding to sustain it as a powerful force.
- As the threat of war increased in the 1930s (see page 139), the BUF's sympathy for Nazi Germany made it very suspect in the eyes of ordinary members of the British public.
- The social and economic breakdown for which the BUF longed never occurred. Mosley was left 'an opportunist for whom no opportunity came'.

Key question

What influence did the Communist Party have in the 1930s?

g) The Communist Party of Great Britain (CPGB)

Many of the limitations from which the BUF suffered also applied to the other extreme political movement in Britain, the Communists. Established in 1920, the Communist Party of Great Britain (CPGB) depended for its funds on secret grants from the Soviet Union. An intriguing detail that has come to light is that the Communist Party received more money in this way than the official Labour Party was able to raise for itself by legitimate means. Yet, in political terms the Soviet payments were largely a waste. As Table 4.6 illustrates, at no point, even in the grimmest days of the Depression, did the Communist Party ever make sufficient ground to be more than a minority pressure group.

Table 4.6: The CPGB's electoral performance

	Candidates	Votes	Seats	% of total votes cast
1924	8	55,346	1	0.3
1929	25	50,614	0	0.3
1931	26	74,824	0	0.3
1935	2	27,117	1	0.1
1945	21	102,780	2	0.4

It is true that the Communists made a bigger impression in local government. Parts of Glasgow, for example, and some London boroughs, saw the Communists play a prominent role in the 1930s in protests over rent payment and housing conditions. But such local following as the party gained never translated into a national movement of note.

The same was true of their efforts in the workplace. Communists were often behind the strikes and industrial disruptions of the time, but, despite the Depression of the 1930s, they failed to exploit the situation well enough to make themselves a major political force or become a real threat to the political order whose overthrow they sought.

Unable to gather support on its own terms, the CPGB tried to affiliate to the Labour Party. It made four separate applications, in 1924, 1935, 1943 and 1946, but was rejected on each occasion. At the time of the first application in 1924 the Labour Party ruled that anyone belonging to the CPGB could not join the Labour Party as an individual member. Consequently, the only way Communists could directly influence Labour was by **'entryism'**, joining the party without declaring their real allegiance.

Such tactics undoubtedly intensified the struggle over policies between the Left and the Right of the Labour Party. Significantly, however, Labour under Attlee, following the pattern established by Ramsay MacDonald, always sought the moderate centre ground when presenting his case to the electorate. One of Attlee's major achievements during his twenty years as leader after 1935 was to prevent the Marxist left from imposing its revolutionary policies on the Labour Party.

Interestingly, the section of society where communist ideas were strong was not among the workers but among the intellectuals. University dons, writers and poets, such as W.H. Auden and Stephen Spender, found Marxist anti-capitalist ideas appealing. Dismayed by the Depression and the rise of fascism, they were beguiled into thinking that Soviet Communism offered a better way. That was why the Spanish Civil War attracted their interest (see page 137).

It was during the 1930s that a coterie of some of the brightest young men at Cambridge University were recruited by the Comintern (page 102) to spy for the Soviet Union. The most notorious of these were Guy Burgess and Donald Maclean who went on to work in the 1940s in the Foreign Office from where they leaked British state secrets before fleeing to the Soviet Union in the 1950s.

It is now clear that British intellectuals turned to communism largely as a reaction against the existence of the right-wing regimes in Hitler's Germany, Mussolini's Italy and Franco's Spain. Fascism and communism are now seen as mirror images, which explains the deep mutual hatred between them as ideologies. But in the 1930s it was their differences that were emphasised by contemporaries. To be a supporter of one was to be the bitter enemy of the other. The aggression and brutality of Nazi Germany gave a form of acceptability to Soviet Communism, which was seen as being intellectually respectable in a way that fascism could not be.

Intellectuals convinced themselves that the viciousness associated with Nazism and fascism was an integral and definitive part of their

'Entryism'
Infiltrating the Labour Party with the aim of pushing it towards the left from within.

Key term

character, whereas the excesses of Communism were occasional lapses brought about by desperate circumstances. This readiness to be forgiving of Communism was boosted by the entry of the Soviet Union into the war as an ally of Britain in 1941 (see page 144).

'A low, dishonest decade'

W.H. Auden memorably described the 1930s as 'a low, dishonest decade', and it is certainly true that historians have tended to find the period of the National Government a dispiriting one. Strong leadership was lacking and the politicians of the day had no answer to the economic difficulties that confronted them. Domestic policies seemed to be a matter of drift rather than direction. However, in the end it was not the National Government's domestic record, but its failure in foreign affairs that has come in for the strongest criticism.

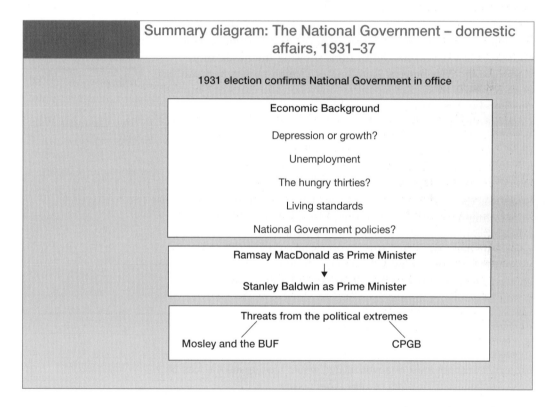

Summary diagram: The National Government – domestic affairs, 1931–37

1931 election confirms National Government in office

Economic Background

Depression or growth?

Unemployment

The hungry thirties?

Living standards

National Government policies?

Ramsay MacDonald as Prime Minister
↓
Stanley Baldwin as Prime Minister

Threats from the political extremes

Mosley and the BUF   CPGB

Key question
What part did public opinion play in the conduct of the National Government's foreign policy?

4 | The National Government – Foreign Affairs, 1935–39

In the first half of its period of office the National Government had to cope with the major economic problems that confronted Britain. In the second half, it was crises in foreign affairs that demanded attention. Arguably, in both cases, the National Government largely failed.

Public opinion

An interesting feature of the foreign policy followed by the National Government was the influence public opinion had upon it. The 1930s were a period when public attitudes began to be measured more accurately and taken more notice of by parties and politicians. The Gallup organisation, an American group, began to make studies of British public opinion in the 1930s. Although the methods and techniques were unsophisticated by later standards, they were obviously the beginning of something significant. Despite never formally admitting it, the National Government was beginning to be aware of public opinion and be influenced by it.

Where this was most noticeable was in the marked reluctance of the public to regard war as a legitimate step in national policy. This derived from a profound terror of military conflict, drawn from memories of the carnage of 1914–18. Moreover, there was a general belief, strengthened by newsreels of the terrible effects of bombing, that a future war would be still more appalling since the civilian population would be at the mercy of aerial bombardment. British audiences had been shocked by films showing the devastation caused by the **Axis powers**' bombing of civilian targets in Spain (see page 137) and by similar Japanese attacks on the cities of China in the **Sino-Japanese War**. Stanley Baldwin put this chillingly in the Commons in November 1932:

> I think it is well also for the man in the street to realise that there is no power on earth that can protect him from being bombed. Whatever people may tell him, the bomber will always get through.

Since war was too horrible to contemplate, its avoidance became a demanding necessity. None of the political parties felt free to advocate a re-armament programme. Furthermore, in a time of economic depression, it was not easy to argue the merits of arms expenditure at the expense of welfare. In November 1936 Baldwin showed how sensitive the decision-makers had become to the power of public opinion:

> I put before the whole House my own views with *appalling frankness* ... supposing I had gone to the country and said that we must rearm, does anybody think that this pacific democracy would have rallied to the cry? I cannot think of anything that would have made the loss of the election from my point of view more certain.

The 'King and Country' debate, 1933

There were striking occasions when the view of the British people was regarded as having been very clearly expressed in its refusal to contemplate war. In February 1933, the Oxford Union voted by a large majority in favour of the resolution 'That this House will in no circumstances fight for its King and Country'. Given that Oxford University supposedly contained some the brightest young

Key terms

Axis powers
Germany and Italy.

**Sino-Japanese War
(1937–45)**
A struggle between China and Japan.

Key date

Oxford Union 'King and Country' debate: 1933

people in the nation from whom would come the next generation of leaders in public life, the debate was interpreted by many in Britain and abroad as evidence of how powerful a hold pacifist feelings had in the country at large.

The Peace Ballot, 1934–35

In a remarkable measurement of public opinion, the first ever attempted on such a scale, a nine-month, house-to-house poll was organised by the **League of Nations Union**. This involved 11.5 million people answering a series of questions regarding their views on disarmament. Most responded strongly in favour of Britain's remaining a member of the League of Nations, and backed the notion of an 'all-round reduction of armaments'. However, to arguably the most important question, whether they supported international armed resistance against an aggressor, nearly seven million replied yes, more than two million said no, with another two million abstaining.

The answers revealed a basic confusion of thought in the majority of those questioned. They were in favour of disarmament while at the same time believing in the legitimacy of international armed resistance to aggression. This was a contradiction to which many held without perhaps realising they were supporting two mutually exclusive positions.

A remarkable example of such thinking were the words of the leader of the Labour Party, Clement Attlee. In 1935 he defined his party's approach to international questions when he told the Commons:

> We stand for collective security through the League of Nations. We reject the use of force as an instrument of policy. Our policy is not one of seeking security through re-armament, but through disarmament.

Attlee's assertion is an interesting expression of the basic paradox in British attitudes at this time. He declared his support for the League of Nations and collective security (see page 104), but at the same time he rejected the use of force and appealed for disarmament. As can now be seen, Attlee's position was logically untenable. If collective security was to be workable, it had to encompass the use of force, albeit internationally organised and employed only as a last resort. It was, therefore, illogical to be for collective security but against the use of force.

Nevertheless, however its logic might be faulted, the anti-war stance was a predominant attitude for much of the 1930s. The Government was conscious of it and largely acted in accordance with it until German aggression finally undermined it.

The Spanish Civil War, 1936–39

How truly anti-war those who believed in collective security and disarmament were was put to the test during the Civil War in Spain (1936–39). In 1936 General Franco led his Nationalist forces, representing Catholic conservative Spain, in rebellion against the

Republican government, which had the support of a combination of anarchists, regional separatists and Communists. A bitter three-year conflict followed. Italy and Germany, eager to test their new weapons and military tactics in a real war, aided Franco's armies, while Stalin's USSR, keen to extend its influence to the other side of Europe, backed the Republicans.

Spanish Civil War: 1936–39

Key date

The National Government in Britain remained officially neutral throughout the struggle. It joined with the French government in formally declaring a policy of non-intervention. But this was an occasion when there was a detectable gap between the governments and the peoples of France and Britain. The Republicans in Spain appealed for help to the peoples rather than the governments of Europe. This provided a great rallying call for those who had been angered by the successes of fascism in Italy and Nazism in Germany and frustrated by the apparent indifference of their governments to all this.

There was a sense in which the war came just at the right moment for such people, trade unionists, Liberals, Marxists and idealists, who can be referred to broadly as the Left. A.J.P. Taylor precisely captured the importance of the conflict for them: 'The Spanish question far transcended politics in the ordinary sense. The controversy provided for the generation of the thirties the emotional experience of their lifetime.' Seeing Spain as a simple struggle of democracy versus fascism, they responded eagerly to the Republican appeal and rushed in their thousands to enlist in the **International Brigades**. Intellectuals such as George Orwell, Stephen Spender and W.H. Auden viewed the Spanish war as the perfect arena for a death struggle with fascism.

International Brigades Pro-Republican forces made up of foreign volunteers.

Key term

The enthusiasm of the idealists could be admired, but they did not receive universal approval. The fact was that the war produced divided responses in Britain. There were those, and not merely those in government, who argued that in their eagerness to fight for a good cause the pro-republican volunteers had disregarded the historical and regional subtleties that had caused the Spanish conflict. It was an over-simplification to interpret it in terms of black and white, good versus evil; the war was much more complex in its origins than that. The strongest criticism was that the Republican supporters had been duped into becoming pawns of the USSR. While it was true that the Soviet Union had given direct assistance to the Republicans, it had done so at a high price. Stalin took the whole of Spain's gold reserves and claimed the right to direct the war strategy. When it became clear to the non-Communist members of the International Brigades that the Soviet Union was as cynically exploitative of the situation in Spain as was Nazi Germany, much of the heart went out of their struggle.

One consequence of the Spanish war was that it compromised the Left. To press for direct British intervention in Spain undermined the Left's claim to base its approach to foreign affairs on the principles of collective security and disarmament. The illogicality of its position did not prevent the Left from fiercely attacking the National Government for its failure to rearm against the growing threat of Germany, but its moral ground had been weakened.

The Spanish Civil War, which was eventually won by the Nationalists after three bitter years of fighting, clearly showed the unwillingness of the National Government to take risks in foreign affairs. No matter how passionately interested in the conflict many of its people were, Britain stood militarily and diplomatically aloof. It was this same reluctance to be involved that was to bedevil its attempts to deal with the mounting threat of Nazi expansionism in Europe.

Chamberlain and appeasement, 1937–39

Key question
Why did Neville Chamberlain persevere for as long as he did with an appeasement policy towards Germany?

In 1937 Neville Chamberlain, the prime minister who was to preside over Britain's entry into war two years later, inherited as his greatest problem a Europe dominated by an expansionist Germany. Until the last moment he continued to believe that war was avoidable and that Hitler and Germany could be pacified if their genuine grievances were met. In taking this line, Chamberlain knew he had the approval of the bulk of the British people. **Appeasement** already existed as the received wisdom of the day. It was one of the clearest examples yet of government policy being in tune with the wishes of the people.

Key term

Appeasement
A policy based on the conviction that the main duty of government is to avoid war. If this means granting an aggressor some of his demands in order to satisfy him that is preferable to armed conflict.

German expansion under Hitler, 1933–39:

1933	Germany withdrew from both the disarmament talks at Geneva and the League of Nations
1935	Hitler re-introduced conscription and began to build up Germany's armed services in direct defiance of the restrictions imposed in 1919
1936	German troops re-occupied the Rhineland
1938	The 'Anschluss' incorporated Austria into the German state, a move expressly forbidden by the Treaty of Versailles
	Sudetenland area of Czechoslovakia occupied by Germany
1939	Remainder of Czechoslovakia seized
	Germany invaded Poland

Key dates

German occupation of the Rhineland: 1936

Chamberlain became prime minister: 1937

The outstanding example of Chamberlain's approach was his handling of the Czech crisis in 1938, the event which may be said to have led directly to the outbreak of war a year later, and the one by which the policy of appeasement is finally judged.

The Czech crisis, 1938

Key question
How did Chamberlain justify Britain's acceptance of the Munich agreement?

Under the Versailles Treaty, an area known as the Sudetenland had been incorporated into the newly created state of Czechoslovakia. However, the Sudetenland was overwhelmingly German in population. Hitler eagerly exploited the demand of the three million Sudeten Germans for 'self-determination', the right to be reincorporated into Germany. He subjected the Czech government to a set of impossible demands, threatening war if they were not accepted.

To avoid war, for which Britain had begun to prepare by digging shelters and distributing gas masks, Chamberlain took it upon himself to engage in summit diplomacy. A series of meetings between him and Hitler, which involved his flying to Germany, culminated in September 1938 in the Munich agreement, signed by the European powers. Britain, France and Italy acknowledged Germany's claims and the Czechs were forced to accept the loss of the Sudetenland. In a radio broadcast Chamberlain justified his sacrifice of the Czechs:

Munich agreement: 1938

German occupation of Czechoslovakia: 1939

British guarantees to Poland: 1939

Key dates

> How horrible, fantastic, incredible it is that we should be digging trenches and trying on gas-masks here because of a quarrel in a faraway country between people of whom we know nothing.
>
> Reported in *The Times*, 28 September 1938

Although those words later came to be regarded as notorious, at the time they were accepted by the majority of the British people as being the only proper response to the crisis. Before Chamberlain entered the plane on his first visit to Hitler, he quoted Shakespeare, declaring to loud cheers that 'out of this nettle, danger, we pluck this flower, safety'. The cheers were even louder on his return from Munich, when he waved a copy of the agreement he had signed with Hitler declaring their nations' commitment never to go to war with each other again. He had brought back, he said, 'peace in our time'. That evening, crowds filled Downing Street to shout Chamberlain's name and applaud him long and enthusiastically when he appeared at the window to acknowledge their thanks. Cinema audiences also broke into spontaneous applause when they saw the newsreels and heard the commentator praise Chamberlain for his consummate statesmanship. Formal prayer services were held in Westminster Abbey and Canterbury Cathedral in which the Prime Minister was lauded as a saviour of world peace.

Appeasement and public opinion

It should be stressed how big a step in the manipulation of public opinion Chamberlain's visits to Hitler were. They were a study in public relations. The whole thing was meant to impress the British people and keep them on the prime minister's side. That was why he was careful to make sure his departure and return were major press occasions, covered by the cameras. He well knew that the newsreels would be shown to the millions of the nation's cinema-goers. What has sometimes been lost sight of is how successful Chamberlain was in this. Because his summit diplomacy with Hitler eventually collapsed, it is too easy to forget how hugely popular it initially was. He carried the people with him.

It all ended in failure, of course; Hitler had no intention of being bound by any of the agreements he made at Munich. Undeterred, he went on to dismember Czechoslovakia and threaten the same to Poland. Reluctantly admitting that Hitler could not be stopped by diplomacy, Britain gave Poland guarantees of protection. It was hoped the guarantees might make

Key date

Britain declared war
on Germany:
September 1939

Hitler pause, but they did not. Chamberlain's capitulation to
German demands over Czechoslovakia had convinced Hitler that
Britain would not be willing or able to fight over Poland. He was
half right. The Polish guarantees were essentially a gesture; Britain
simply did not have the physical means to defend Poland in 1939.
Nonetheless, it was in accordance with these guarantees that
Britain, its appeasement policy in tatters and its patience
exhausted, declared war on Germany in September 1939.

The failed outcome of appeasement made Chamberlain appear
foolish and inept, an image that was quickly spread by his
opponents and has remained the common view taken of him by
posterity. Yet what has to be emphasised is that until appeasement
became an obvious and tragic failure, it had expressed the will of
the great majority of the British people. In seeking by all means to
avoid war, Chamberlain was pursuing a policy that matched the
public mood.

Sympathy for Germany

A further key consideration is that until the post-Munich period,
moderate political opinion was markedly sympathetic towards
Germany. The harshness of the Versailles settlement in regard to
Germany was commonly acknowledged as giving that country the
right to redress its legitimate grievances. Winston Churchill was
one of the most outspoken critics of German re-armament in the
1930s, yet even he acknowledged that the re-occupation of the
Rhineland in 1936, the Anschluss and the reclamation of the
Sudetenland were all in keeping with the principle of self-
determination which the Allies had made the basis of the
Versailles Treaty in 1919.

Fear of Soviet Communism

Key question
What influence did
British distrust of the
USSR have on
appeasement?

There was also an ideological dimension to the problem. Since
1917 Bolshevik Russia had called for the violent overthrow of the
capitalist nations of Europe. It is now known that there had been
no possibility of this. The Soviet Union did not have the strength,
even if it had had the will. But at the time the threat seemed real
enough and it was taken seriously in western Europe. That was why
many in Britain welcomed the growth of a strong, anti-Communist
Germany. They saw it as a barrier to the spread of Bolshevism
westward. The perceived Soviet menace predisposed Britain to
being conciliatory towards Nazi Germany. It was only when the
USSR became perforce an ally of Britain following the German
invasion of Russia in June 1941 that suspicion of Soviet
Communism lifted, and then only for the duration of the war.

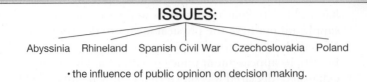

Summary diagram: The National Government – foreign affairs, 1935–39

ISSUES:

Abyssinia   Rhineland   Spanish Civil War   Czechoslovakia   Poland

• the influence of public opinion on decision making.

REASONS FOR BRITAIN'S APPEASEMENT POLICY:

- Memories of the slaughter of 1914–18 created a powerful anti-war feeling in Britain.
- Many people put their faith in the League of Nations and backed the concept of collective security.
- A growing belief between the wars that Germany had been harshly treated in the Versailles settlement.
- A similar belief that, in accordance with the principle of self-determination, Germany had the right to recover the German territories taken from it.
- Fear of Soviet Russia made Britain more tolerant of Nazi Germany.
- The same fear made it attractive to have Germany as a buffer state in central Europe.
- Anglo-French mutual suspicions made effective co-operation difficult.
- The cost of Britain's existing defence commitments discouraged further military expenditure.
- The armed services chiefs warned the government in the mid-1930s that Britain was already overstretched militarily and was incapable of fighting a major European war.
- The severe economic Depression made welfare spending a priority before rearmament.

Study Guide: AS Questions

In the style of AQA

(a) Explain why Ramsay MacDonald became leader of a National Government in 1931. (12 marks)

(b) How successful were the National Governments of 1931–39 in combating the problem of unemployment? (24 marks)

Exam tips

The cross-references are intended to take you straight to the material that will help you to answer the questions.

(a) Re-read pages 118–20. In order to answer this question you would need to explain the financial crisis brought about by the Wall Street Crash of 1929 and its impact on Britain. The issue of the balanced budget and the division over the May Committee proposals are crucial, but so, too, is MacDonald's own attitude and that of the other political leaders. You should comment on whether he put country before party or simply took leadership of a coalition government in order to retain personal power. This question is primarily concerned with the range of factors involved, but consideration of such issues will allow you to show your own ability to form a supported judgement.

(b) Don't be tempted to spend too long discussing the problem of unemployment. This answer should focus on the measures taken to deal with it and provide a balanced evaluation. Government actions would include: the return of protective tariffs, deflationary measures and the 1935 Housing Act. Other factors affecting employment might include the growth in the consumer and service industries, the gradual recovery in world trade from the mid-1930s (and re-armament) and the reorganisation of industry. It is unlikely you will suggest the National Governments were particularly successful, but in conclusion you may want to consider whether they did the best they could in the circumstances or whether their failures, for example, to apply Keynesian economics, deserves condemnation.

In the style of OCR

Domestic issues, 1918–51

How successful were the National Governments in dealing with
domestic problems between 1931 and 1939?   (50 marks)

Exam tips

*The cross-references are intended to take you straight to the material
that will help you to answer the question.*

You need to show that you have understood the focus of the
question and that you can select an appropriate range and depth of
evidence to support your argument. This question requires an
evaluation of the problems, policies and results in the 1930s. Your
answer should focus on explanation rather than description or
narrative. You could organise your answer according to particular
problems or to the Governments' success and failure at tackling
them. Some of the problems you are likely to assess are:

- the Depression (pages 123–25), unemployment (pages 124–25),
  limited investment and trade unions
- housing (page 127), poverty, welfare and living standards
  (pages 126–28)
- finances and deflation (page 128)
- the abdication crisis (page 130)
- political parties – BUF (page 131), CPGB (page 133)
- rearmament (page 128).

Ensure that you prioritise your arguments and in your conclusion
reach a judgement on the most important factors.

5 Britain at War, 1939–45

Key dates

1939	Conscription introduced
1940 May	Churchill became PM
1940–41	The Blitz
1942	The Beveridge Report published
	Fall of Singapore
	British defeat at Tobruk
1944	Normandy landings
	V weapons launched
1945	Yalta Conference
	German surrender

1 | The Impact of the War on the British People

a) The scale of involvement

The twentieth century has been described as the era of total war. So advanced had the world become technologically that warfare could no longer be limited to a military front only. Modern war was now fought on an industrial scale. This meant that every citizen, combatant or not, became involved in the struggle. The civilian home front which provided the vast array of armaments and materials that sustained the war effort was equal in importance to the military front – a reason, incidentally, why all sides in the Second World War felt themselves morally justified in attacking civilian targets.

In Britain, the 1939–45 war was the greatest collective experience that the nation had yet undergone. War and its effects reached into every home and affected all sections of society. There was scarcely a family that was spared the anxieties that war entailed. Nearly everyone had a close relative in the armed services. The pain and worry of enforced separation between serving men and their families were a common experience. Fearful uncertainty about the fate of loved ones at home or at the front was an everyday shared reality. People carried on as best they could, but at home the war brought serious disruption to family and community life, to education and to employment.

Britain was the only country in Europe to avoid enemy occupation during the war. But there was another trauma it did not escape. It was subjected to long periods of bombing from the air. Before the war, there had been a deep dread that aerial bombardment of the civilian population would be so deadly and disruptive that it would prove insufferable. In the event, the bomb and rocket attacks directed on London and other cities proved less destructive than had been anticipated, but the constant threat to life and property that they created imposed barely tolerable strains on domestic and economic life and tested the emergency services to the limit.

To fight a six-year war on the scale of the 1939–45 struggle placed huge demands on Britain and its people. From the beginning it was realised and accepted that the war effort necessitated centralised direction. This resulted in an unprecedented extension of State authority, involving the sacrifice of legal and civil rights in the cause of national security. Between 1939 and 1945 the British government introduced conscription, rationing, the direction of labour, restrictions on the right to travel, and evacuation. It is interesting to observe that Churchill's Coalition government moved so far towards a regulated economy that the post-war Labour government, rather than being radical, was simply continuing the established pattern (see page 162).

The war had a lasting impact on social attitudes. Britain's collective effort as a nation in wartime narrowed the gap between the classes, or at least led to an understanding of how arbitrary and, by extension, how unacceptable class differences were. Privilege and deprivation would, of course, continue after the war, but the years 1939–45 proved a vitally formative period in the advancement of notions of political, social and economic equality. The war stimulated a widespread feeling that the people deserved something better than the grim economic uncertainties that had been the lot of so many in the 1920s and 1930s.

The statistics of Britain's total war

At the end of the war the Ministry of Information proudly declared: 'Britain has radically transformed her national existence by the extent of her mobilisation for war.' It is certainly true that nothing illustrates the totality of the British war effort more clearly than the statistics of the ways in which ordinary citizens were mobilised militarily, economically and socially during the six years, 1939–45:

- UK's overall population – 51 million (32 million adults)
- of the 15.9 million males aged between 14 and 64, 14.9 million (ninety-three per cent) were registered for war service

- of the 16 million females aged between 14 and 58, 7.1 million (forty-five per cent) performed some type of war service.

The war service in which adults were engaged took the following main forms:

- 5.5 million were called up into the serving forces
- 3.2 million worked in the munitions industries
- 4 million performed in other essential war work
- 225,000 in full-time civil defence.

To be added to these figures were the 1.75 million in the **Home Guard** and 1.25 million in part-time civil defence. There were also many thousands involved in fire watching (see page 172), an activity that was compulsory for men who worked fewer than 60 hours a week and women who worked fewer than 50 hours.

During the war the government issued over eight-and-a-half million Essential Work Orders. These were legal controls that directed workers to particular employment within designated vital industries and denied them the right to change their jobs or employers to dismiss them. Registration for employment was made compulsory in 1941.

b) Conscription

One of the divisive political debates at the beginning of the 1914–18 War had been over the morality of conscription (see page 55). The discussion in 1939 was much more muted; there was a widespread, if resigned, acceptance that the call-up was a necessity. From early 1938, growing fears of German expansion had led Britain to take some preliminary steps towards supplementing its 200,000 strong peacetime army. Under the terms of the Emergency Powers (Defence Act) of August 1938, physically fit males aged 20 and 21 had been obliged to undergo six months' military training. When war broke out in September 1939, Britain had 900,000 men available, a number which included the volunteers who came forward as soon as war was declared.

However, judging that this fell well below Britain's troop needs, the government in October rushed through a National Service Act, which required all able-bodied males between 18 and 41 to register for armed service. Registration began with the youngest and continued in stages over the next ten months until it reached the 40-year-olds. Exempted from the call-up were men defined as being in **reserved occupations**, performing work that was crucial to the war effort. Those conscripted were allowed to choose to join one of the three services: army, navy or air force. By the end of 1939, over one-and-a-half million had joined up: one million in the army and 250,000 in each of the other two services.

By the war's end, some five-and-a-half million Britons had been called up and over four-and-a-half million had seen active service. This represented nearly sixty per cent of all males aged between 18 and 40. As in the First World War, there were a number of conscientious objectors who asked to be exempted from military service on moral grounds. They were treated with greater

Key term

Home Guard
Local defence units largely made up of service veterans and those too old for the call-up; the movement was later lovingly, and not wholly inaccurately, caricatured in the BBC television series, *Dad's Army*.

Key question
How was conscription organised in wartime?

Key date

Conscription introduced: 1939

Key term

Reserved occupations
The main workers exempted from call-up were: dockers, farmers, merchant seamen, miners, scientists engaged in war projects, key transport workers (e.g. railwaymen) and workers in the vital utilities (i.e. water, gas and electricity).

understanding than 25 years earlier, though they still tended to be regarded with disdain by the bulk of the population. Of the 60,000 who went in front of tribunals to plead their cause, 42,000 had their appeals against military service upheld.

British wartime victims

It was revealed in May 1945 that the total number of casualties was very close to a million. This was broken down into the following categories:

- armed services: 746,109 casualties; 287,859 killed, 274,148 seriously wounded, 184,102 prisoners of war
- merchant navy: 43,582 casualties, 30,589 killed, 12,993 missing or wounded
- civilians: 146,760 casualties (80,307 of these occurring in London); 60,585 killed (27,570 men, 25,392 women, 7,623 children), 86,175 seriously injured.

Although Britain did not suffer the scale of war casualties experienced, for example, by Germany and the Soviet Union, the losses were deeply tragic and affected many millions beyond the immediate victims. Loss and bereavement occasioned by violent enemy action became a widely shared common experience.

c) Rationing

Food rationing

Key question
Did rationing have a cohesive or disruptive influence on wartime Britain?

On the eve of war in 1939 Britain was importing around 55 million tons of food annually. This represented approximately a ton of imported food for each member of the population. Since the greater proportion of these supplies came via long sea journeys from regions as distant as Australia, the Caribbean, South Africa and North America, it soon became apparent that the German submarines would easily be able to disrupt the flow of imports. With vivid memories of the crisis produced by the German blockade during the 1914–18 war (see page 58), the government responded in two ways:

- It began a campaign to encourage increased production of home-grown food on the existing farms and by bringing unused land into cultivation. The population was urged to plant and tend allotments on every available space. 'Dig for Victory' was one of the government's slogans.
- It immediately drew up plans for food rationing.

Of all the hardships that war brought to the civilian population, rationing was arguably the one that was most consistently felt since it imposed itself on everybody's daily lives. It has been calculated that the topic that dominated the conversation of ordinary people was not the progress of the war, important though that obviously was, but rationing. This is not surprising; the food queues which formed daily, largely composed of housewives, were a constant reminder that putting food on the table was the most demanding need facing ordinary families.

It had been hoped that rationing itself would eliminate the need for long queues, since everybody would be entitled to a prescribed allowance. However, in practice, food supplies were never so regular as to guarantee that the shops had what people wanted, when they wanted it. Butchers, bakers and greengrocers could sell only what they were delivered. Queues often formed in anticipation of deliveries. A common joke among housewives was that if you saw a queue you joined it. It did not matter what it was for; it was bound to be for something you needed or could use.

A montage of wartime Ministry of Information posters which became the backdrop to everyday life in the towns and villages. How do these posters help to give an impression of what the government regarded as the key issues and themes that the public should be informed about and urged to act upon? How would the constant presence of such propaganda posters stimulate a feeling of solidarity among the public?

The following list shows how food rationing was steadily extended:

- January 1940 – bacon, butter and sugar
- March 1940 – meat
- July 1940 – tea and margarine
- March 1941 – jam
- May 1941 – cheese
- June 1941 – eggs
- January 1942 – rice and dried fruit
- February 1942 – tinned tomatoes and peas
- July 1942 – sweets and chocolate
- August 1942 – biscuits
- 1943 – sausages.

Vegetables and fruit were not put on ration, which meant they were invariably in short supply and occasioned some of the longest queues. Bread was also exempt but, since white bread flour was scarce, wholemeal loaves became the main type available. Milk was unrationed, which resulted in frequent shortages. Milk and egg powder in Ministry of Food tins was produced in an effort to make up for the shortfall in what many people regarded, along with tea, as the food they just could not do without. The government made a particular effort to supply children with essential vitamins. Infants and their mothers were entitled to cod liver oil, concentrated orange juice and powdered milk. In 1941 state schools began to provide each individual pupil with a third of a pint of milk a day, free of charge, a practice which continued to operate until the 1970s.

The actual amounts of the rations to which each person was entitled varied slightly during the course of the war. Expectant or nursing mothers, infants and people with special medical conditions were entitled to extra rations. The following list suggests the typical weekly allowances for the ordinary individual:

- bacon: 4 ounces (100g) initially only 2 ounces (50g)
- cheese: 4 ounces (100g)
- eggs: 1
- fats (butter, margarine and lard): 4 ounces (100g)
- meat: 6 ounces (150g)
- sugar: 8 ounces (200g), initially 12 ounces (300g)
- sweets: 2 ounces (50g)
- tea: 2 ounces (50g).

Meat was often supplemented by Spam, a cheap processed form of ham, which a later generation of comedians found highly comical, but which at the time was a godsend to families who concocted ingenious recipes to make it palatable. Pigs, cattle and sheep provided Britain's traditional meats. But since wartime shortages had turned pork, beef and mutton into luxuries, the Ministry of Food urged people to consider alternative animal meats. Horse flesh was declared to be nutritious and, despite its toughness, fit for human consumption. A more notorious recommendation was snoek, a South African fish, which proved tasteless and inedible.

The famous luncheon meat. How would one account for the wartime popularity of this particular commodity?

The public declined to be attracted by either of these strange delicacies and the government found itself with unsellable stocks on its hands.

The story goes that Churchill once asked to see an actual example of what a typical ration for one actually looked like. He was duly shown a set of plates with the various items on them. He remarked approvingly that he could comfortably survive for a day on that amount, only to be told that what he was looking at were the rations for a whole week.

Other rationing

Food was far from being the only commodity to be rationed. Petrol sales were restricted immediately after war was declared in 1939. Fuel shortages led to coal being rationed from July 1941. This was followed in March 1942 by the placing of severe restrictions on household consumption of gas and electricity. To save vital oil and fat supplies, soap was also put on ration in February 1942. To make rationing fair and acceptable, the government exercised price controls. The cost of rationed goods was fixed at a level that made them available even to the poorest families. There were protests from retailers who regarded this as an interference with the right to determine their own profits, but the government countered this by suggesting that in a time of national shortage rationing gave the shopkeepers guaranteed sales.

In a further effort to conserve materials needed for the war effort, rationing was extended to cover clothes in June 1941. As with the system for food, each individual was issued with a ration book containing colour-coded sets of coupons, denoting various amounts, which had to be presented to the shopkeeper when goods were being bought. The coupons were either cut out or marked with indelible pencil to prevent their being re-used. At its lowest, the annual clothing allowance for each individual was 48 points. How restrictive that was is evident from the following examples:

Points needed to buy:

gent's overcoat – 18
pair of shoes – 7
vest and pants – 8
pair of socks – 3
pyjamas – 8
shirt – 8

lady's coat – 14
dress – 11
skirt –7
stockings – 2
nightdress – 6
blouse – 5

Appreciating that rationing made it hard for ordinary families to buy new clothes, the government urged them 'to make do and mend' as a way of contributing to the war effort. The official line was that it was one's patriotic duty not to discard anything that could be re-used. Women found ingenious ways of using old curtains to run up an apparently new dresses. To give the impression they were wearing stockings some girls applied watered-down gravy powder to their legs and then got someone they knew well to draw a 'seam' from the back of the thigh to the heel with an eyebrow liner.

People of course grumbled about the ever-present strain and irritation of rationing. Yet given the genuine national shortages that existed, the form of rationing that was introduced was probably as fair and efficient as could be achieved in the circumstances of war. It was based on the notion of fair shares and equality of sacrifice in a time of national emergency. One beneficial result of food rationing was that it encouraged an understanding of what constituted a proper balanced diet. In working out the necessary contents of the basic ration, the Ministry of Food's experts provided ordinary Britons with a valuable lessen in nutrition.

The black market

As with all rationing systems, there are always those who exploit the situation for personal gain. A trade in forged ration books became widespread as people sought to circumvent the restrictions. This was one example of the illegal trafficking in food and goods that enabled people to buy more that their ration allowance permitted. Supplying and selling surplus goods became a highly organised and lucrative activity since the price asked was always highly inflated. Every city and town had its black marketeers – 'spivs' – and a large and eager clientele. How widespread the system was is evident in the statistic that during the war over 100,000 people were prosecuted by the Ministry of Food for black market offences, and these were only the ones who were caught. The inspectors whose task it was to oversee the rationing system worked with the police in making arrests and bringing charges against wrongdoers. Though as government officials they were acting for the general good, they were often resented by the public as snoopers whose activities added to the cares and burdens of life in wartime.

d) The effects of bombing

In twentieth-century warfare, the line between combatant and non-combatant became increasingly blurred. The concept of total war and the technology of aerial bombardment made the terrorising of the civilian population both legitimate and possible. Yet one reason why the London **Blitz** proved bearable was that, grim though the bombing was, it never reached the scale anticipated in the gloomier pre-war forecasts. German and Japanese cities were later to experience Allied bombardment that carried civilian suffering way beyond that undergone in British cities. The death toll of 60,000 Britons killed as a result of bombing during the war was truly fearful, but it was smaller than expected.

There was, however, greater destruction of property. Three-and-a-half million houses were bombed out, forcing 22.5 million people, nearly half the population, to move house. The social disruption is further shown by the record of 60 million changes of address in Britain between 1939 and 1945.

Damage to factories and production centres in cities such as London and Coventry was severe, but the use of make-shift premises and the dispersal of industrial plants meant that production was not severely curtailed. Interestingly, worker absenteeism fell during the Blitz and again during the V1 and V2 attacks in 1944–45, which suggested that the systematic bombing had strengthened rather than weakened civilian morale. There was some panic, particularly at the beginning of the Blitz, but this was not widespread and a mixture of resolution and resignation appears to have been the general response. The normal pattern of life and work was disrupted but not destroyed. People adjusted to the undoubted horror of it all and the sense of a shared common danger tended to maintain morale. A London journalist recorded in his diary in October 1941:

> ... we have got accustomed now to knowing we may be blown to bits at any moment ... A woman of ninety-four with six daughters in a large expensive house are taking shelter in the basement when the house is hit. Two of the daughters die. What a picture! A family creeps out of its garden dug-out to get some supper. They sit down at table. Next minute they are all dead. We know this may happen to any of us. Yet we go about as usual. Life goes on.

Hitler's terror weapons

Later in the war the civilian population faced a new horror from the skies. In what proved to be Hitler's last desperate attempt to stave off defeat, he launched his terror weapons against Britain. The attacks by the **V1 flying bombs** which began in June 1944, were followed in September by the launching of the **V2**. The weapons caused widespread death and damage in and around London and led to the evacuation of one-and-a-half million people. But, owing to sabotage by resistance groups and Allied bombing of the launch sites, the destruction was never on the scale Hitler had originally planned.

Key question
How was civilian morale affected by the war?

Key terms

The Blitz, September 1940–May 1941
Sustained, mainly nightly, German bombing raids on London and other selected English cities.

V1 flying bomb
A pilotless jet-propelled plane loaded with explosives.

V2
An armed rocket, launched from mobile sites.

Key dates

The Blitz: 1940–41

V weapons launched: 1944

The total number of V1s fired was 10,000. Of these 3,676 hit London, 2,600 failed to reach their target, 1,878 were shot down by anti-aircraft batteries and 1,846 were destroyed by fighters. The total number of people killed by the V1s was 6,184. The total number of V2s launched was 1,115, killing 2,754 people.

e) Evacuation

An interesting feature of the collective war effort in Britain was the way it increased social perception. The shared experience of the dangers of war helped make people aware of each other in ways that had not happened before. Knowledge of 'how the other half lives' led to a questioning of the class differences that existed. Evacuation was especially influential in this respect.

At the outbreak of the war, the Government, fearing large-scale air attacks on major urban centres, organised a migration of primary school children from the danger zones to the relatively safer rural areas. Although four million were planned for, only one-and-a-half million actually made the move. During the **phoney war** period most evacuees drifted back home, only to migrate again when the Blitz began late in 1940. A further evacuation occurred in 1944 at the time of the rocket attacks on London.

It was one of the largest movements of people in such a short time in British history; in terms of getting vast numbers of children from A to B and settled away from danger it was a huge success. However, the research that has gone into the effects of evacuation suggests that the majority of children suffered significant psychological disturbance as a result of being uprooted from home, family and environment. Acute homesickness was the lot of most of the children. A sense of the loneliness and disorientation comes through in the following recollection of an evacuee:

> Suddenly the white council house was remote, the country cruel, home the other side of the world. We went to strange beds and lay with fists clenched. Our toes found tepid hot water bottles and our fingers silk bags of old lavender inside the pillows. An owl hooted, wings brushed the window. I remembered the London sounds of distant trains and motor cycles, the creaking limbs of the mountain ash, next door's dog, the droning radio, the fifth stair groaning and the ten-thirty throat clearing; I remembered the familiar wallpaper and the curve of the bedstead rail which had seemed as permanent as evening cocoa. We sobbed in awful desolation but never again mentioned those first war tears to each other.
>
> Derek Lambert, *Wartime Reminiscences*, 1960

Evacuation meant that town and country met for the first time. This came through strongly in the invaluable reports of the Women's Institute (WI) which organised much of the resettlement of the uprooted children. The astonishment of the country people at the habits of the evacuees they took in suggests that for the first time the middle and wealthier classes were learning how the other

Key question
How did evacuation help to alter social perceptions?

Phoney war
An American description, applied to the period from September 1939 to April 1940 when, although the population was busily preparing for hostilities, nothing of military significance actually happened.

Key term

half lived. The WI's recording of the malnourishment and lack of social graces of the evacuees helped create an awareness of the poverty and deprivation from which large sections of the urban population suffered.

> Grimsby. 'Their chief food at home was in most cases fish and chips, more often the latter without the fish. Milk puddings were unheard of and some did not even know what a pudding was.'

> Manchester. 'Few children would eat food that demanded the use of teeth, in almost every case could only eat with a teaspoon. Practically all disliked fresh vegetables and pies and puddings of fresh fruit were quite unknown to them.'

> Liverpool. 'One little girl of 5 remarked one day that she would like to have beer and cheese for supper. Most of the children seemed under-nourished when they arrived, yet some were troublesome to feed, not liking stewed fruit, vegetables and jam. Children had been used to receiving a penny at home to buy their own dinners. One used to buy broken biscuits, the other Oxo cubes. Most of them seemed quite unaccustomed to ordinary everyday food and preferred a "piece" or bag of chips on the doorstep.'

> 'Town Children Through Country Eyes', a pamphlet of National Federation of Women's Institutes, 1940

Evacuation proved to be a remarkable social experiment. Designed as a protective measure for the young children of the cities, it led to a rethinking in social attitudes. In many instances, criticism and revulsion among the better-off turned into sympathy and brought a new sense of social concern. It was no coincidence that a major Education Act, aimed at widening educational opportunity for all children, was introduced in 1944 (see page 186). However, social concern was not a universal response. While acknowledging that evacuation opened the eyes of many to the deprivation existing in Britain, a number of historians have stressed that there was an equal likelihood that it confirmed the prejudices of some:

> For conservative social observers, [evacuation] confirmed the view that the bulk of the problems were caused by an incorrigible underclass of personally inadequate 'cultural orphans' for whom a Welfare State could do little. Evacuation thus shows us that the ideological consensus of wartime, so stressed by ... some historians was something of a myth.

> John Macnicol, quoted in *Britain 1918–1951*, 1994

Privilege and deprivation would, of course, continue after the war but, insofar as Britain became a less class-divided society in the twentieth century, the impact of the Second World War was a major factor in making it so. This is not to argue that everybody pulled together as suggested by the Ministry of Information propaganda films or the patriotic BBC broadcasts. As the flourishing black market indicated, people in Britain were far from being selfless saints totally committed to a united cause. Nevertheless, there was sufficient sense of common purpose engendered by the experience of war for historians to judge the period 1939–45 as having been a critical stage in Britain's development as a **socially cohesive state**.

> Bombs, unlike employment, knew no social distinctions, and so rich and poor alike were affected in the need for shelter and protection. Food rationing produced common shortages and even the royal family ate Spam ... the so-called **Dunkirk spirit** did bring the nation together in a common united purpose.

f) Industrial unrest

Another factor that challenged the notion of Britain as a wholly united society was the frequency of industrial disputes. Although these fell in number with the outbreak of war, by 1942 they were back at pre-war level. The disputes were over the traditional issues of pay and conditions. The workers being fully aware, as they had been in 1914–18, that the war had made them an indispensable part of the war effort, felt entitled to press their claims. This was not lack of patriotism or disregard of those risking their lives at the front; it arose from a determination not to allow war needs to become an excuse for worker exploitation.

Table 5.1: Industrial strikes, 1939–45

	Working days lost	Number of strikes	Number of strikers
1939	1,356,000	940	337,000
1940	940,000	972	299,000
1941	1,079,000	1,251	360,000
1942	1,527,000	1,303	456,000
1943	1,808,000	1,785	557,000
1944	3,714,000	2,194	821,000
1945	2,835,000	2,293	531,000

g) Women's role in the war

The remarkable contribution of women to Britain's war effort is immediately evident from the figures of their involvement:

- 1.85 million worked in the munitions industries
- 1.64 million were employed in other essential war work
- 3.1 million took up other full-time employment
- 467,000 entered the auxillary armed services
- 56,000 served in full-time civil defence
- 350,000 served as part-time civil defence workers.

Women were not conscripted directly into the fighting services, but in December 1941 the compulsory enlistment of women into the **Uniformed Auxillary Services** was introduced. Britain was the first of the countries at war to do this. Those liable for call-up were

Key terms

Socially cohesive state
A nation whose people broadly agree on fundamental social principles, e.g. welfare.

Dunkirk spirit
In June 1940, an armada of small private vessels, manned by volunteers, had helped transport 300,000 besieged British troops to safety from the beach at Dunkirk. It was common thereafter to refer to this as an example of the collective purpose that would carry Britain successfully through the war.

Key question
How extensive was the role of women in the war effort?

Key term

Uniformed Auxiliary Services
Auxiliary Territorial Service (ATTs), Women's Auxiliary Air Force (WAAFs), Women's Royal Navy Service (WRENs).

widows without dependent children and single women aged between 20 and 30, later widened to between 19 and 49 years.

Enlisted women could also opt to serve in the civilian Women's Land Army. By 1943 there were 80,000 'Land Girls' working, in effect, as poorly paid farm labourers in an unglamorous but vital part of the war economy.

On the industrial front, women workers were brought in to bridge the gap created by the conscription of millions of male factory workers. By 1943, nearly half of the females in Britain between the ages of 14 and 59 were employed in war work. A year later, women made up these percentages of the workforce:

- forty per cent in aircraft manufacturing
- thirty-five per cent in the engineering industries
- fifty per cent in the chemical industries
- thirty-three per cent in heavy industry (e.g. munitions and ship building).

This development appeared to give women increased status. Yet within a few months of the war's end seventy-five per cent of the female workers had left their jobs to return to their traditional role in the home. This makes it questionable whether the war had permanently altered traditional patterns of social behaviour. However, these things are sometimes difficult to measure: the contribution of women to the war effort had been enormous. Without their work in the factories Britain could not have sustained itself.

Equally important, though less immediately visible, was the way they had been the principal agents in the maintenance of social stability as effective heads of the family in their husbands' absence, a role thrust upon them by the disruption of war. It was wives and mothers who experienced the daily strain of trying to preserve family normality in a time of danger and shortages. Sadly, the strains did not necessarily end when the war ended. Indeed, wives, husbands and children who had been separated by war often found it difficult to return to ordinary family life. David Kynaston, a modern social historian, describes the problem:

> The strains on marriage were severe. A couple might not have seen each other for several years; he expected to return to his family position as the undisputed head; she had become more independent (often working in a factory as well as running the home) – the possibilities for tension and strife, even when both were emotionally committed to each other, were endless.
>
> David Kynaston, *Austerity Britain 1945–51*, 2007

Table 5.2: Number of divorces in Britain

1939	7,012
1944	12,314
1947	60,190

The divorce figures may be taken as a mark of the disruption war had brought to ordinary people.

It remains a matter of lively controversy whether the war actually improved the lot of women. A group of distinguished French analysts have suggested that the abuse of women as industrial fodder far outweighed any gains from apparent emancipation.

Great though their contribution to the national effort was, it may be that in all countries, Britain included, they were more exploited than elevated: Women were liberated socially only to be enslaved economically.

h) The financial and economic burdens of the war

The most immediate effect of the war was that it finally ended the Depression. Even before hostilities began in 1939 the threat of war in the late 1930s (see page 128) had led Britain to embark on a major rearmament programme. This recreated a huge demand for industrial products, which in turn led to a demand for workers. The problem was no longer a surplus of labour, but a shortage. By 1941 an extra two million workers were needed to cope with the demands of war.

The impact of the war on Britain's finances:

- Government expenditure rose from £1.4 billion in 1939 to £6.1 billion in 1945.
- Income tax was levied from most workers by **PAYE** at the rate of twenty-five per cent of earnings in 1939, fifty per cent of earnings in 1945.
- Government borrowings by direct loans and **lend lease** from the USA. Between 1941 and 1945 Britain received $30 million worth of supplies under the lend lease scheme.
- In 1945 Britain owed £4 billion to overseas creditors.
- The National Debt rose from £500 million in 1939 to £3,500 million in 1945.
- The **balance of payments** deficit in 1945 was £1 billion.

i) The Beveridge Report, 1942

Since the nineteenth century, a basic issue in British politics had been how far, if at all, the State was responsible for the well-being of its citizens. The Second World War put the answer to that question beyond doubt. The war won the argument for all those who believed that the prime function of politics was to provide for the welfare of the people. All the parties came to accept that the efforts made by the British people in wartime required that reconstruction and welfare were now prime considerations. It is true that the parties would disagree about the speed with which welfare schemes should be implemented, and about how they were to be funded, but for the rest of the twentieth century that government existed to serve the economic and social interests of the people became the accepted motive of politics.

It is arguable that Britain would in any case have moved towards a welfare state in peacetime. But what the war did was to increase the understanding of the inequalities and deprivation and to heighten the feeling that changes had to be made. Britain owed its people protection and welfare. Economic well-being should not be left to chance. The provision of a decent standard of living was the least that could be expected of a civilised nation duty-bound to reward its people for their heroic efforts. The

Key question
How did the economy adjust to the demands of war?

Key term

PAYE (Pay As You Earn)
A sophisticated form of government theft by which the tax due from workers is extracted from their wages before they have received them.

Key question
Why was the Beveridge Report such a significant social document?

Key term

Lend lease
An arrangement that operated from 1941, under which Britain imported war materials from the United States with no obligation to pay for them until the war was over.

Key date

The Beveridge Report published: 1942

Key terms

Balance of payments (trade balance)
A measurement of the profit or loss on trade in a given period; when the price of imports outstrips the income from exports, financial crisis follows.

Atlantic Charter, August 1941
An agreement signed by Churchill and Franklin Roosevelt, the American president, laying out the principles on which a better world could be constructed once the Allies had won the war. It became the basis for the later United Nations Organisation.

Key figure

Sir William Beveridge (1879–1963)
Had a long experience as a civil servant specialising in social security provision; he was an MP 1944–45.

constant refrain of the government's message through its propaganda agencies was that the nation was fighting for a better world.

The wartime Coalition under Churchill gave considerable thought to post-war reconstruction. In political circles, guilt was still felt over how short of providing a land fit for heroes Britain had fallen in the 1920s and 1930s (see page 82). There was a general determination not to fail a second time. By the end of 1940, despite the terror of the Blitz, the danger of an invasion of Britain had considerably lessened. Morale had risen and made planning for peacetime seem not wholly unrealistic. The presence in the government of a number of Labour Party leaders was a guarantee that social issues would be kept to the fore.

Indeed, planning was not a matter of political dispute at this stage; all the parties accepted the need to extend social welfare in the post-war world. In the words of Paul Addison, a modern authority, 'welfare took its place as the highest common denominator between the parties'. Significantly, the **Atlantic Charter** had, thanks to the insistence of Ernest Bevin, included in its peace aims a commitment to raise the level of social welfare.

It was in this atmosphere that Britain saw the preparation and presentation of one of the great social documents of the twentieth century – the Beveridge Report. Late in 1940, Arthur Greenwood, who had been health minister in the Labour government of 1929–31 (see page 115), was instructed by Churchill to take the preliminary steps towards post-war re-organisation. In June 1941, Greenwood set up an Interdepartmental Committee to study the existing schemes of social insurance and make recommendations for their improvement. **William Beveridge** was appointed Chairman of this committee of senior civil servants. Taking his remit very seriously, Beveridge immersed himself totally in his work. His role in the drafting of the report containing the committee's proposals was so central that it was considered appropriate that he alone should sign the document which bore his name and which was presented to the House of Commons in November 1942.

The following is a key passage expressing the vision that inspired Beveridge's proposals:

This is first and foremost a plan of insurance – of giving, in return for contributions, benefits up to a subsistence level, as of right and without means test, so that individuals may build freely upon it. Organisation of social insurance should be treated as one part only of a comprehensive policy of social progress. Social insurance fully developed may provide income security; it is an attack upon Want. But Want is only one of five giants on the road of reconstruction, and in some ways the easiest to attack. The others are Disease, Ignorance, Squalor and Idleness.

A cartoon by George Whitelaw published in the *Daily Herald* in 1944. A cartoon welcoming the Beveridge plan, but suggesting that, like the proverbial curate's egg, it might be good only in parts. Why should the *Daily Herald*, a pro-Labour newspaper, have had reservations about the Beveridge plan?

Beveridge's aims

Beveridge aimed at the abolition of material want. He believed that it was possible to establish a national minimum level of welfare without recourse to extreme methods. He proposed a universal scheme of insurance which would provide protection against the distress that invariably accompanied sickness, injury and unemployment.

Additionally, there would be grants to ease the financial hardships that came with maternity, parenthood and bereavement. The term 'protection from the cradle to the grave', although not Beveridge's own, was an appropriate description of the envisaged scale of welfare provision. The plan was to replace the current unsystematic pattern of welfare with a centrally funded and regulated system. Since it would be based on insurance, it would avoid being associated with the hated **means test** or the Poor Law.

Insurance was to form the base with welfare organisations providing the superstructure. Beveridge's 'five giants' to be defeated on the road to reconstruction were a figurative representation of the major ills afflicting society.

Want – to be ended by national insurance.
Disease – to be ended by a comprehensive health service.
Ignorance – to be ended by an effective education system.
Squalor – to be ended by slum clearance and re-housing.
Idleness – to be ended by full employment.

Beveridge's scheme pointed toward 'the welfare state', a term which pre-dated the report by some ten years, but which began to be widely used during the war years. Hardly any of Beveridge's proposals were new. What made them significant in 1942 was their integration into a comprehensive scheme. Beveridge had laid the theoretical foundations for all subsequent developments in the field of social welfare provision.

Key term

Means test
In the 1930s, to qualify for dole or relief individuals or families had to give precise details of all the money they had coming in.

Cartoon by George Whitelaw published in the *Daily Herald* on the 2nd December 1942. Beveridge's 'Five Giants'. What was the cartoonist's view of the problems facing Beveridge?

Key question
What were the Report's basic social principles?

Beveridge proposed to take the best aspects of the existing welfare systems and integrate them into a universal plan. It was no mere coincidence that as a younger man Beveridge had been directly involved in the introduction of the social service programme of the pre-1914 Liberal governments. In his proposals Beveridge, true to his Liberal background, insisted on the principle of insurance. He specifically denied that his plan aimed at 'giving everybody something for nothing'. Freedom from want could not be 'forced on or given to a democracy'; it had to be wanted by the people. Beveridge stressed that a good society depended not on the State but on the individual. He spoke of the retention of 'personal responsibilities'. Individuals would be encouraged to save as private citizens. These ideas were very much in the Liberal tradition, as was his belief that his proposals would not involve an increase in government expenditure.

As a good Liberal, Beveridge at every point assumed the continuation of capitalism. The political movement called socialism can be defined in various ways, but one attitude common to all its forms is a conviction that the capitalist system is exploitative and unjust and, therefore, ultimately indefensible. Throughout the Beveridge Report there is an essential understanding that welfare reconstruction will take place within the framework of continuing capitalism. It is for that reason that historically the Report has to be seen as belonging to the mainstream of liberal rather than socialist thinking and planning.

William Beveridge stood as a Liberal candidate in the 1945 election, hoping to retain the seat he had won a year earlier. But his defeat meant that he was unable to oversee the progress of his plan through parliament. Nevertheless, he had provided the essential basis on which Clement Attlee's government between 1945 and 1951 (see page 184) would build the welfare state, both a fulfilment of the Beveridge plan and a fitting tribute to its creator.

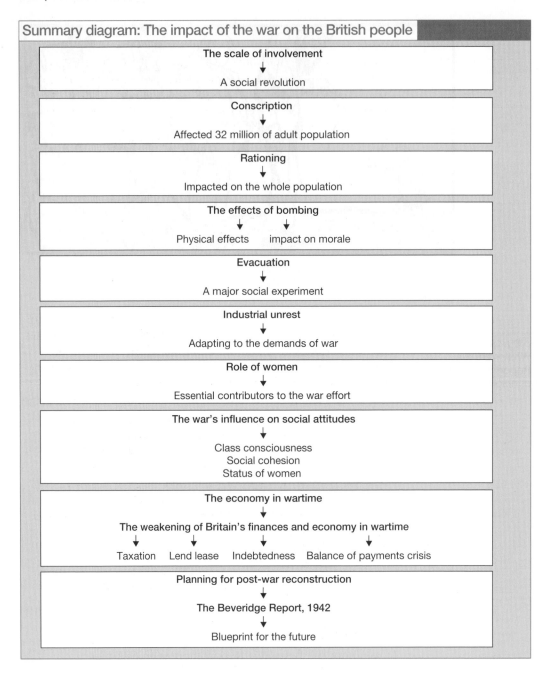

Summary diagram: The impact of the war on the British people

The scale of involvement
↓
A social revolution

Conscription
↓
Affected 32 million of adult population

Rationing
↓
Impacted on the whole population

The effects of bombing
↓   ↓
Physical effects   impact on morale

Evacuation
↓
A major social experiment

Industrial unrest
↓
Adapting to the demands of war

Role of women
↓
Essential contributors to the war effort

The war's influence on social attitudes
↓
Class consciousness
Social cohesion
Status of women

The economy in wartime
↓
The weakening of Britain's finances and economy in wartime
↓   ↓   ↓   ↓
Taxation   Lend lease   Indebtedness   Balance of payments crisis

Planning for post-war reconstruction
↓
The Beveridge Report, 1942
↓
Blueprint for the future

2 | The Growth in the Power of the State

A striking feature of war in the twentieth century was the encouragement it gave to centralist tendencies in government. Faced with the strains of total war, nations without exception showed a readiness to accept extension of State control as a means of creating the maximum war effort. This was as evident in democratic countries as in totalitarian regimes. Britain's Coalition Government moved so far towards regulation that the post-war

Key question
How did government control increase in wartime?

Collectivist
Describing a society in which the individual is less important than the group. In times of need, therefore, the rights of the individual must be subordinated to the greater good of the group.

Internment
The holding in detention of those members of the population whose nationality or political views made them a potential risk to national security.

Labour government inherited an established pattern of centralised control.

Britain, in effect, became a **collectivist** state during the Second World War. Rationing, conscription, direction of labour and the suspension of many traditional legal and constitutional freedoms: these were accepted by the British public, if not readily, at least without open signs of resistance.

Extension of State power in Britain during the war:

• food and fuel rationing
• restrictions on press freedom
• suspension of legal rights
• conscription of men and women into the armed services
• direction of workers to undertake specific work in nominated areas
• control of rates of pay and hours of employment
• subjection of employers to ministerial control
• control over exchange rates and import–export dealings
• right to arrest and detain citizens without trial.

New government departments were established covering such areas as: food supply, information, economic warfare, civilian aviation and town and country planning. The Emergency Powers Act, passed through parliament in 1939 soon after the start of the war, granted an extraordinary degree of authority to the Home Secretary and the Minister of Labour. It is instructive to quote the term of the Act:

> Such persons may be detained whose detention appears to the Secretary of State [the Home Secretary] to be expedient in the interests of public safety or the defence of the realm. The Secretary of State, the Minister of Labour, has the authority to oblige any person in the United Kingdom to perform any service required in any place. He may prescribe the remuneration of such services and the hours of work. He may require such persons to register particulars of themselves; he might order employers to keep and produce any records and books.

These were unprecedented powers for British ministers and the fact that they were exercised with discretion and moderation did not lessen their significance or, in the opinion of some, their danger.

Internment

The state's power was seen at its most direct in regard to **internment**. On the grounds that they represented a potential threat to the war effort, many thousands of German aliens were interned in special camps. Tragically, these even included Jewish refugees who had fled to Britain to escape Nazi persecution. Although the camps were often surrounded by barbed wire and patrolled by armed guards, conditions inside were not notably severe; it was deprivation of liberty and livelihood that was the hardest thing for the innocent to bear.

Some 1,800 British subjects were also interned – 763 of these were members of the BUF and included Oswald Mosley, the leader (see page 131). Nearly all internees had been released by the end of the war.

Libertarians were unhappy about the legal and economic powers that the government exercised. However, as had happened during the First World War when a similar extension of government authority had occurred, the argument of national security carried the day. Necessity justified the increase in government power. Legal niceties took second place to the struggle for survival. As its title was meant to convey, the Emergency Powers Act was a temporary measure, not a permanent enlargement of State power. To survive the war, the nation had to be organised at its most effective. If this required a massive spread of government power, that was the price that had to be paid. This in essence was the case put forward by government and parliament and accepted by the mass of the people.

Key question
How was the growth in state power justified?

A far-reaching consequence of the 1939–45 war was that it made the idea of government direction of the economy seem perfectly logical and reasonable. The six-year struggle was a national effort led by a coalition Government which introduced a range of measures which would have been unacceptable in peacetime. For example, thousands of farmers were dispossessed of their land during the war for failing to conform to the production levels laid down by the government.

The concept of necessity helped to create an atmosphere in which it was accepted that government knew best. In 1944 the Government formally announced that it was now responsible for the 'maintenance of a high and stable level of employment'. A.J.P. Taylor, a provocative English historian, wrote that the war 'produced a revolution in British economic life, until in the end direction and control turned Great Britain into a country more fully socialist than anything achieved by the conscious planners of Soviet Russia'.

Keynesianism

By an interesting coincidence it so happened that a powerful theory was available to justify the government's intrusion into the running of economic affairs. Every so often a particular financial or economic theory arrives to dominate its time and appears to oblige governments to structure their policies in accordance with it. For most of the period between the late 1930s and the late 1970s the ideas of **John Maynard Keynes** provided the basic frame of reference. The National Government had chosen to ignore Keynes' ideas but they began to appear increasingly relevant in wartime.

Key question
According to Keynes, what role should government play in the economy?

Dismayed by the Depression in the 1930s, Keynes had written a number of works suggesting ways of tackling unemployment. He believed that economic depressions were avoidable if particular steps were taken. His starting point was demand. He calculated that it was a fall in demand for manufactured products that caused industrial economies to slip into recession. If demand could be sustained, decline could be prevented and jobs preserved. Keynes maintained that the only agency with sufficient power and influence to keep demand high enough was the Government itself. He urged, therefore, that:

John Maynard Keynes (1883–1946) A Cambridge don, had been a director of the Bank of England during the war and the Government's chief economic adviser.

Key figure

- The Government should use its budgets and revenue powers to raise capital, which it could then reinvest in the economy to keep it at a high level of activity.
- This artificial boost to the economy would lead to genuine recovery and growth. Companies and firms would have full order books and the workers would have jobs and earnings.
- Those earnings would be spent on goods and services with the result that the forces of supply and demand would be stimulated.

Key term

Norwegian Campaign, April 1940
Responding to the German invasion of Norway, Britain sent a task force there, but it proved too small to prevent the Germans overrunning the country.

Keynes argued that the Government should be prepared to overspend in the short term, even if this meant borrowing to do so. It would eventually be able to repay the debts by taxing the companies and workers whose profits and wages would rise considerably in a flourishing economy.

The six years of government-directed war effort, during which Keynes was an influential figure at the Treasury, helped to give strength to his arguments. What is interesting is that although Keynes thought in terms of limited government action, it was the notion of government being an *essential* part of economic planning that become widely accepted. The Labour Governments under Clement Attlee after 1945 were to benefit from this new conviction (see page 185).

Summary diagram: The growth in the power of the state

> The extension of State power in Britain during the war
> ↓
> Britain a collectivist state?

> The new economic thinking of the day
> ↓
> Keynesianism

Key question
What was Winston Churchill's personal contribution to Britain's survival in the Second World War?

3 | Churchill's Coalition Government, 1940–45
Churchill becomes prime minister, May 1940

The **Norwegian campaign**, the first major engagement of the war for Britain, went badly in April 1940. In a heated Commons' debate Neville Chamberlain was condemned not merely for the failure in Norway but for his Government's uninspiring handling of the war since it started. The most cutting attacks came from his own Conservative side. Leo Amery ended his speech by quoting Oliver Cromwell's words from three centuries before: 'You have sat here long enough for all the good that you may do. In the name of God, go'. Chamberlain still tried to carry on. He asked whether the Liberals and Labour party would be willing to serve in a new coalition under him. But the prime minister was roundly condemned by all parties in parliament, including a large section of his own Conservatives. He resigned to be replaced by Winston Churchill, 'the man of the hour'. Churchill was to preside over government for the next five years.

The outbreak of war with Germany had placed Churchill in a strong position politically. Not being sufficiently trusted by his own Conservative party to be offered a government post during the 1930s, he had used his time to warn the nation against the growing dangers of expansionist Nazi Germany and to mount a campaign urging Britain to rearm. This had led to his being dismissed by some on both sides of the Commons as a war-monger. But the war that came in 1939 as a climax to German aggression vindicated his call for rearmament and his denunciation of appeasement. Should Chamberlain mishandle the war, Churchill was now ideally placed to succeed him. The only thing that could stop him would be if a serious rival contender for the premiership emerged or if a majority of the MPs refused to accept him. In the event neither challenge materialised.

Key date

Churchill became PM: May 1940

There was only one possible alternative leader, Lord Halifax, an uninspiring figure who did not really want the job, and whose chances were effectively destroyed when the Labour party declared it would not enter a coalition government if he were its head. Churchill remained in office as Prime Minister throughout the war against Germany.

Reasons for Churchill's becoming prime minister

- His being in the political wilderness in the 1930s worked in his favour. Since he had not held office in the Conservative-dominated National Government, he was not associated with its failures.
- His opposition to Nazism and his call for Britain to re-arm vindicated his stand and suggested his sense of realism in foreign affairs.
- In 1940 he had no real challenger. Once Chamberlain had been disgraced over the failed Norwegian campaign, there was no possibility of him rallying enough Commons' support to carry on.
- Lord Halifax, the only possible alternative, did not have the quality or character to lead the nation in war time. Moreover, Halifax genuinely did want to be prime minister.
- The refusal of the Labour party to enter a coalition if was led by Chamberlain or Halifax meant a government of national unity could not be formed unless it was led by Churchill.
- With the French and British armies on the verge of defeat in Northern France, the crisis facing Britain was so grave that, whatever their misgivings about Churchill's previous record, the majority of MPs agreed that his bullish qualities and self belief made him the 'man of the hour'.

Profile: Winston Churchill (1874–1965)

1874	– Born the son of Randolph Churchill, a leading Tory radical
1898	– Fought in the Sudan under Kitchener
1900	– Taken prisoner by the Boers in South Africa
	– Entered the Commons as a Conservative MP
1904	– Left the Conservatives to join the Liberals
1908–09	– President of the Board of Trade – showed himself to be a progressive social reformer
1910–11	– Home Secretary
1911	– Used troops against striking Welsh miners
1911–15	– First Lord of the Admiralty
1916	– Served on the Western Front
1917–19	– Minister of Munitions
1919	– Fiercely anti-Bolshevik, he supported British intervention in Russia
1921–22	– Secretary for the Colonies
1924	– Left the Liberals and declared himself a 'Constitutionalist'
1924–29	– Chancellor of the Exchequer
1926	– Strongly opposed the General Strike
1929	– Formally rejoined the Conservatives
1939–40	– First Lord of the Admiralty
1940–45	– Prime Minister and Minister of Defence
1945	– His party heavily defeated in the general election
1947	– Helped to define the Cold War by his 'iron curtain' speech
1951–55	– Prime Minister
1965	– Died

In many ways Churchill was a radical, but he was loathed by the left because of his strike-breaking and fierce anti-Bolshevism. He was too individualistic to be entirely at ease in any one party. In 1904, after only four years as a Unionist MP, he left the party to join the Liberals. His radical approach to social questions made him the great ally of Lloyd George in their creation of the pre-1914 social service state.

Twenty years later, having established an impressive record as a Liberal social reformer, he returned to the Conservative fold, but in a strange relationship. He called himself a 'constitutionalist', and, despite being Chancellor of the Exchequer in Baldwin's government between 1924 and 1929, did not formally rejoin the Conservatives until 1929. Churchill remained out of office for the next ten years. His demand that Britain re-arm, and his outspoken attacks on appeasement and on the idea of independence for India made him unpopular with the Conservative establishment and he despaired of ever playing a major role in politics again. It is certainly hard to think that, had the Second World War not intervened, he would have reached the pre-eminence he then did.

Clement Attlee described him as 'the greatest citizen of the world of our time'. As well as making history, Churchill also wrote it. His deep historical sense was evident in his many books and in his brilliant speeches in which he used his speech impediment to great effect. One example was his deliberate mispronunciation of the word 'Nazi', with a long 'a' and a soft 'z', in order to show his contempt for the movement to which it referred. His feel for the dramatic and his ability to use elevated language without losing the common touch is evident in the extract from his first broadcast to the nation as prime minister.

> This is one of the most awe-inspiring periods in the long history of France and Britain. It is also beyond doubt the most sublime. Side by side, unaided except by their kith and kin in the Great Dominions and by the wide Empires which rest beneath their shield – side by side, the British and French peoples have advanced to rescue not only Europe but mankind from the foulest and most soul-destroying tyranny which has ever darkened and stained the page of history. Behind them – behind us – behind the Armies and fleets of Britain – gather a group of shattered states and bludgeoned races: the Czechs, the Poles, the Norwegians, the Danes, the Dutch, the Belgians – upon all of whom the long night of barbarism will descend, unbroken even by a star of hope, unless we conquer, as conquer we must, as conquer we will.
>
> A BBC broadcast, 19 May 1940

Churchill wrote in his war memoirs that on becoming prime minister in 1940 he felt that the whole of his previous life had been a preparation 'for this hour and this trial'. As Lloyd George had done in 1916, he devoted himself totally to the task of winning the war. Every other consideration took second place. Despite the deep depression from which he frequently suffered, the 'black dog' as he called it, he never wavered in his conviction that Britain would prevail. His inexhaustible capacity for work, his rousing oratory and his extraordinary gift for inspiring others were used to rally the nation to a supreme effort. He later wrote that the British people were the lions; he merely provided the roar.

Key debate

> Did Churchill's wartime leadership strengthen or weaken Britain's position as an international power?

The traditional view of Churchill as war leader

Such was his personal contribution to Britain's survival during the darkest days of war that A.J.P. Taylor described him as 'the saviour of his country'. This is very much the traditional picture of Churchill in wartime. His chief biographer, Martin Gilbert, paints him as an inspiring leader guiding a united nation through peril to victory over a deadly enemy and, in so doing, establishing himself as an outstanding world figure.

Revisionist challenges

But there have been challenges to that view. Interestingly, these have come not from the Left, but from the Right. Revisionist historians, such as Alan Clark and John Charmley, have advanced interesting alternative interpretations. They criticise Churchill on three counts.

One is that Churchill as a war leader clung to the notion of victory when he had the opportunity to make peace with Germany. The irony of that charge is that there was at least one moment when Churchill appeared to give serious thought to negotiating a settlement with Germany. Although he suppressed the fact in his memoirs, it is now known that in late May 1940 he discussed a compromise peace with a small group of his cabinet. He even said that he might consider pulling Britain out of the war, but only after it had fought on for a time so as to win better terms.

However, whatever consideration Churchill may have given to these ideas, he certainly did not act upon them. Nothing came of the War Cabinet discussions. Although Halifax was keen to pursue the notion of a settlement, Churchill, sure of Labour's support, overruled him and thereafter would not entertain talk of negotiations with Germany. That is why revisionists are able to sustain the accusation that Churchill, despite being a dedicated imperialist, prolonged the struggle for five years, thereby unintentionally weakening Britain to such an extent that it was no longer able to keep its empire after the war was over.

The other charge also has irony. Throughout his career Churchill opposed socialism, yet, critics say, it was during his Coalition government that measures were introduced that prepared the way for the socialist policies followed by British governments after 1945 (see page 162).

A third gloss on the Churchill record has been provided by David Carlton, who has argued that what motivated Churchill during the later war years was the same thing that had consistently inspired him since 1917 – hatred and fear of Soviet Communism. Carlton's argument is that, despite being Stalin's ally, Churchill, as his private correspondence has revealed, believed that by 1944 the Soviet Union was as great a threat to British interests as ever Nazi Germany had been.

Churchill became obsessed with the Communist threat and thereafter saw the struggle to defeat Germany as no more than a second-order crusade. Increasingly he devoted attention to frustrating Soviet expansionist aims. Accordingly he struck a brutal but realistic bargain with Stalin in 1944 with respect to Bulgaria, Romania and anti-communist POWs, but Britain was able to intervene in Greece to prevent communists seizing power.

'Churchill's Secret War with Stalin', *Daily Telegraph*, 11 Feb 2000

The 'brutal bargain' between Stalin and Churchill to which Carlton refers was the agreement by which the Soviet Union was given a free hand in Bulgaria and Romania and allowed to deal as it chose with any Soviet citizens who, after being captured by the Germans, had fought against the USSR. In return, the Soviet Union would not enforce a Communist takeover in Greece. This is an aspect of what may be called Churchill's appeasement of Stalin at the end of the war. In order to limit Soviet ambitions, Churchill, at the **Yalta Conference**, joined with the USA in accepting the USSR's right to remain in control of the territories in eastern Europe that it had taken in its push westwards against Germany. By a bitter irony this included Poland, the country whose independence Britain had gone to war in 1939 to defend.

Interestingly, the charge levelled against Lloyd George over his leadership as prime minister in the First World War (see page 59) was also raised against Churchill in the Second. Paul Addison wrote in 1992: 'Churchill was a profoundly egocentric statesman for whom parties were vehicles for ambition rather than causes to be served.'

Some key books in the debate:
Paul Addison, *The Road to 1945* (Cape, 1992)
David Carlton, *Churchill and the Soviet Union* (MUP, 2000)
John Charmley, *Churchill: The End of Glory* (Hodder & Stoughton, 1993)
Alan Clark, *The Suicide of Empires* (CUP, 1971)
Peter Clarke, *Hope and Glory: Britain 1900–1990* (Allen Lane, 1996)
Martin Gilbert, *Churchill, a Life* (Heinemann, 2000)
Richard Holmes, *In the Footsteps of Churchill* (BBC Books, 2005)
Kevin Jefferys, *The Churchill Coalition and Wartime Politics 1940–45* (Manchester University Press, 1991)
A.J.P. Taylor, *English History, 1914–45* (OUP, 1965)

a) Churchill's wartime coalition colleagues

As Lloyd George had done in the First World War, Churchill chose to govern through a war cabinet, but remained the dominant figure throughout. He later admitted: 'All I wanted was compliance with my wishes after reasonable discussion.' It was a benign dictatorship. There were mutterings against Churchill among backbenchers in parliament at various times during the war, but no sustained opposition.

His worse moments came in 1942 when a number of military reverses, including the loss of **Singapore** to Japan and **Tobruk** to the Germans, increased the pressure on him. There were strong criticisms of his conduct of war policy at this point. In July 1942 Aneurin Bevan complained in the House that, while the Soviet Union was able to resist the enemy for months at a time in various campaigns, badly led British forces capitulated too easily. Yet opinion polls showed that Churchill's popularity with the public was at times as high as eighty-eight per cent, and even at the darkest moments never dropped below seventy-eight per cent.

ALL BEHIND YOU, WINSTON

'All Behind You, Winston.' Cartoon by David Low published in the *Evening Standard* on the 14th May 1940. To Churchill's left are Attlee, Bevin, Morrison and Beaverbrook. Among those in the second row are Chamberlain, Halifax and Eden. How justified was Low's caption?

The following were among Churchill's most notable wartime government colleagues.

Ernest Bevin (1881–1951; Minister of Labour and National Service, 1940–45)

Bevin ranks alongside Churchill and Attlee as one of the most influential British statesman of the age. Between the wars, as a moderate Labour Party member and trade unionist, he fought against the communist infiltration of the party and the unions. As minister of labour in the wartime Government he had the enormous task of organising British industry to meet the demands of war (see page 163). This involved him drafting output targets and negotiating with the bosses, managers and trade unions to reach compromises that adequately rewarded the workers, to whose interests all his experience as a union official predisposed him, while maintaining the war effort at its fullest.

The powers Bevin had over workers and industry were unprecedented. Yet it is a striking tribute to the sparing and responsible way in which Bevin used them that he was criticised in some quarters for being too cautious in his approach.

Stafford Cripps (1889–1952; Ambassador to USSR 1940–42, Minister of Aircraft Production, 1942–45)

Cripps was regarded as the most intellectually gifted member of the Labour Party. Hoping that Cripps' Marxist sympathies, which had led to his temporary expulsion from the party for attempting to impose Stalin's popular front policy on it after 1937, equipped him for the task, Churchill sent him as Ambassador to Moscow. The hope was that Cripps would use his influence to undermine the Nazi–Soviet alliance. Cripps' strong pro-communist leanings obviously became more acceptable after the USSR entered the war in 1941.

To keep India in the war on the British side and to help protect it against possible Japanese invasion, Churchill then sent Cripps on a special mission to India in 1942 to discuss the possibility of independence. The move showed how expedient the Prime Minister was prepared to be in wartime. To maintain the war effort, he was willing to accept the possible weakening of Britain's imperial links with India and swallow his distaste for Cripps' politics. On his return from India, Cripps was side-lined as minister of aircraft production, an office he performed without panache but with competence, building on the work laid down by his predecessor Lord Beaverbrook, the dynamic newspaper magnate Churchill had brought into the government.

Herbert Morrison (1888–65; Leader of the LCC, 1934–40, Minister of Supply, 1940, Home Secretary, 1940–45)

Morrison's invaluable experience in local government politics and administration as leader of the London County Council during the previous six years was put to very effective use when he became home secretary under Churchill in 1940. Morrison served with distinction as home secretary throughout the war. Like Bevin's, his powers were extensive but his duties huge and formidable. To him fell the responsibility of organising home security. He was responsible for the policy of internment and oversaw the defence of London during the Blitz, which included the recruitment and training of **fire watchers** and **ARP** officers. An interesting personal note is that the protective indoor shelters that in 1941 he ordered to be built in every appropriate house became known as Morrison shelters.

Again, like Bevin, he exercised his wartime powers with marked restraint during the five years he was home secretary. This did not, however, prevent his coming under attack on occasion. One row was over his threat to close down the *Daily Mirror* for publishing a particular cartoon in March 1942 (see next page). Churchill and Morrison chose to view the cartoon not as a tribute to the heroism of British seamen, but as an undermining of the war effort by implying that British lives were being sacrificed to make money for the oil producers. Morrison described it as a 'wicked cartoon' and ordered **MI5** to investigate whether Zec, the cartoonist, was a subversive. M15 found only that Zec, as a Jew, was a passionate anti-Nazi.

Common sense prevailed and Churchill and Morrison, realising they had misread the cartoon's intention, called off the dogs and withdrew their threat to the *Mirror*, a newspaper which is now seen as having been unfailingly patriotic and supportive of the war effort.

Key terms

Fire watchers
Members of the public who took up vantage points on high buildings to report outbreaks of fire.

ARP
Air Raid Precautions.

M15
Britain's counter-espionage agency.

'The price of petrol has been increased by one penny.' Official. Why might the
cartoon have been open to an interpretation opposite to the one intended?

Despite the fuss this particular incident caused, it was not typical of
Morrison's policies at the Home Office. Although his security
measures were often unpopular because of their necessarily
restrictive nature they were intended to be as fair and as widely
protective of the civilian population as the circumstances of war
allowed. However, at a personal level Morrison tended to make
enemies. Neither Ernest Bevin nor Aneurin Bevan could get on
with him. On hearing someone describe Morrison as being his own
worst enemy, Bevin jumped in with, 'Not while I'm alive, he ain't.'

Hugh Dalton (1887–1962: Minister of Economic Warfare, 1940–42, President of the Board of Trade, 1942–45)

Dalton's time as economics minister under Churchill is fascinating
for the example it gave of the way in which politics could interfere
with war planning. The great domestic demand was for coal to fuel
the factories and plants that produced the hardware of war. Yet
coal production actually fell between 1939 and 1942, from 227
million tons to 200 million. A mixture of poor wage levels and the
conscription of 80,000 young miners into the services saw the
number of mine workers drop alarmingly.

Dalton's response was to prepare a national scheme of rationing
intended to reduce the amount of coal available to domestic
consumers so that the armaments factories would not go short. News
of the plan leaked out, however, and there was a Conservative revolt.

Judging the scheme to be a move towards nationalisation, since it would subject the mine owners to direct government control, the Conservatives threatened an all-out attack. Dalton backed down in the face of the threat and rationing was formally abandoned.

The affair has been described as the 'only successful Conservative revolt of the war'. Yet not a great deal was lost. Dalton asked a series of committees and advisers to find other ways round the problem. The eventual answer, which largely worked, was simply to reduce the amount of coal that consumers could buy – rationing by other means. At the same time the miners were awarded an across-the-board wage increase and the promise of a minimum wage. Although this brought workers back to the mines, it did not lead to a significant increase in coal production. Nevertheless, supplies to the factories were maintained, which had been Dalton's basic intention.

Anthony Eden (1897–1977; Secretary of State for War, 1940, Foreign Secretary, 1940–45)

It was Eden's fate to live the greater part of his political life in the shadow of Winston Churchill, the man he admired and whom he was destined to succeed, but not until 1955 when he himself was ageing and past his best. In the late 1930s Eden had supported Churchill in his attacks on the National Government's appeasement policies. When Churchill became prime minister in 1940, he made Eden his war secretary and later in the year his foreign secretary.

Given that Churchill, in effect, acted as foreign secretary, attending all the key international conferences himself and conducting his own brand of summitry with President Roosevelt and Joseph Stalin, Eden's role was reduced to that of the ever-present, loyal confidant and background figure.

b) The extremist parties in wartime

The BUF and the war

The war destroyed such credibility as Oswald Mosley had in his claims to speak for Britain (see page 132). His argument before 1939 had been that he was an honest politician defending Britain's interests in the face of the incompetence and ignorance of the established political class represented by the National Government. This became impossible to maintain when his natural sympathy for Britain's enemies, Germany and Italy, made him appear a traitor to the land he supposedly loved. For security reasons, Mosley, his wife Diana and a number of other fascists were interned in May 1940 and the BUF was declared an illegal organisation.

Three years later, believing that the war was going well enough to render Mosley no longer a danger, Herbert Morrison, as home secretary, authorised the release of Mosley and his wife on humanitarian grounds. It was around this time that many of the other internees were also set free.

Key question
What was the impact of the war on the BUF and the CPGB?

If ever Mosley's brand of fascism had been a threat to Britain, the war and its outcome finally removed the danger. Mosley would try to resurrect the fascist party in the post-war period but the war had brought his loyalty into question and ended any hopes he may still have harboured of making fascism part of the mainstream of British politics.

The CPGB and the war

The Communists in Britain had an odd war. For the first two years of the struggle, the CPGB under its secretary, Harry Pollitt, spent its time protesting against the war and seeking to slow down Britain's war effort. This was not from love of Germany but from devotion to the Soviet Union. Of all the communist parties in Europe, the British one was the most subservient to the demands of Moscow and the Comintern. Between 1939 and 1941 Hitler's Germany and Stalin's Soviet Union were not the deadly enemies they were soon to become; having signed the Nazi–Soviet Pact, in August 1939, they were allies (see page 171). Soviet instructions to the CPGB, therefore, were for it to obstruct the war effort where possible. This had been the reason why the government had closed down the party's newspaper, the *Daily Worker*, and interned some of the more outspoken communists.

But this all changed on 22 June 1941 when Hitler launched the invasion of the USSR. Germany was now the deadly enemy and British Communists, doing a U-turn, now rushed to support the war. As poachers turned gamekeepers, they now used their influence to prevent strikes and industrial disruption. This gave an immediate lift to the CPGB. Its opposition to the war had seen it lose 12,000 of its 17,000 members by the end of 1939. Its commitment to the war after June 1941 saw its membership rise to over 30,000.

However, its twists and turns did it considerable damage in the longer term. Workers in Britain could clearly see that they came second in the CPGB's order of priorities. It was its subordination to the orders of the Soviet Union that determined the policy and behaviour of the CPGB. This became increasingly apparent when the party directed all its energies into a 'start a second front now' campaign. To take the pressure off the Soviet forces in their desperate struggle on the Eastern Front between 1941 and 1943, Stalin continually appealed to Britain and the USA to open a second front by a major invasion of some part of German-occupied western Europe. To Stalin's disgust, the Allies claimed they could not do this successfully until they were fully ready, which in the event was not until the **Normandy landings** of June 1944.

The communists obviously rejoiced in the final victory over Germany in 1945, but their assertion that from the beginning they had taken part in a great anti-fascist crusade on Britain's behalf, rang hollow. This claim conveniently overlooked the fact that they had taken up the fight only after Nazi Germany had ceased to be an ally of the Soviet Union and become its enemy.

Key dates

Normandy landings: 1944

German surrender: 1945

Key term

Normandy landings, June 1944
A massive Anglo-American invasion of occupied western France which proved the starting point of the defeat of Germany by May 1945. A fascinating detail is that when the Government, anxious to map the landing areas, asked people to send in any holiday snaps they had of the French coast, a total of ten million photos were received.

The truth was that the CPGB had compromised itself by its changes of policy during the war. It would continue with its efforts to infiltrate the Labour Party, but its support of the Soviet Union in the Cold War, that began as the German war closed, put its loyalty to Britain in doubt. Unlike the Labour Party, which grew in strength and confidence because of its contribution to the war effort, the CPGB condemned itself by its wartime behaviour to remaining a fringe party.

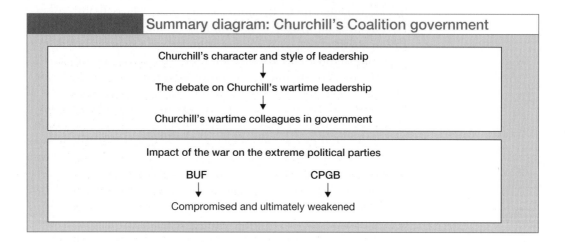

Summary diagram: Churchill's Coalition government

Churchill's character and style of leadership

↓

The debate on Churchill's wartime leadership

↓

Churchill's wartime colleagues in government

Impact of the war on the extreme political parties

BUF   CPGB

↓   ↓

Compromised and ultimately weakened

Study Guide: AS Questions

In the style of AQA

(a) Why did Churchill become prime minister in May 1940?

(12 marks)

(b) How far did the experience of the Second World War help erode class divisions in Britain? (24 marks)

Exam tips

The cross-references are intended to take you straight to the material that will help you to answer the question.

(a) This is a fairly straightforward question and you should ensure the reasons you give are clear and organised without them becoming a chronological narrative. Consider the short-term reasons linking Churchill's appointment to the attack on Norway, the position of the British armies and the imminent fall of the Low Countries and fears about France, and balance these against the longer-term factors working in Churchill's favour – his long-standing opposition to appeasement, his 'bullish' character, and the personalities/weaknesses of both Chamberlain and Lord Halifax. Try to prioritise between the various reasons to provide a supported conclusion. (Re-read pages 165–66).

(b) You should show how many of the wartime changes, such as rationing, evacuation, war work, the Blitz and increased government control, served to weaken the class divide and emphasise the similarities between the British people rather than their social differences. It is no coincidence that the war years saw the publication of the Beveridge report and that a number of moves were taken before 1945 to introduce wide-ranging welfare reforms to reduce the difference between the haves and have-nots. However, you should also be aware of the ways in which class divisions were perpetuated – for example, in the type of work women were called upon to do and, in the ability of the wealthy to obtain rationed goods more easily or to escape the cities and the worst of the bombing. Britain did not emerge from the war as a classless society! You must try to assess the social impact of war and should try to support your views throughout your answer. (Re-read pages 145–56).

In the style of OCR
Domestic issues, 1918–51

How much did the social reforms of the Labour governments of 1945–51 owe to wartime reports? (50 marks)

Exam tips

The cross-references are intended to take you straight to the material that will help you to answer the question.

You need to show that you have understood the focus of the question and that you can select an appropriate range and depth of evidence to support your argument. This question requires you to assess the role of the Beveridge and Butler Reports in influencing the social reforms after 1945. Your answer should focus on explanation rather than description or narrative although you are likely to refer to the main features of these reports in your evaluation. You might begin by comparing the aims and principles of the Beveridge and Butler Reports and refer to their influence on changes in National Insurance, National Assistance, Industrial Injuries, education, the NHS and Family Allowances (page 158, see also Chapter 6, page 186).

A counter-argument needs to be established to show the extent to which social reforms were influenced by other factors. For example:

- liberal and socialist ideologies (Chapter 6, pages 187–88)
- the impact of the Second World War (pages 145–58)
- collectivism and nationalisation of industries (pages 162, and Chapter 6, pages 185 and 195).

Ensure you prioritise your arguments and in your conclusion reach a balanced judgement that refers directly to the question set.

6 The Labour Party in Power, 1945–51

POINTS TO CONSIDER

The period 1945–51, following directly on from the Second World War, was one of the most formative in the whole century. Labour came into power with a large majority after an impressive victory in the 1945 election. During the next six years it introduced the welfare state and nationalised a significant part of the industrial economy. In doing so, the Labour Government set a pattern that was largely followed by all succeeding governments until 1979. This chapter describes the domestic achievements of Clement Attlee's post-war Governments and examines the historical debate over those achievements:

• Labour's victory in 1945
• Labour's creation of the welfare state
• The economy under Labour, 1945–51
• The Labour Governments' achievements

Key dates

1945	Start of Cold War
	Overwhelming election victory for Labour
	Family Allowances Act
1946	National Insurance Act
	NHS Act
	Nationalisation of coal, civil aviation, cable and wireless, the Bank of England
1946–47	A severe winter intensified the Government's austerity measures
1947	Government undertook to develop Britain's independent nuclear deterrent
	Nationalisation of road transport and electricity services
	Independence of India
1948	NHS began
	Industrial Injuries Act

	National Assistance Act
	Britain began to receive substantial Marshall aid
1949	Nationalisation of Iron and Steel Act
	Government forced to devalue the pound sterling
	Parliamentary Reform Act
1950	Start of Korean War
	Election reduced Labour majority to five
1951	Bevanite rebellion over prescription charges
	Election success for Conservatives, but Labour gained highest popular vote yet

1 | Labour's Victory in 1945

The size of the election victory in 1945 surprised even the Labour Party. It had gained a massive majority of 180 over the Conservatives and one of 148 overall.

Key question
Why was the Labour party so successful in the 1945 election?

Table 6.1: July 1945 election results

	Votes	Seats	% of total votes cast
Labour	11,995,152	393	47.8
Conservative	9,988,306	213	39.8
Liberal	2,248,226	12	9.0
Communist	102,780	2	0.4
Others	751,514	20	3.0

In proportional terms, the victory is less impressive; Labour was over two per cent short of winning half the total vote, and the opposition parties collectively polled more votes and had a greater percentage of popular support. Despite its overwhelming number of seats, Labour was a minority government. The disparity that the electoral system had once again produced is evident in the following figures:

Key date

Overwhelming election victory for Labour: 1945

- For each seat Labour won, it had polled 30,522 votes.
- For each seat the Conservative Party won, it had polled 46,893 votes.
- For each seat the Liberal Party won, it had polled 187,352.

However, the observations made above apply to all subsequent general elections; none of the parties which came to power did so with the majority of the electorate having voted for them. In all their future election victories the Conservatives would similarly gain from the inbuilt imbalance of the system. It was only the Liberals who missed out because they could not convert their popular following into seats in parliament. Political commentators are fond of talking, as in regard to 1945, of landslides and crushing defeats, but these things rarely happen. What does occur is a marginal shift in a range of closely fought constituencies, sufficient to give the winning party the edge over its opponents.

With that said, it is undeniable that Labour had performed extraordinarily well. Ten years earlier it had gained 37.9 per cent of the overall vote but had won only 154 seats (see page 128). In 1945 it gained ten per cent more of the vote, increased its support by three-and-half million and won 393 seats.

In hindsight, the reasons for this are not difficult to find. Churchill's great popularity as a wartime leader did not carry over into peacetime. In the minds of a good part of the electorate, his Conservative Party was associated with the grim Depression years of the 1930s and with the failure either to prevent war or to prepare for it adequately.

In 1945 there was also a widespread feeling in Britain that effective post-war social and economic reconstruction was both vital and deserved, and that the tired old Conservative-dominated establishment that had governed during the inter-war years would be incapable of providing it. People could remember clearly how, a generation earlier, the Lloyd George Coalition and the Conservative governments of the 1920s had failed to deliver 'the land fit for heroes' that the nation had been promised. It was not so much that Labour won the election as that the Conservatives lost it.

Another important factor was the Conservatives' poor electioneering. Confident of victory, Churchill misread the mood of the nation. On one notorious occasion he suggested that the Labour Party's proposed reform programme would require 'a Gestapo' to enforce it. He had failed to appreciate the reputation that had been gained by the leading Labour figures who had served in his own wartime Coalition. The ministerial record of such men as Attlee, Cripps, Bevin, Dalton and Morrison had destroyed any doubts there might have been about their ability or loyalty.

It used to be claimed that the size of Labour's victory was due to the pro-Labour teaching in the education services of the armed forces. The argument was that the teachers conscripted into the education corps during the war were predominantly left-wing and gave slanted talks and instruction in the classes they put on for the troops. When the soldiers cast their vote in the election, therefore, they had already been indoctrinated into supporting Labour.

It is a difficult claim to sustain. Even if one could know precisely how the armed services voted, it would still not be possible to know their motives. The personnel in education may indeed have leaned to the left, but to ascribe Labour's victory to their efforts would be an exaggeration. What is more likely to have had an impact on the voters' attitudes was the work of the government's wartime propaganda department. The documentary films that it put on regularly in the cinemas were not simply anti-German. A recurring theme was the need for the people to look beyond the war and think in terms of acting together to reconstruct a better nation. Such films were not overtly supportive of the Labour Party, and were probably not deliberately intended to be, but their message was much more in tune with the ideas of Labour than any of the other parties.

Reasons for Labour's large-scale victory in 1945

Conservative handicaps:

- a broad feeling that the inter-war political establishment had not understood the needs of ordinary people and had outlived its time
- Churchill's inability to carry his wartime popularity into peacetime
- the inability of Conservative politicians to manage the economy and deal with unemployment in the 1930s
- the inglorious appeasement policy of the Conservative-dominated National Government which had failed to prevent war occurring
- the memories of the failure of the inter-war governments to provide 'a land fit for heroes'
- the Conservative Party's ill-judged and unconvincing election campaign.

Labour advantages:

- the attractive image of the Labour Party as representing the progressive **zeitgeist** that encouraged reform and reconstruction
- the general view that Labour was better fitted to carry out post-war construction, despite the Conservatives' acceptance of the need for it.
- the invaluable experience gained by leading Labour figures as ministers in the wartime Coalition, which had gained the respect of the electorate
- a willingness among voters to overlook Labour's own failings in 1924 and 1929–31 or to attribute them to Labour's difficulties as a minority government
- the imbalance in the electoral system in 1945 that worked in Labour's favour.

Zeitgeist
Spirit of the times, i.e. dominant prevailing attitude.

Key term

The leading members of Attlee's governments

In forming his government, Clement Attlee could call on the services of a remarkable set of politicians, most of whom had already proved themselves in public office as loyal and successful members of Churchill's wartime coalition (see pages 171–74).

Key question
What qualities distinguished the members of Attlee's government?

Ernest Bevin

Bevin's contribution to international affairs was hugely significant. As foreign secretary between 1945 and 1950, in a critical period of Cold War diplomacy, he established the basic lines of British foreign policy for the next half century. His pro-American and anti-Soviet stance was the essential position adopted by Britain throughout the Cold War.

Stafford Cripps

His lean features and joyless manner seemed perfectly fitted to his role as Chancellor of the Exchequer, under Attlee, after 1947, calling on the nation to make sacrifices and put up with shortages and restrictions. In an unfortunate, but not altogether inappropriate, slip of the tongue, a BBC radio announcer once introduced him as 'Sir Stifford Craps'.

Herbert Morrison

Morrison was Attlee's dedicated second-in-command after 1945. He had a running feud with Aneurin Bevan whose left-wing views he regarded as dangerous. Having lost to Attlee in the leadership election in 1935, Morrison seemed to be permanently sidelined within the party. He served as deputy prime minister between 1945–51 and, after a brief spell as foreign secretary in 1951, as Deputy Leader of the party between 1951 and 1955.

Hugh Dalton

Dalton made a major contribution to the planning of Labour's nationalisation programme. A loud, self-opinionated academic whom Attlee tolerated only because of his talents, Dalton had to resign as Chancellor of the Exchequer in 1947 after incautiously leaking some of his budget plans.

Aneurin Bevan

Bevan was the dominant figure on the left of the Labour Party in Attlee's time. He came from a Welsh mining background and represented the Ebbw Vale constituency continuously from 1929 until his death in 1960. Like Churchill, he overcame a speech impediment to become an outstanding hustings and parliamentary speaker. His greatest achievement as a minister was the creation of the National Health Service, which came into operation in 1948. He was defeated for the leadership of the party after Attlee's retirement in 1955 by Hugh Gaitskell.

Hugh Gaitskell

One of the most able of the younger Labour MPs who entered parliament in 1945, Gaitskell served as Attlee's minister of fuel and power (1947–50), before becoming Chancellor of the Exchequer in 1950. It was as Chancellor that Gaitskell introduced the controversial cuts in NHS expenditure that led to the revolt of the Bevanites in 1951 (see page 196).

History suggests that Attlee himself may now be regarded as the outstanding figure in his government.

Profile: Clement Attlee (1883–1967)

1883	– Born in London into a comfortable middle-class family
1901–04	– Read law at Oxford
1907	– Became manager of a boys' settlement in London's East End
1914–18	– Served as an officer in the War
1919	– Became Mayor of Stepney
1922	– Elected Labour MP for Limehouse
1930–31	– Served in Ramsay MacDonald's Labour government
1935–55	– Leader of the Labour Party
1940–45	– Deputy PM in Churchill's Coalition Government
1945–51	– Prime Minister
1955	– Retired as party leader and went to the House of Lords
1967	– Died

In his own time and for years afterwards, Clement Attlee tended to be underrated. He suffered by comparison with Winston Churchill. Attlee's unprepossessing physical presence and limited skills as a public speaker did not create the grand image. However, in the 1970s, Attlee began to be reassessed. Stress was laid upon his skill in surviving six years of one of the most difficult periods of twentieth-century government. Nor was it merely survival. His record as prime minister was truly remarkable. Nationalisation, the welfare state, NATO, Indian independence: these were the striking successes of this unassuming man. His ordinariness was a positive virtue in that he came to typify the very people whose well-being he did so much to advance. Attlee's achievements would have been impressive at any time, but when it is appreciated that they were accomplished in a post-war period dominated by the most demanding of domestic and international crises, they appear even more striking.

In an interview in 1960, Attlee summed up his own practical, down-to-earth style of conducting government business:

> A Prime Minister has to know when to ask for an opinion. He can't always stop ministers offering theirs; you always have some people who'll talk on everything. But he can make sure to extract the opinion of those he wants when he needs them. The job of the Prime Minister is to get the general feeling – collect the voices. And then, when everything reasonable has been said, to get on with the job and say, 'Well, I think the decision of the Cabinet is this, that or the other. Any objections?' Usually there aren't.
>
> Harold Wilson, *A Prime Minister on Prime Ministers*, 1977

Stories are often told of Churchill's withering comments on Attlee's lack of personality. The stories are apocryphal; Churchill always denied them. Despite their party differences, Churchill had the deepest respect for the talent and integrity of the man who had been his committed and loyal wartime deputy, regarding him as 'a gallant English gentleman'.

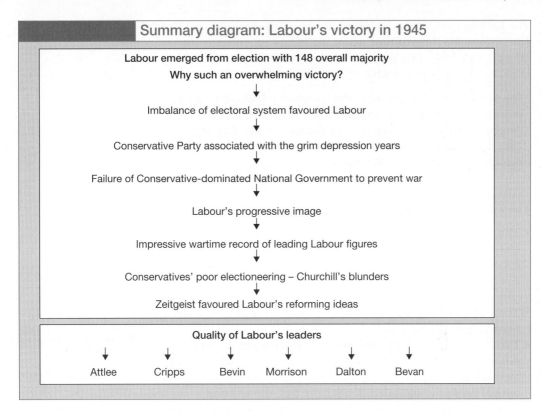

Summary diagram: Labour's victory in 1945

Labour emerged from election with 148 overall majority
Why such an overwhelming victory?
↓
Imbalance of electoral system favoured Labour
↓
Conservative Party associated with the grim depression years
↓
Failure of Conservative-dominated National Government to prevent war
↓
Labour's progressive image
↓
Impressive wartime record of leading Labour figures
↓
Conservatives' poor electioneering – Churchill's blunders
↓
Zeitgeist favoured Labour's reforming ideas

Quality of Labour's leaders
↓   ↓   ↓   ↓   ↓   ↓
Attlee   Cripps   Bevin   Morrison Dalton   Bevan

2 | Labour's Creation of the Welfare State

Key question
What were the main features of the welfare state introduced under Attlee?

Key term

Collectivism
The people and the state acting together with a common sense of purpose, which necessarily means a restriction on individual rights.

When Beveridge's Report (see page 158) first appeared in 1942 it met an eager response from the Labour Party. But the fact was, all the parties accepted the report's basic objectives. There was broad agreement that social reconstruction would be a post-war necessity in Britain. This showed how much ground had been made in Britain by the principle of **collectivism**. This in turn was evidence of the influence of the moderate socialism that the Labour Party espoused. Yet Churchill did not regard the Report as socialist; his reluctance to put the Report into practice was on the grounds of cost rather than principle. It is noteworthy that the Labour members of his war cabinet supported him in 1942 and 1943 in defeating Commons motions demanding legislation to implement the Report.

However, in office after 1945 with a massive majority, the Labour government turned its attention to applying the main proposals of the Beveridge Report. Labour's election campaign had promoted the notion that after six years of monumental effort the people were entitled to a just reward. It would also be a fitting recompense for the sufferings of the nation during the depression of the inter-war years. The Beveridge plan had provided the new government with its blueprint for social reconstruction.

The Labour government's strategy for an integrated social welfare system took the form of four major measures, which came into effect in July 1948. In a prime ministerial broadcast Attlee explained in plain terms what the intention was:

> The four Acts which come into force tomorrow – National Insurance, Industrial Injuries, National Assistance and the National Health Service – represent the main body of the army of social security. They are comprehensive and available to every citizen. They give security to all members of the family.
>
> A BBC broadcast by Clement Attlee, 4 July 1948

The main features of the measures to which Attlee referred were:

- **The National Insurance Act** of 1946 built upon the Act of 1911 (see page 24) by creating a system of universal and compulsory government/employer/employee contributions to provide against unemployment, sickness, maternity expenses, widowhood and retirement.
- **The Industrial Injuries Act** of 1948 provided cover for accidents occurring in the workplace.
- **The National Health Service Act** of 1946 brought the whole population, regardless of status or income, into a scheme of free medical and hospital treatment. Drug prescriptions, dental and optical care were included. Under the Act, the existing voluntary and local authority hospitals were co-ordinated into a single, national system, to be operated at local level by appointed health boards.
- **The National Assistance Act** of 1948 complemented National Insurance by establishing National Assistance Boards to deal directly and financially with cases of hardship and poverty.

Two other measures need to be added to the four listed by Attlee: the Education Act of 1944 and the Family Allowances Act of 1945. These were introduced before Labour came into office but were implemented by Attlee's Government.

- **The Education Act** of 1944 (the Butler Act) was introduced by R.A. Butler, a Conservative, and may be regarded as the first organised attack on one of Beveridge's five giants – ignorance. It provided compulsory free education within a tripartite secondary education system. At the age of eleven pupils were to take an examination ('the eleven plus') to determine whether they were to attend a secondary grammar (for the academically inclined), a secondary technical (for the vocationally gifted) or a secondary modern (for those not fitted for either of the former two categories).
- **The Family Allowances Act** of 1945 provided a weekly payment of 5 shillings (25p) for every child after the first. The money was paid directly to the mother and did not require a means test.

Key dates

National Insurance Act: 1946

Industrial Injuries Act: 1948

NHS Act: 1946

National Assistance Act: 1948

Family Allowances Act: 1945

Key question
How far was Attlee's government's introduction of the welfare state the implementation of socialist principles?

Key debate – the principles of the welfare state

The Labour government's implementation of the welfare state has been described as a social revolution. It was certainly an event of major significance, but it is important to see it in context. It was a not a revolution forced on an unwilling people and it was not a revolution that pushed down existing structures. Quite the opposite; it built upon what was already there. Beveridge had, indeed, described his plan as a revolution, but he had been keen to stress that it was a British revolution, by which he meant it was not destructive but constructive, built upon precedent not on the introduction of sweepingly novel ideas. He said it was 'a natural development from the past'; the nation was ready for such a revolution.

Interestingly, Attlee's Government, when introducing the welfare measures, was also careful to point out that, far from representing revolutionary socialism, the implementation of the welfare state was a responsible act of social reconstruction. Ernest Bevin expressed the government's basic view in a speech in the Commons in June 1949:

> From the point of view of what is called the welfare State and social services, I beg the House not to drag this business into a kind of partisan warfare. This so-called welfare State has developed everywhere. The United States is as much a welfare State as we are, only in a different form.

In saying this, Bevin was responding to the criticism of the Conservative opposition who voted against nearly all the major clauses of the various welfare measures. He was hoping to take the question out of the political arena, arguing that the welfare state was not peculiar to Britain. This now looks a trifle naïve; it had become a political issue and the American system at the time bore little relation to the one that Britain was adopting.

The welfare state – fulfilment of socialism or liberalism?

Bevin's view is instructive since it shows that the Labour government was not hell-bent on pursuing revolutionary socialist policies. In the light of such views, it is perhaps best to see Labour's impressive achievement in the field of social services not as an entirely new departure, but as the implementation of welfare policies that represented progressive thinking in all parties. Although Churchill and the Conservatives opposed the measures at every turn, subsequent events were to show that this was purely tactical. All the Conservative governments that were to follow between 1951 and 1997 committed themselves to the preservation and, indeed, the extension of the welfare state in all its main aspects. It is true that the main parties would continually row about how it was funded and how efficiently it was managed, but there was no serious difference between them over the need to keep the welfare state in existence.

It can now be seen that rather than being the advent of reconstructive socialism, Labour's moves towards a welfare state marked the high point of reforming liberalism. It was very much in the tradition begun by the Liberal governments between 1906 and 1914. Although the Liberal Party had ceased to be a major political force long before 1945, it could be argued that the coming of the welfare state marked the final great triumph of liberalism as a set of ideas. It had set the agenda for the foreseeable future.

Key date

NHS began: 1948

Resistance to the introduction of the NHS

Yet when due note has been taken of Liberal influence and of the ultimate consensus between the parties over welfare, the clear historical fact remains that it was the Labour Party under Attlee that between 1945 and 1951 found the commitment and consistency of purpose to turn good intentions into workable and permanent structures. This was often, moreover, achieved in the face of determined opposition. One of the most striking examples of this was the resistance of the **British Medical Association (BMA)** to the introduction of the National Health Service.

Professions are notoriously reluctant to put the public first. George Bernard Shaw once memorably described them as 'conspiracies against the people', suggesting that all professions always put their members' interests above the needs of the public they supposedly exist to serve. It was certainly the case that the majority of the consultants and senior doctors, fearing a loss of their privileges and a reduction in their income, initially refused to co-operate with Aneurin Bevan who, as minister of health, was responsible for the introduction of the NHS.

Key term

British Medical Association (BMA) The professional association and registered trade union for doctors in the United Kingdom.

DOTHEBOYS HALL

"It still tastes awful."

A cartoon showing 'Matron' Bevan forcing the doctors to take the nasty medicine of the NHS. How accurately does the cartoon depict the relationship between the BMA and Aneurin Bevan?

Dandruff syndrome
Describes the tendency that affects all systems that are provided free to the consumer. Since all medical treatment was free there was no limit to the number of people entitled to call on the services of doctors and nurses. This led to time and many resources being wasted on trivial or non existent conditions, e.g. dandruff.

Gross Domestic Product (GDP)
The annual total value of goods produced and services provided by Britain at home.

In the end, after protracted negotiations, he had to buy off the BMA. In return for a guarantee that they would not lose financially and would be allowed to keep their private practices, the doctors agreed to enter the NHS. Bevan remarked bitterly that he had won them over only by 'stuffing their mouths with gold'.

Regardless of his long and often bitter struggle with the medical profession, Bevan still believed that the NHS would not only solve the nation's major social problems, but that it would also pay for itself. A healthy society would mean far fewer workers being absent. Efficiency and wages would rise. Higher wages would produce higher tax yields. From that increased revenue, the State would be able to finance its welfare provision.

Such thinking now seems sadly unrealistic. Bevan declined to listen when he was told that the demand for treatment would outstrip supply and that the cost of drugs and medical appliances and machinery would spiral beyond the capacity of the Government to match it from revenue. But he was less culpable in regard to another development that undermined the NHS. He could not know that there would be a major population shift in the second half of the century caused by people living longer and in old age making demands on a service that could be financed only by a dwindling proportion of people of working age paying tax. Nor was he aware that his scheme would fall foul of the **dandruff syndrome**.

The gap between Bevan's estimation of cost and the reality is clear from these figures:

Health and social security budget:

- 1949 – £597 million (equivalent to 4.7 per cent of **GDP**)
- 1990 – £91 billion (equivalent to 14 per cent of GDP).

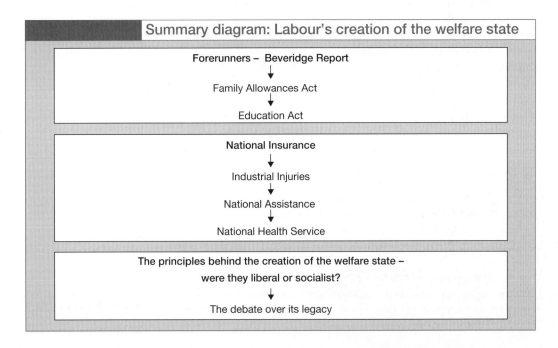

Summary diagram: Labour's creation of the welfare state

Forerunners – Beveridge Report
↓
Family Allowances Act
↓
Education Act

National Insurance
↓
Industrial Injuries
↓
National Assistance
↓
National Health Service

The principles behind the creation of the welfare state –
were they liberal or socialist?
↓
The debate over its legacy

3 | The Economy under Labour, 1945–51

From its earliest days the Labour Party had advanced the principle that government had the right to direct the key aspects of the economy in order to create efficiency and social justice. When it came into office with an overwhelming majority in 1945, the times were ripe for it to fulfil its aims. In its election manifesto, *Let us Face the Future*, the party promised to implement an ambitious programme for the **nationalisation** of Britain's major industries. These were specified as:

• the fuel and power industries
• iron and steel
• inland transport, which included rail, road and air services.

The nationalisation programme

Labour's public ownership programme makes impressive reading.

Chief industries and institutions nationalised under Labour:

1946   Coal, civil aviation, cable and wireless, the Bank of England
1947   Road transport, electricity
1948   Gas
1949   Iron and steel

Coal, Britain's most vital industry, yet one which for decades had been subject to disruption and under-production (see page 105), was the first ear-marked for public ownership. The government considered that the modernisation that this would bring could also be achieved in the gas and electricity undertakings. Nationalisation would mean greater safety, productivity and efficiency, with the result that all the other industries associated with fuel and power production would benefit. It was also reckoned that the ending of private ownership in transport, which would be the prelude to the co-ordination of the road, rail and canal system, would similarly improve the quality of the nation's essential services.

Iron and steel

The odd-man-out in the list of enterprises scheduled for nationalisation was the iron and steel industry. It had in fact been included only because of a Labour Conference decision of 1944 which had imposed it on the unwilling Labour leaders. Since steel was the only profit-making industry, it had stout defenders willing to fight against nationalisation. This made the legislation relating to its takeover by the State a fierce battle ground.

The key factor here was that nationalisation involved compensating the former owners of the concerns that were taken into public ownership. In a declining industry, coal for example, nationalisation might well be a blessed relief to the owners since it bought them out at a price that cut their losses. However, in a concern that was still profit-making, compensation was a much

Key question
How extensive was the Labour governments' restructuring of the economy?

Key term

Nationalisation (public ownership) Clause IV of the Labour Party's constitution committed it to achieving 'the common ownership of the means of production, distribution and exchange'. In effect, common ownership or public control meant government control.

Key dates

Nationalisation of coal, civil aviation, cable and wireless, the Bank of England: 1946

Nationalisation of road transport and electricity services: 1947

Key dates

Nationalisation of iron and steel: 1949

Start of Cold War: 1945

Government undertook to develop Britain's independent nuclear deterrent: 1947

Parliamentary Reform Act: 1949

more difficult issue to resolve. It raised the question of what was a fair settlement, but, more significantly still, it opened up the larger issue of whether the State had the right to overrule the declared objections of the owners and shareholders. It became an argument over justice in a free society.

Opponents of the nationalisation of iron and steel protested on four main grounds:

- it was not a public utility but a privately owned manufacturing industry
- it was successfully run and making profits
- large investments had recently been made into it
- it had an excellent record of employer–employee relations.

Conservative resistance

The row over iron and steel proved a godsend to the Conservatives. They had been badly damaged by their heavy defeat in 1945 and their morale and reputation were low. Now in 1948 the proposal to nationalise iron and steel created a rallying ground for them. Until that point the Conservative opposition had offered only token resistance to nationalisation. There was a sense in which the war seemed to have won the argument for State direction. The principle of public ownership itself had rarely been discussed; most of the debates were taken up with the dry detail of the methods for making the change and the levels of compensation. The iron and steel bill changed all that. The Conservatives now had a cause to defend. In the Commons they launched their salvoes against the government's nationalisation programme as an abuse of government power.

Key term

Invisible exports
The sale of financial and insurance services to foreign buyers, traditionally one of Britain's major sources of income from abroad.

Government victory over iron and steel

However, in the end the government was able to push through the nationalisation of iron and steel in 1950. The path to success was greatly eased by the passing of the Parliamentary Reform Act of 1949, a measure which effectively prevented the Conservatives from using their majority in the House of Lords to block the steel nationalisation bill and so allowed nationalisation to become law before the scheduled end of the Labour term in office in 1950.

Key question
Why did the Labour government experience serious financial difficulties?

The government's financial problems

It was not simply Conservative opposition that prevented Attlee's Governments from going further down the road of reform. The main barrier was the sheer scale of the financial problem they inherited. By the end of the war Britain carried the following burdens:

- debts of £4,198 million
- balance of payments deficit of nearly £1 billion
- exports of manufactures that had dropped by sixty per cent in wartime
- shrinkage of **invisible exports** from £248 million in 1938 to £120 million in 1946

- costs of maintaining overseas military commitments had quintupled between 1938 and 1946

To deal with this dire situation, Hugh Dalton, the Chancellor of the Exchequer (1945–47), negotiated a loan of $6 billion from the USA and Canada. The Government's hope was that, in accordance with Keynesian theory (see page 164), the loan would provide the basis of an industrial recovery which would then produce the revenue which could be used to pay off the debt. But such recovery as did occur was never enough to meet expectations.

Part of the problem was that the American dollar was so strong at the end of the war that it dominated international commerce. The consequence was that Britain began to suffer from what was known as the **'dollar gap'**. This drained Britain of a substantial part of the loan it had negotiated, while at the same time making it harder to meet the repayments.

What made the situation still worse was that Britain had agreed with the USA, its **Cold War** ally, to increase its spending on defence from £2.3 billion to £4.7 billion. Despite demobilisation in 1945, Britain, as one of the occupying forces in Europe and as a member of the United Nations Security Council, continued to maintain a large peacetime army. In 1950 this stood at nearly one million men. Adding to the costs of this was the further financial burden Britain had shouldered when Attlee's Government in 1947 committed Britain to the development of its own **independent nuclear deterrent**. Ernest Bevin, the foreign secretary, declared: 'We've got to have it and it's got to have a bloody Union Jack on it.'

By the late 1940s Britain was spending fourteen per cent of its GNP on defence. To maintain this level of commitment, the Labour Government's only recourse under Dalton and his successor, Stafford Cripps, was to adopt a policy of **austerity**. The basic aim was to use rationing and tight economic controls to prevent **inflation**. Such measures, it was hoped, would keep employment high and allow the Government to continue with its welfare programme. Controls on imports were imposed to keep dollar spending to a minimum. But this led to further shortages and rationing. In 1949, in an effort to relieve the situation and make British goods easier to sell abroad, the pound sterling was devalued from $4.03 to $2.80.

Key terms

'Dollar gap'
Since sterling was weaker than the dollar, the goods that Britain desperately needed from North America had to be paid for in dollars.

Cold War
The period of tension between the USSR and its allies and the USA and its allies, 1945–91.

Independent nuclear deterrent
In 1947, to the anger of the left wing of the Labour Party, the Government initiated a research programme that led to the detonation of a British atom bomb in 1952 and a hydrogen bomb in 1957.

Austerity
A time of rationing and shortages.

Inflation
A decline in the value of money, which would mean Britain's having to spend more dollars to buy its imports; devaluation was intended to slow down inflation.

Freezing cold, accompanied by heavy snowfalls affecting large parts of Britain, persisted between January and March 1947, leading to fuel shortages and regular cuts in domestic and industrial electricity supplies. Some four million workers were laid off as a direct result of the weather conditions. Why was the country so poorly prepared for dealing with the situation?

Key term

Wage freeze
An undertaking not to press for higher wages until Britain's economy had improved.

Key dates

Government forced to devalue the pound sterling: 1949

Severe winter intensified the government's austerity measures: 1946–47

Britain began to receive Marshall aid: 1948

The Government's anti-inflationary policies did not please the trade unions, particularly when they were asked to show restraint in the difficult times and operate a **wage freeze**. There were thinly veiled threats from the Government that if the unions did not do this voluntarily, wage restrictions would have to be legally imposed. Despite being the Government's natural supporters and the chief provider of funds, the unions were not prepared to be docile. As they saw it, a Labour Government was in power to provide for the needs of the workers first, not to involve itself in financial deals which kept the USA happy but left British workers vulnerable. Arthur Deakin, general secretary of the large and influential TGWU, had warned the government in its first year of office of where the unions stood:

> We shall go forward building up our wage claims in conformity with our understanding of the people we are representing ... Any attempt to interfere with that position would have disastrous consequences
>
> Quoted in David Kynaston, *Austerity Britain, 1945–51*, 2007

The hard times were made harder by the coinciding of this period of austerity with Labour's creation of the welfare state, which placed further heavy financial burdens on an already strained economy. Yet Britain's financial problems would have been even greater had it not been for the relief provided by the Marshall Plan, which began to operate from 1948.

Britain and the Marshall Plan

After 1945 the world's trading nations all experienced severe balance of payments difficulties. Worried that this would destroy international commerce, the USA, the only economy with sufficient resources, adopted a programme in 1947 to provide dollars to any country willing to receive them in return for granting trade concessions to the United States. Whatever America's self-interest may have been, it is difficult to see how Europe could have recovered without a massive inflow of American capital. Under the Plan, which bore the name of the US secretary of state, **George Marshall**, Europe received $15 billion, Britain's share being ten per cent of that.

The Marshall Plan ranks as one of the major achievements of Ernest Bevin as foreign secretary. It was he who did so much to convince the USA of the necessity of such a plan, both for shoring up Europe against the threat from the USSR and for sustaining an international economy without which the USA itself could not maintain its strength as the world's greatest industrial power.

Desperate though Britain was for Marshall aid, the left of the Labour Party was frustrated and angered by the government's acceptance of it. For many Labour MPs the financial arrangement tied Britain to the USA in the relationship of beggar and master, and so denied the government any chance of acting independently in the post-war, Cold War world.

George Marshall (1880–1959)
One of America's most distinguished soldier-statesmen of the twentieth century.

Key figure

Summary diagram: The economy under Labour, 1945–51

THE NATIONALISATION PROGRAMME

1946 – coal, civil aviation, cable and wireless, the Bank of England
1947 – road transport, electricity
1948 – gas
1949 – iron and steel

THE GOVERNMENT'S FINANCIAL PROBLEMS

Wartime debts
Balance of payments crises
Declining exports
Dollar gap
Defence expenditure
Heavy demands on fuel and power supplies

The government's response
Austerity measures
↓
Rationing of essential items
Deflationary budgets
Financial controls
Wage freeze
Devaluation of £ sterling
Access to Marshall aid

Key question
What did Labour achieve during its six years of office, 1945–51?

Key date

Independence of India: 1947

Key question
How radical were the policies of Attlee's governments?

Key terms

Indian independence
In 1947 Attlee's government gave independence to the sub-continent in the form of the separate sovereign states of India and Pakistan.

North Atlantic Treaty Organisation (NATO)
A defensive alliance formed in 1949 by Britain, France and the Benelux countries as a safeguard against Soviet expansion. The USA eagerly accepted the invitation to join.

4 | The Labour Governments' Achievements

Key debate

How successful were the Labour governments of 1945–51?

The record of Attlee's Governments showed that despite working throughout under the shadow of serious economic and financial difficulties, they achieved a high degree of activity and success. This was a tribute to the enthusiasm and to the administrative and political skills of their leading ministers.

Main achievements of the Attlee governments, 1945–51:

- implemented a large-scale nationalisation programme
- created the Welfare State
- helped convince the USA of the need for the Marshall Plan
- granted **Indian independence**
- a major housing programme, resulting in one million new homes being built
- played a key role in the formation of the **North Atlantic Treaty Organisation**
- started the programme that turned Britain into a nuclear power.

So large was Labour's majority in the 1945 election that its opponents feared it would leave the new Government free to subject Britain to sweeping socialist changes. It is true that during the next six years many significant and lasting reforms were introduced, but the Labour Governments made no attempt either to disrupt the capitalist system in Britain or to destroy the social structure.

That indeed was the complaint of the left of the Labour Party, who argued that the Government, with its unassailable majority, was in a position to bring about a genuine transformation of British society. But instead, they asserted, it threw away the opportunity by settling for half measures. Its nationalisation programme was not really an attempt to take central control of the economy. With the exception of steel, it was restricted to non-profit-making concerns and it made no effort to take over the private banks or insurance companies.

Another accusation from left-wing critics was that, by borrowing heavily from the USA in order to lessen its financial difficulties, Attlee's Government lost its freedom of action in foreign policy. Dependent on America, Britain found itself locked into a lasting Cold War hostility towards the Soviet Union.

A powerful argument from an opposite political viewpoint was that the Labour government had indeed thrown away a historic opportunity to reform Britain – not, however, by doing too little, but by doing too much. Writers, such as Corelli Barnett, have claimed that after the war Britain should have given priority to financial recovery and investment in the nation's **infrastructure**. This would have provided the means for Britain to re-establish itself as a major manufacturing economy, able to respond to the post-war international demand for commodity goods.

Instead, runs Barnett's argument, Britain made a priority not of industrial recovery, but of social welfare. However, welfare was costly and Britain, being practically bankrupt at the end of the war, had to borrow heavily to fund it. Saddled with large debts, Britain was able to achieve only low economic growth. To strengthen his case, Barnett quoted the example of West Germany, which, by delaying its welfare state until it had achieved industrial recovery, put itself on the path to an economic miracle.

From time to time there have also been suggestions that Labour failed to make an impact in areas where it should have been at its most influential. In 1951, despite six years of government by a supposedly radical party with an unassailable majority:

- Britain's class structure remained largely unaltered.
- Social reform had not greatly raised the conditions and status of women.

The Bevanite revolt over the NHS

An even more telling criticism is that the National Health Service, Labour's proudest creation and the one which best defined its character as a party of the working class, failed to fulfil the expectations invested in it. This charge is that it was not the poorer and disadvantaged sections of the population who benefited most from the introduction of the NHS but the already privileged middle classes. It was they who no longer had to pay for medical treatment but who could now call on the services of the best qualified GPs whose practices tended to be in the more prosperous areas where the middle classes lived. In contrast, the underprivileged still lacked access to the best treatment and were worst hit when the Labour Government, backtracking on its promise to maintain free healthcare, introduced prescription charges.

It was this issue that produced the most serious challenge to Attlee yet from within the Labour Party. In 1951, forced by its financial difficulties to make savings in public expenditure, his Government imposed charges on dental treatment and the provision of spectacles as well as on prescriptions. Aneurin Bevan, the man who had constructed the NHS, led a number of ministers, including **Harold Wilson**, in resigning from the Cabinet. Those who followed him in this became known as Bevanites; they protested that the charges contravened the founding principle that the NHS should be free to all at the point of treatment and were thus a betrayal of basic Labour values.

Infrastructure
The interlocking systems and installations which enable a nation's industrial economy to operate, e.g. transport, power supply, sewerage and communications.

Key term

Bevanite rebellion over prescription charges: 1951

Key date

Harold Wilson (1916–95)
MP, 1945–83; leader of the Labour party; 1963–76; PM, 1964–70, 1974–76.

Key figure

Table 6.2: 1950 election results

	Votes	Seats	% of total votes cast
Labour	13,266,592	315	46.1
Conservative	12,502,567	298	43.5
Liberal	2,621,548	9	9.1
Others	381,964	3	1.3

The end of the Attlee Government

The Bevanite rebellion helped to sound the death knell of Attlee's Government. Reduced by the 1950 election to an overall majority of only five, a majority that was so tight that, when there was a close vote in the Commons, sick Labour MPs had to be brought from their hospital beds and helped through the division lobby, the Government now had to contend with mounting dissatisfaction within its own ranks. The open challenge to prescription charges encouraged those Labour MPs and members of the party who had previously swallowed their grievances to voice their doubts over the direction the Government had taken over economic, welfare and foreign policy.

Such divisions stimulated the Conservatives and sharpened their attacks. In such an atmosphere, another election could not be long delayed. The 1951 election was a close-run thing, with the Conservatives gaining a narrow victory. It was doubtless with some relief that a weary and beleaguered Labour government left office.

Reasons for Labour's 1951 defeat:

- Attlee's government was worn down by heavy economic and financial difficulties.
- Collectively and individually, the government was exhausted after six troubled years in office.
- A number of its ministers, e.g. Attlee himself, Herbert Morrison and Ernest Bevin, had been working continuously since 1940.
- Serious divisions had developed between the right and left of the party over economic, welfare and foreign policies.
- There was resentment among some trade unions at Labour's slowness in responding to workers' demands.
- The shrinking in the 1950 election of its large majority made governing difficult and damaged party morale.
- Labour found it difficult to shake off its image as a party of rationing and high taxation.
- In their call for the austerity that they claimed the times demanded, leading ministers such as the ascetic Stafford Cripps as Chancellor of the Exchequer and the aggressive Manny Shinwell, minister of fuel and power, did not present an attractive picture to the electorate.
- Britain's entry into the **Korean War** in 1950 made Labour's left wing unhappy; they argued that although technically British forces fought as part of a United Nations body, in reality the Labour Government was sheepishly following the USA in a Cold War engagement.
- The Conservatives had begun to recover from the shock of their defeat in 1945.
- The 1950 election had seen an influx of bright young Conservative MPs eager for battle against a tiring government.
- Under the direction of the dynamic **Lord Woolton**, 'a cheerful cove' as a colleague put it, the Conservative Party had reformed its finances and constituency organisation and was much better fitted to fight for seats and votes than in 1945.

- The attack on the Government's nationalisation of iron and steel provided a strong platform for the Conservative opposition.

The explanation for Attlee's losing office in 1951 is not so much Labour decline as Conservative recovery. While Labour had gained an extra two million votes between 1945 and 1951, the Conservatives had added nearly four million. Yet they only just squeezed into power. What benefited them was the Liberal Party's decision to put up only 109 candidates, a drop of 366 compared with 1950. The nearly two million ex-Liberal votes that became available went largely to the Conservatives.

Election success for Conservatives: 1951

Key date

Table 6.3: 1951 election

	Votes	Seats	% of total votes cast
Conservative	13,717,538	321	48.0
Labour	13,948,605	295	48.8
Liberal	730,556	6	2.5
Others	198,969	3	0.7

The election figures for 1951 reveal one of the oddest aspects of British electoral politics. It is possible for a party to poll more votes than its opponents yet still be defeated. After six years of government Labour had in fact more than held its share of the vote. Remarkably, the 1951 election saw Labour gain the highest aggregate vote ever achieved by any party up to that point. It outnumbered the Conservatives by a quarter of a million and had nearly one per cent more of the vote. The ratio of votes to seats was: Labour 47,283:1, Conservatives 42,733:1, Liberals 121,759:1. It was clearly not the case that Labour had been dumped out of office by a disillusioned electorate. It was more a matter this time of Labour's being the victim, not the beneficiary, of the unfairness of the British electoral system.

The legacy of the Attlee governments, 1945–51

While there may be legitimate criticisms of the Labour government regarding particular policy failures, there is a broader significance to the years 1945–51. In government in that period the Labour party laid down the policies that were to be followed in all essentials by successive Labour and Conservative governments over the next 35 years. Until Margaret Thatcher came into power in 1979 and deliberately challenged this **consensus**, there was a broad level of agreement on what were the major domestic and foreign issues and how they were to be handled.

Conservative and Labour policies were based on:

- economic policies based on Keynesian principles of public expenditure and state direction
- welfare policies based on the implementation of the Beveridge Report
- foreign policies based on a pro-American, anti-Soviet stance
- imperial policies based on the principle of independence for Britain's former colonies.

Key question
How important were Attlee's governments in the long term?

Consensus
Common agreement between the parties on basic policies.

Key term

This common area of agreement did not prevent serious political rivalry, but, when in government, the Labour and Conservative parties followed fundamentally similar policies.

Whatever the later questions concerning the Labour Governments' performance, there was little doubt among contemporaries that something momentous had occurred between 1945 and 1951. They were conscious that Labour had created the welfare state, that it had carried into peacetime the notion of State-directed planning, which had always been one of its basic socialist objectives, and that in so doing it had established Keynesianism as the basic British approach to economic planning. R.A. Butler, a leading Conservative, put the Labour reforms into historical perspective by describing them as 'the greatest social revolution in our history'. What gives particular significance to Butler's words is that the Conservative Party came in all major respects to accept that revolution.

The distinctive characteristic of the policies followed by Conservative governments from 1951 was how closely they coincided with those introduced by the Attlee governments. In the words of a modern historian, Dilwyn Porter, 'Attlee's patriotic socialists gave way to Churchill's social patriots'. Just as Labour had moved to the right by accepting capitalism and the mixed economy, so the Conservatives moved to the left by accepting Keynesianism and the managed economy.

In opposition, the Conservatives had opposed every nationalisation measure and many of the welfare proposals. Yet, in government themselves after 1951, they fully denationalised only one industry – steel – and built upon the welfare programme which they had inherited. Labour could justly claim that it had converted the Conservative Party to welfarism. This was perhaps one of Attlee's most enduring legacies.

Some key books in the debate:
Stuart Ball, *The Conservative Party and British Politics 1902–51* (Longman, 1995)
Corelli Barnett, *The Audit of War* (Macmillan, 1986)
Peter Catterall (ed.), *Britain 1918–1951* (Heinemann, 1994)
Peter Clarke, *A Question of Leadership: From Gladstone to Thatcher* (Penguin, 1992)
Peter Clarke, *Hope and Glory: Britain 1900–1990* (Penguin, 1996)
Dennis Kavanagh and Peter Morris, *Consensus Politics From Attlee to Major* (Blackwell, 1994)
David Kynaston, *Austerity Britain 1945–51* (Bloomsbury, 2007)
Andrew Marr, *A History of Modern Britain* (Macmillan, 2007)
Kenneth Morgan, *The People's Peace, British History 1945–90* (OUP, 1999)
Robert Pearce, *Attlee's Labour Governments 1945–51* (Longman, 1998)
Alan Sked and Chris Cook, *Post War Britain* (Penguin, 1992)
Nick Tiratsoo (ed.), *From Blitz to Blair A New History of Britain Since 1939* (Phoenix, 1997)

Summary diagram: The Labour Governments' Achievements

MAIN ACHIEVEMENTS:
↓
the Welfare State
↓
nationalisation
↓
Indian independence
↓
NATO
↓
nuclear weapons.

REASONS FOR ITS FALL
↓
Attlee's government worn down by heavy economic and financial difficulties
↓
Serious divisions between the right and left of the party
↓
Resentment among some trade unions at Labour's policies
↓
Labour's image as a party of rationing and high taxation
↓
Britain's entry into the Korean War in 1950 upset the Labour left
↓
The Bevanite rebellion, 1951
↓
Conservative recovery of morale.

LABOUR'S LEGACY
↓
Pushed Britain towards consensus politics in:
↓
economics
↓
welfare
↓
foreign affairs

Study Guide: AS Questions

In the style of AQA

(a) Explain why the Labour Party won the general election in
1945. (12 marks)

(b) How successful was the Labour government of 1945–1951 in
addressing Britain's economic problems? (24 marks)

Exam tips

*The cross-references are intended to take you straight to the material
that will help you to answer the questions.*

(a) Read pages 179–82. Labour's apparently surprising election
success needs to be explained with references not only to
Labour's strengths but also the Conservatives' (and Churchill's)
weaknesses. You will need to explain how the Labour Party had
benefited from involvement in the wartime Coalition and had had
time to formulate proposals for social reconstruction while
Churchill was preoccupied with the battle for victory. Labour's
resurgence can be linked to wartime social trends and the
Beveridge Report. You should also consider the election
campaigns of the two sides, Churchill's over-reliance on his wartime reputation and the Conservatives' association with the
'hungry' (and appeasing) thirties. Try to offer some supported
judgement as to which reasons were the most crucial ones.

(b) Read pages 189–194. You will obviously need to identify what
Britain's economic problems were, but the main focus of the
essay should be on the various measures taken by Labour and
their success, both individually and collectively. You should
evaluate:

- nationalisation
- austerity – rationing, controls, wage freeze and other anti-
  inflationary policies
- the devaluation of sterling
- Bevin and the Marshall Plan.

You will need to decide on your viewpoint before you begin
writing and should use the evidence to provide a clearly
sustained argument about the extent of success.

In the style of OCR

Domestic issues, 1918–51

To what extent were the Labour Party's internal divisions the main reason for its defeat in the 1951 general election?   (50 marks)

Exam tips

The cross-references are intended to take you straight to the material that will help you to answer the question.

You need to show that you have understood the focus of the question and that you can select an appropriate range and depth of evidence to support your argument. This is a comparative question and you should begin by analysing how the Labour Party's divisions contributed to its defeat. Your answer should focus on explanation rather than description or narrative. You might argue that:

- It was this issue that produced the most serious challenge to Attlee yet from within the Labour party. In 1951, forced by its financial difficulties to make savings in public expenditure, his government imposed charges on dental treatment and the provision of spectacles as well as on prescriptions. Aneurin Bevan, the man who had constructed the NHS, led a number of ministers in resigning from the Cabinet. These included Harold Wilson, who was to succeed Attlee as Labour Party leader and prime minister. Those who followed Bevan in this became known as Bevanites; they protested that the charges contravened the founding principle that the NHS should be free to all at the point of treatment and were thus a betrayal of basic Labour values (page 195).
- Nationalisation was a contentious issue and the proposal to nationalise iron and steel divided the Commons (page 189).
- Many Labour MPs felt literally exhausted and voters felt that ministers had run out of ideas (pages 197–98).
- Disagreements between Bevin and Morrison, which Atlee had hitherto contained, worsened and surfaced in 1951.

Counter-arguments are that:

- The Conservatives attacked the continuation of 'austerity' policies, Labour's mishandling of finances and social problems (pages 190–93).
- The Conservatives called for a reduction in state regulation and nationalisation (page 191).
- Since 1945 the Conservative Party had been regenerated with new leaders and reformed policies that were well received by the electorate (page 197).

Ensure you prioritise your arguments and in your conclusion reach a judgement on the most important factors. You might point out that Labour only just lost the election and actually won a larger share of the vote, so a combination of factors probably explains its defeat.

Glossary

Affiliated   Formally joined to an organisation.

Allied struggle   The main Allies fighting against the Central Powers.

Anglican   The established English Protestant Church, the nation's official religion.

Appeasement   The policy of avoiding war by granting concessions to an aggressor.

ARP   Air Raid Precautions.

Atlantic Charter, August 1941   An agreement laying out the principles on which the Allies planned to construct a better world once the war was won.

Austerity   A time of rationing and shortages.

Axis powers   Germany and Italy.

Balance of payments (trade balance) The equilibrium between the cost of imports and the profits from exports.

Balanced budgets   Keeping a balance between the revenue received by the government and the amount it spends (public expenditure).

BBC   The British Broadcasting Corporation.

Black and Tans   Irregular auxiliary British force sent to Ireland by Lloyd George in 1920.

Blitz, September 1940–May 1941 Sustained, mainly nightly, German bombing raids on London and other selected English cities.

Boer   Afrikaans (Dutch) word for farmer.

'Bright young things'   The young people of the privileged classes of the 1920s and 1930s.

British Communist Party   Set up in 1920, it was always subservient to the Comintern, which provided the bulk of its funds.

British debts   Britain had borrowed heavily from the USA during the war. At the end of his negotiations with the Americans in 1923, Baldwin, the Chancellor of the Exchequer, had committed Britain to repaying £46 million annually for 62 years.

British Medical Association (BMA)   The professional association and registered trade union for doctors in the United Kingdom.

Building societies   Finance companies that advance mortgages over long periods of time.

Chief Whips   The MPs who perform the vital function of organising the party in parliament.

Cold War   The period of tension between the USSR and its allies and the USA and its allies, 1945–91.

Collective security   The concept of all nations of good will acting together to stop an aggressor nation.

Collectivism   The people and the state acting together with a common sense of purpose, which necessarily means a restriction on individual rights.

Collectivist   Describing a society in which the individual is less important than the group. In times of need, therefore, the rights of the individual must be subordinated to the greater good of the group.

Comintern   The Communist International, the Soviet agency for fomenting revolution in other countries.

Conciliation Bill, 1910   A cross-party compromise on women's suffrage which came to nothing.

Consensus   Common agreement between the parties on basic policies.

Consensus politics   Parties suspending their differences and working together on policies they agreed on.

Conservative and Unionist Party   The Conservative party added Unionist to its title after 1886 in order to indicate the strength of its opposition to Home Rule for Ireland.

Constitutional   Issues relating to the conventions and methods by which Britain was governed.

Conurbations   Concentrated urban areas of high population density.

Convention   Since Britain does not have a written constitution, matters are decided by referring to traditional practice or convention.

Convoy system   The sailing of merchant ships in close groups protected by a ring of accompanying warships.

Co-operative societies   Formed in the nineteenth century to run shops and stores as non-profit-making ventures providing workers with food at affordable prices.

Corporate state   Power concentrated at the centre, entitling the government to direct the running of society and the economy.

Dail   Parliament.

Dail Eireann   Irish parliament.

Dandruff Syndrome   The wasting of time and resources on trivial conditions such as dandruff.

Dawes Plan, August 1925   Scheme devised by General Dawes, an American banker, for dealing with the reparations problem.

Deflationary gestures   The cutting of public expenditure in the hope that this would limit inflation and so encourage manufacturers to continue producing and, therefore, employing workers.

Differentials   Separate rates of pay for different levels of skill.

'Dilution'   The employment of unskilled workers in jobs previously restricted to skilled workers.

'Ditchers'   Those peers who, in 1911, were prepared to defend their power of absolute veto to the last ditch.

'Dollar gap'   Since sterling was weaker than the dollar, the goods that Britain desperately needed from North America had to be paid for in dollars.

Dunkirk spirit   A reference to the volunteers who had helped transport 300,000 besieged British troops from Dunkirk to safety in June 1940.

Edwardian   Strictly speaking, the adjective 'Edwardian' refers to the reign of Edward VII (1901–10). However, the term is often extended to include the early years of George V's reign between his accession in 1910 and the outbreak of the First World War in 1914.

Elective tyranny   The notion that an all-powerful House of Commons would not mean greater democracy but would simply allow the government of the day to use its majority to do as it wished.

Emergency Powers Act, 1920, 1939   Granted the Executive wide authority and extraordinary powers in the event of a major disruption of essential services.

'Entryism'   Infiltrating the Labour Party with the aim of pushing it towards the left from within.

Eugenics   The science of improving the quality of a race by allowing only couples of a high level of physical and mental health to produce children.

February Revolution   In February 1917 the Russian tsar, Nicholas II, abdicated and was replaced by a provisional government.

Fire watchers   Members of the public who volunteered to take up vantage points on high buildings and report outbreaks of fire over a given area.

First past the post   A candidate winning an election simply by gaining more votes than any of his challengers individually.

Franchise   The right to vote in parliamentary elections.

Free vote   Individual MPs are allowed to vote without instructions from their party.

Friendly societies   Non-profit making bodies which pooled contributions from members and paid out when members were in need.

Gallipoli Campaign   The unsuccessful Allied landings in Gallipoli in southern Turkey in April 1915.

Garden Suburb   The gardens of 10 Downing Street where Lloyd George had his own special War Cabinet centre.

'Geddes Axe'   Named after Sir Eric Campbell-Geddes, Chairman of a special government committee that recommended spending cuts in 1922.

General Strike   The idea of all the unions affiliated to the TUC coming out together.

Gold standard   The position in which a nation's currency is tied to the price of gold.

Great crash   The collapse of the American stock market in 1929.

Gross Domestic Product (GDP)   The annual total value of goods produced and services provided by Britain at home.

Gross National Product (GNP)   The annual total value of goods produced and services provided by Britain at home and in trade with other countries.

Home Guard   Local defence units largely made up of service veterans and those too old for the call-up.

Home Rule   An independent government in Dublin responsible for Irish affairs.

Hung parliament   A situation in which no single party has an overall majority in the House of Commons.

Independent nuclear deterrent   Britain's own nuclear weapon.

Indian Congress party   The main nationalist party in India, dedicated between 1858 and 1947 to ending British rule.

Indian independence   In 1947 Attlee's government gave independence to the sub-continent in the form of the separate sovereign states of India and Pakistan.

Industrialisation   The spread of manufacturing plants and factories, invariably accompanied by urbanisation.

Inflation   A decline in the purchasing power of money.

Infrastructure   The interlocking systems and installations that enable a nation's industrial economy to operate.

International Brigades   The foreign volunteers who fought for the Republicans in the Spanish Civil War, 1936–39.

Internment   The holding in detention of those members of the population whose nationality or political views made them a potential risk to national security.

Invergordon Mutiny, September 1931   In protest against scheduled cuts in service pay, sailors of the Atlantic fleet declared that they would not obey orders.

Invisible exports   The sale of financial and insurance services to foreign buyers.

Khaki   British forces adopted this as the colour of their standard uniform during the Boer War.

'King's party'   An unofficial grouping of some 60 MPs, who, during the 1936 Abdication Crisis, argued that Edward VIII should be allowed to make his own decision, free from political pressure.

Korean War (1950–53)   American-dominated UN armies resisted the takeover of South Korea by the Chinese-backed Communists of North Korea.

League of Nations   The body, to which all nations were entitled to belong, set up in 1919, as part of the Versailles settlement, with the aim of resolving all future international disputes.

League of Nations Union   Formed in October 1918 with the aim of educating the public to the need for supporting the League as the only guarantor of peace through collective security.

Left-wing intellectuals   Writers and thinkers who believed in radical social and economic change.

Lend lease   An arrangement that operated from 1941 under which Britain imported war materials from the United States with no obligation to pay for them until the war was over.

Lib–Lab pact, 1903   An agreement between the Labour and Liberal parties that their constituency candidates would not stand against each other in parliamentary elections.

Lobby fodder   MPs going through the division lobbies (i.e. voting) at their party's command, regardless of the merits of the case.

Lock-outs   Employers locking out the workers by closing the factory gates.

M15   Britain's counter-espionage agency.

Mandate   Authority granted by the people to the government to follow a particular set of policies.

Marconi scandal   The row in 1913 over Lloyd George's use of his inside knowledge as Chancellor of the Exchequer to buy and sell shares in the Marconi Company for a large profit.

Means test   In the 1930s, to qualify for dole or relief individuals or families had to give precise details of all the money they had coming in.

Middle class   The comfortable, moneyed section of society.

Military Service Act, 1916   Imposed compulsory enlistment on single males between the ages of 18 and 41.

Ministry of Reconstruction   A body which drew together the various committees that had come into being during the war; its main task being the improvement of standards of living and working.

Mod cons   Short for modern conveniences, i.e. household accessories such as vacuum cleaners, refrigerators and radios.

National Debt   The total amount owed by the government to its domestic and international creditors.

National Grid   A nationwide network of high-voltage lines carrying electricity from generating stations to homes and factories.

Nationalisation   The common ownership of the means of production, distribution and exchange.

NATO (North Atlantic Treaty Organisation)   A defensive alliance formed in 1949 by the USA, Britain, France and the Benelux countries as a safeguard against Soviet expansion.

Nazi–Soviet Pact 1939   A non-aggression agreement between Germany and the USSR, signed in August 1939.

Nazism   The German National Socialist movement led by Hitler.

New Liberalism   The movement among progressive Liberals who wanted their party to commit itself fully to social reform.

'New' unions   Represented large groups of workers, such as dockers, transport workers and miners.

No-Conscription Fellowship   A body set up in 1914, devoted to resisting any attempt by the State to introduce a general call-up.

Nonconformist   Those Protestant churches which refused to accept the doctrines and authority of the Anglican Church.

Normandy landings, June 1944   A massive Anglo-American invasion of occupied western France.

Norwegian Campaign, April 1940   Responding to the German invasion of Norway, Britain sent a task force there, but it proved too small to prevent the Germans overrunning the country.

OBE   Order of the British Empire.

'Old' unions   Established organisations representing skilled workers.

Osborne Judgment, 1910   A legal ruling that it was improper for a trade union to use its funds for political purposes, i.e. to support a political party or to pay candidates or MPs.

Parliamentary Reform Act, 1949   Reduced the delaying power of the House of Lords over a Commons Bill to two sessions and one year.

Pawnbroking   Exchanging items for money in the hope that they can be reclaimed later by paying back the original sum with interest added.

PAYE (Pay As You Earn)   A system under which the tax due from workers is extracted from their wages before they have received them.

Peace   The avoidance of war and unnecessary foreign entanglements by embracing the concepts of internationalism and anti-imperialism.

Phoney war   The period from September 1939 to April 1940 when nothing of military significance actually happened.

Picketing   'Strikers' station themselves at the gates of a factory or workplace so as to deter other workers from entering.

'Political levy'   The portion of a member's union subscription that went to the Labour Party.

Poor Law   A scheme dating from 1834 for providing relief by taking the destitute into workhouses.

'Popular front'   An alliance of the socialist and progressive parties of the Left.

Protectionist trading bloc   A set of nations that operates free trade among themselves, but raise protective barriers against outside competitors.

Rapprochement   Resumption of working relations.

Rates   Taxes levied on householders to pay for local government services.

Ratio principle   For every five American vessels there would be five British and three Japanese.

Real wages   The purchasing power of earnings when set against prices.

Recession   A slowing down of economic growth, usually caused by a fall in demand for manufactures.

Reform   Allowing for necessary changes to be introduced by Government so long as they did not encroach on the freedom of the individuals.

Re-nationalised   Brought back into public ownership (i.e. government control).

Reparations   Payments required of Germany to compensate for the war damage it had caused.

Reserved occupations   Those doing work defined as crucial to the war effort were exempted from call up.

Retail prices   The price paid for goods by the purchaser in the shops.

Retrenchment   Saving public money by tightly controlling central-government expenditure.

Revisionist historians   Those who challenge the accepted interpretation of events.

Revolutionary Russia   In October 1917, the Russian Communist revolutionaries had taken power under Lenin and then called on workers everywhere to do the same and overthrow their governments.

Revolutionary socialism   A radical movement which wanted to overthrow the existing state and replace it with a worker-led government.

Salvation Army   A religious movement founded in 1878 to put Christian values into practical form by directly helping the unfortunates of society.

Samuel Commission   A body set up in 1925 to report on the problems of the mining industry and put forward solutions.

Scramble for Africa   Between the 1870s and 1914 the major European colonial powers took over large areas of the African continent.

Self-determination   The right of peoples to be free of domination by an outside power, and to form a nation and government of their own choice.

Service industries Those enterprises that directly cater for consumer demand.

Seven-year rule The law requiring that a general election be held at least once very seven years.

Shell crisis A shortage of shells required for artillery barrages on the Western Front.

Singapore, February 1942 The surrender of the 70,000 British forces stationed there to the invading Japanese, who thereby gained control of South East Asia, was one of the most shattering defeats of the war for Britain. Some historians see it as marking the end of the British Empire.

Sinn Fein Gaelic for 'Ourselves Alone'.

Sino-Japanese War (1937–45) A struggle between China and Japan.

Socially cohesive state A nation whose people broadly agree on fundamental social principles, e.g. welfare.

Somme offensive, 1 June–October 1916 A major but ultimately unsuccessful British attack on the Western Front, resulting in 420,000 casualties.

Stalemate The situation on the Western Front between two massive sets of entrenched armies, neither being able to inflict a decisive defeat on the other.

Staple industries The enterprises on which Britain's industrial strength had traditionally been based, e.g. textiles, coal mining, iron and steel production and ship building.

Starred workers After 1914, volunteers who were thought to be already doing vital war work had a star put against their name and were exempted from military service.

Suffrage The right to vote.

Suffragettes Advocates of votes for women, who were prepared to use violence.

Suffragists Advocates of votes for women, who were opposed to violent methods being used.

'Sweated' Describing unhealthy, overcrowded premises where unscrupulous employers exploited cheap labour.

Syndicalism A revolutionary movement calling on workers to smash the industrial-capitalist system by violent action.

Temperance Opposition to the taking of alcoholic drink.

'Terrible beauty' Term used by W.B. Yeats to describe the 'terrible' nature of violence and the uplifting 'beauty' of sacrifice.

TGWU Transport and General Workers Union.

Tobruk, June 1942 The surrender of 33,000 British troops to Rommel's army.

Total war A struggle that directly and indirectly involves the whole population.

Treaty of Sevres, 1920 The agreement that formally ended the war between the Allies and defeated Turkey.

TUC (Trades Union Congress) The body created in 1868 to represent the unions collectively.

Two-chamber structure The elected House of Commons and the unelected House of Lords.

Two nations The division of Britain between the rich and the poor, and between the areas of Britain which were flourishing and those which were in decline.

Uniformed Auxiliary Services Auxiliary Territorial Service (ATTs), Women's Auxiliary Air Force (WAAFs), Women's Royal Navy Service (WRENs).

Union of Democratic Control, 1914–18   A pressure group set up to protest against the war and urge a negotiated peace.

US dollar   As the world's strongest currency, the dollar was taken as the financial benchmark. All other currencies were measured in terms of their exchange value against the dollar.

USSR   Union of Soviet Socialist Republics (often shortened to Soviet Union).

V1 flying bomb   A pilotless jet-propelled plane loaded with explosives.

V2   An armed rocket launched from mobile sites.

Versailles Treaty, 1919   The major post-war peace settlement.

Victorian   Relating to the years of Queen Victoria's reign (1837–1901).

Wage freeze   An undertaking not to press for higher wages until Britain's economy had improved.

War of attrition   Wearing the enemy down by sheer persistence and willingness to suffer casualties.

War indemnities   Reparations paid by the losing side for the cost of the war.

Wartime blockade   Between 1914 and 1918, in an attempt to inflict economic damage on each other, Britain and Germany imposed blockades to prevent supplies being imported or exported.

Welfare state   A fully funded state programme to provide the essential social, health and educational needs of all its people, regardless of their income or social status.

White Russians   The Communists' (Reds') main opponents.

Wyndham's Act   Named after George Wyndham, Secretary for Ireland, 1900–05.

Yalta Conference   Held in February 1945 and attended by the USSR, Britain and the USA to consider the post-war settlement.

Young Plan, August 1929   The proposal to reduce Germany's reparation payments and advanced it a loan of $300 million.

Zeitgeist   The spirit of the times.

Index